LEGACIES
OF THE HOMELAND

100 Must Read Books by
Punjabi Authors

Paramjeet Singh

INDIA • SINGAPORE • MALAYSIA

Notion Press

Old No. 38, New No. 6
McNichols Road, Chetpet
Chennai - 600 031

First Published by Notion Press 2018
Copyright © Paramjeet Singh 2018
All Rights Reserved.

ISBN 978-1-64249-423-5

This book has been published with all reasonable efforts taken to make the material error-free after the consent of the author. No part of this book shall be used, reproduced in any manner whatsoever without written permission from the author, except in the case of brief quotations embodied in critical articles and reviews.

The Author of this book is solely responsible and liable for its content including but not limited to the views, representations, descriptions, statements, information, opinions and references ["Content"]. The Content of this book shall not constitute or be construed or deemed to reflect the opinion or expression of the Publisher or Editor. Neither the Publisher nor Editor endorse or approve the Content of this book or guarantee the reliability, accuracy or completeness of the Content published herein and do not make any representations or warranties of any kind, express or implied, including but not limited to the implied warranties of merchantability, fitness for a particular purpose. The Publisher and Editor shall not be liable whatsoever for any errors, omissions, whether such errors or omissions result from negligence, accident, or any other cause or claims for loss or damages of any kind, including without limitation, indirect or consequential loss or damage arising out of use, inability to use, or about the reliability, accuracy or sufficiency of the information contained in this book.

Dedicated to…

My Parents, Sohan Singh and Jasbir Kaur

This book is a labour of love for our *ma-boli*, Punjabi.
My parents, voracious readers both,
inculcated in me the love of the language,
as well the love of the written word.

Some books are undeservedly forgotten;

none are undeservedly remembered.

W. H. Auden

Contents

Foreword	ix
Acknowledgements	xiii
Introduction: About this Book	xv
Punjabi Literature: The Journey So Far	xxv

Autobiographies

Ajeet Cour	2
Amrita Pritam	5
Bachint Kaur	8
Dalip Kaur Tiwana	11
Gian Singh 'Shatir'	13
Gurdial Singh	16

Novels

Amrita Pritam	22
Amrita and Imroz	26
Baldev Singh	29
Bhai Vir Singh	32
Bhisham Sahni	36
Dalip Kaur Tiwana	39
Fakhar Zaman	42
Fauzia Rafiq	45
Gurdial Singh	48
Gulzar Singh Sandhu	50
Gurmukh Singh Sehgal	53
Inder Singh Khamosh	56

Contents

Jaswant Singh Kanwal	58
Kartar Singh Duggal	61
Krishna Sobti	65
Krishna Sobti	68
Nanak Singh	70
Nanak Singh	73
Niranjan S. Tasneem	76
Om Prakash Gasso	78
Rajinder Singh Bedi	81
Rajinder Singh	85
Ram Sarup Ankhi	88
Ram Sarup Ankhi	91
Sant Singh Sekhon	94
Satnam	97
Shivcharan Jaggi Kussa	100
Sohan Singh Seetal	103
Sohinder Singh Wanjara Bedi	106
Swaran Chandan	109
Yashpal	112
Yashpal	114

Poetry

Amarjit Chandan	118
Baba Farid	121
Beeba Balwant	125
Bulleh Shah	128
Dev	132
Faiz Ahmed Faiz	135
Gagan Gill	138
Harbhajan Halwarvi	140
Harbhajan Singh	143
Harbhajan Singh	146
Jaswant Deed	148
Jaswant Zafar	151
Lal Singh Dil	154
Manjit Tiwana	158

Contents | vii

Mohan Singh — 160
Munir Niazi — 163
Pash — 166
Santokh Singh Dheer — 169
Shah Hussain — 172
Shah Mohammed — 175
Shiv Kumar Batalvi — 179
Sultan Bahu — 183
Surjit Patar — 186
Waris Shah — 189

Plays

Atamjit — 194
Kartar Singh Duggal — 198
Manjit Pal Kaur — 201
Mazhar Tirmazi — 204
Sant Singh Sekhon — 207

Short Stories

Ajeet Cour — 210
Amrik Singh Kanda — 213
Baldev Singh Dhaliwal — 216
Balwant Singh — 219
Bushra Ejaz — 222
Gurnam Gill — 225
Harbans Singh — 228
Hina Nandrajog & Madhuri Chawla — 230
Jarnail Singh — 233
Jasjit Mansingh — 237
Jaswinder Singh — 239
Khushwant Singh — 241
Krishan Chander — 244
Kulwant Singh Virk — 247
Manjit Inder Singh — 250
Mohan Bhandari — 253
Mohinder Singh Sarna — 256

NarinderJit Kaur	259
Nirupama Dutt	261
Prem Prakash	264
Raghubir Dhand	266
Rajendra Awasthy	269
Rajinder Singh Bedi	272
Ranjit Singh	275
Ranjit Singh	277
Rana Nayar	280
Saadat Hasan Manto	283
Sadhu Binning	287
Sujan Singh	290
Waryam Singh Sandhu	293
Note on Exclusive Anthologies	
Dedicated to Punjabi Writers Settled Abroad	297
Rana Nayar	299
Rita Chaudhry and Harbir S Manku	302
Puran Singh	305
Appendix 1: Translation	309
Appendix 2: The Monolingual Dystopia – Power Dynamics of Literary Translation – Change Magazine – 10 March 2017	
By Anvita Budhraja	311
Appendix 3: What Ails Punjabi Writing?	315
Appendix 4: Reclaiming Punjabi by Mahmood Awan	319
About the Translators'	323
Bibliography	345
Index	347

Foreword

100 Must-Read Books by Punjabi Authors is a compilation by Paramjeet Singh, who is an IRS by profession, but an avid reader by choice. A self-taught reader, he has, of late, discovered his interest in Punjabi literature and has come up with this collection for other readers, who share his literary tastes and cultural proclivities.

It is certainly not an easy task to compile a collection of this nature. It involves wading through an endless sea of literary works, reading them, sifting them, preparing notes and then documenting them in some discernible order. Of course, this also involves an extremely important process of selection, which though intensely personal and highly individualistic, has to be made in such a way that it appears to be both fair and objective to others as well.

One may question the very notion of 'must read books.' Let us accept that we are living in the times of extreme relativism, where our choices in all spheres of life, including our selection of books and the acts or modes of reading, have become egregiously personal and individualistic. One may even feel offended if someone takes it upon himself to suggest 'Well, these books you must read.' But there is no denying the fact that it is this very age of extreme relativism that demands from us a certain commitment to the ideals of stability, continuity and rootedness.

Though in books, as in fashions, the styles of authors differ as much the choices of readers do, some books continue to enjoy the privilege of being 'permanent travellers.' Such books travel with us through time, fascinating us, engaging us, entertaining us and even sustaining us. Such books provide us glimpses into the best that has ever been thought or expressed by human mind. Such books contain the collective wisdom of our culture and come to our rescue in the best, or even the worst of times.

No wonder, such books easily assume the appellation of 'classics,' and we all know that classics are for all times and all seasons. I have no hesitation in saying that most of the books selected for discussion in this collection have either already become 'modern classics' or are likely to become so, in times to come. Mr. Singh has been extremely careful and judicious in his selection of 100 books, and in this respect, he has allowed himself to be guided more by the considerations of aesthetics than those of ideology.

One doesn't come across any ideological bias in his selection of books. Mr. Singh has only selected those books, which have, over the years, created a permanent niche for themselves in the cultural space of Punjab and also in the heart of the Punjabi readers. In fact, his effort, as he states candidly in his introduction, is mainly to share his personal joy of reading Punjabi authors with those who don't have access to literature available in this great language.

Starting from Baba Farid to the present times, Punjabi language and literature have had a long, established history of over 900 years, if not more. All genres, conventions, styles and literary codes have flourished in this language, that too, with aplomb. Often the richness and vitality of Punjabi literature is lost on those who are unable to read this language. To that extent, Mr. Singh's effort is commendable as he is making available some of the rarest of gems of Punjabi literature to the non-Punjabi readers.

The last few decades have witnessed a phenomenal increase in the number of good, reliable translations of Punjabi authors into English. Slowly, Punjabi literature is breaking the barriers of language, region and geography and making forays into the international markets. This is in recognition of the universal presence of Punjabis across the globe. There is a growing need and demand to understand the cultural dynamics of Punjabis, who have contributed significantly to the growth of several multicultural societies in the world. Of course, when it comes to understanding the problematics of a culture, literature is perhaps the best source available.

I congratulate Mr. Singh on putting together this selection and hope that non-Punjabi readers of this book would find new horizons of cultural experience opening up before them. Of course, for Punjabi readers, it may be yet another opportunity to experience a sense of genuine pride in their rich legacy of language, literature and culture.

– **Prof. Rana Nayar**

Acknowledgements

This book turned out to be a mammoth exercise. It required a lot of research and help from many people and it was very heartening to see that most of them were very generous in offering information and other help and assistance required.

I am indebted to Nirupama Dutt and Professor Rana Nayar for their help, guidance and encouragement. For offering valuable suggestions in selecting books and authors as well as allowing me to access and use their highly erudite and well-researched papers, I thank them. I am grateful to Nirupamaji for introducing me to some valuable contacts and to Rana Nayar Sahab for agreeing to write the foreword of the book.

Heartfelt gratitude to Rupinderpal Singh Dhillon and Mahmood Awan, who graciously allowed me to use their brilliant articles that have added indispensable perspective to the book. I am also thankful to NarinderJit Kaur and Moitrayee Bhaduri for helping me in reviewing some of the books. Thanks also to many of the writers and translators who, despite being busy, responded immediately to queries and requests: Harjeet Atwal, Sadhu Binning, Tejwant Singh Gill, Ishmeet Kaur Chaudhry, Hina Nandrajog, Fauzia Rafique, Amandeep Sandhu, Khushwant Singh, Parminder Sodhi, Arvinder Kaur, Amarjit Chandan, Zubair Ahmad, Gurshminder Singh Jagpal, Gurdev Singh Rupana, Swarajbir, Ranjit Singh, Ravinder Ravi, Rajinder Singh and Atamjit. I would also like to acknowledge Harish Jain of Unistar Books Pvt. Ltd. and my colleague, Tarun Doshi for their help in locating and obtaining many books. I am also extremely thankful to my colleague, Farheen for her invaluable help in researching for the book and to my friend, Geetali Tare for her valuable inputs and corrections.

My children, Archit and Anvita – wordsmiths in their own right – helped me review the manuscript for grammar and diction. A huge thank you to Gurjeet, my wife, who gave me the time and space needed to indulge in this passion and for putting up with my long hours spent in reading books and writing about them. The wholehearted encouragement of my family was very inspiring.

Introduction: About This Book

This book is not intended to provide a list of the 100 'best' books ever written and published by Punjabi authors. Given the sheer range of books written by Punjabi authors and the unpredictability of individual taste, any such definitive list is quite impossible. Secondly, the choice has been restricted to books that were written by them either in Punjabi, Hindi or Urdu but have been translated into English. Thus, personal choice restricted by availability has dictated this selection. The choice of books includes autobiographies, novels, short stories, poems and plays. Research books, religious books and books written originally in English have not been included. Books written in English by Punjabi authors may be featured in the second edition to this book, if all goes well.

The quest for this book came from a desire to showcase the vast variety of subjects that Punjabis have written about. As author Harish Dhillon writes in the preface to his book *Love Stories from Punjab*, the purpose of undertaking the project was that he was commissioned by a person who had a special love for Punjab and all things Punjabi, and who was saddened by the fact that a whole generation of English-speaking Punjabis – and, by extension, a whole generation of Indians – had grown up with no knowledge of the beautiful love stories of Punjab. I share the same sentiment; only mine extends to showcase the entire gamut of Punjabi books and not just the love stories that have emerged out of this rich culture.

The books are organized according to genre. Within the genres, the books are arranged alphabetically by the author's name. Short story anthologies are also organized alphabetically by the author's name; however, in the case of anthologies that contain stories by multiple authors, I have used the translator's name in the alphabetical order. They describe the plot of each title, offer some value judgements, and say something brief about the author's place in the history of literature and/or about their other works. Additionally, 'Read on' lists are provided, which are other books by the same author, books on a theme relevant to the main text, and details of films, plays and other adaptations made on the primary text.

Most authors receive only one entry. The original intention was to have 100 authors and 100 books but it soon became clear that this was impractical. How can the richness and variety of authors like Amrita Pritam, Nanak Singh, Gurdial Singh, Ajeet Cour, K.S. Duggal, Krishna Sobti, Yashpal and so many others be represented by merely one book? Yet, if every masterpiece by a dozen or so writers were to be included, there would be room for very few other authors. In the end, I decided (again, more or less arbitrarily) that the most an author could have is two titles.

Finally, because of the anthologies included, more than 100 authors are being introduced. In these cases, the emphasis is laid on the book and not on the author's biography. The attempt is to introduce these wonderful stories written by Punjabi authors. Some of the authors are giants of Punjabi literature, while others are professionals who have also written books. But, ultimately, all of these books are must-reads.

Since the target audience of this book is English readers, some of the most excellent Punjabi works have been left out, because they have not been translated into English. For instance, there is no book in English by a pioneering author like Gurbaksh Singh 'Preetlari,' a man whose magazine *Preetlari* published the major

Punjabi works and forwarded the career of so many upcoming Punjabi authors. Preetlari continues to do an exemplary job – it is still being published as a monthly magazine and now has an online Punjabi version too. Similarly, there are no English translations available of the works of authors like Dhani Ram Chatrik, Balwant Gargi, Gurmukh Singh Musafir, Devendra Satyarthi, Dr. Jagtar, Buta Singh, Mohan Singh Diwana, Prabhjot Kaur (just to name a few) and even that of diaspora writers like Harjeet Atwal, Veena Verma, Ajmer Rode, Surjit Kalsi and Roop Dhillon. Even a giant of Punjabi Literature like Nanak Singh does not have many of his books translated.

Punjabi plays are the least translated works, for reasons not immediately understandable. There is a rich tradition of Punjabi drama and it enjoys a respectable appreciation. But none of the works of even the foremost Punjabi dramatist, Balwant Gargi, are available in English. Poetry has received a better treatment from the translators and many works of the leading poets are fortunately available in English. Despite this, there still exist inconsistencies. For instance, none of the works of Shiv Kumar Batalvi, except *Luna*, have been translated into English. The same is the position in West Punjab. It is clear then that a lot of work needs to be done in the area of translating Punjabi works.

A lot of writers are not very happy with the quality of translations, so they refuse to get their works translated and are also quite wary of the publishers. Sahitya Akademi, which is tasked with promoting Indian Literature, also needs to do a lot in relation to promoting Punjabi. It has four regional offices to oversee the publication work in various languages – Kolkatta (for Assamese, Bengali, Bodo, Manipuri, Oriya, English, Tibetan and other North-Eastern languages) Bangalore (for Kannada, Malayalam, Tamil and Telugu; in fact, it has a sub-regional office in Chennai that is focused on Tamil works), Mumbai (for Gujarati, Konkani, Marathi and Sindhi) and Agartala (for unrecognized languages of the North-East). Clearly, a regional office in Punjab for Punjabi and other North Indian languages would go a long way in the promotion of Punjabi language and literature.

There have always been more English and other language works that are being translated into Punjabi than the other way around. So this book is a tribute to all the translators who have served the cause of Punjabi Literature by translating books into English and giving them a pan-India or even a global readership. Only Amrita Pritam, Dalip Kaur Tiwana, Gurdial Singh and Sant Singh Sekhon have been fortunate that many of their works have been translated in English. Similar is the plight of writers from West Punjab where even a prolific writer like Najm Hosain Syed does not have any of his books translated into English.

Fortunately, English readers can get a taste of these as yet inaccessible writers through the anthologies of short stories included in this book. Short story as a genre enjoys a certain popularity with Punjabi authors, and a lot of authors whose full-length books may not have been translated into English do have their stories translated. So, after much thought, anthologies have been included and we get to read the works of a large number of Punjabi writers who would have otherwise been left out. Translators like Tejwant Singh Gill, Paramjeet Singh Ramana, Rana Nayar, Narinder Jit Kaur, Nirupama Dutt, Jai Ratan, Hina Nandrajog, Madhumeet and even full time authors like Khushwant Singh, Harbans Singh and K. S. Duggal have done a commendable job by bringing to the readers the works of writers like Sujan Singh, Balwant Singh, Raghubir Dhand, Kulwant Singh Virk, Gurmukh Singh Musafir, Ahmed Salim, Ajmer Rode, Mohammad Mansa Yaad and contemporary writers like Veena Verma, Prem Gorkhi, Chandan Negi, Nachhatar, Sukhwant Kaur Mann, Bhagwant Rasulpuri and many more. Punjabi University, Patiala, and Sahitya Academy have done a great job in having the works of Punjabi authors translated into English. National Book Trust of India; Punjabi Academy, Delhi; Guru Nanak Dev University, Amritsar; and publishers like Unistar Books Pvt. Ltd. too have played a very important part.

I have chosen these 100 books because I think they will provide some sense of the enormous range of subjects that Punjabi authors have tackled – from Partition to agriculture, from naxalism and militancy to wider diasporic concerns. There are two surprising omissions in the topics covered. First, most of the authors who write originally in Punjabi have not written anything about the pogroms against Sikhs, variously described as Sikh Massacre or Sikh Genocide of 1984…it is as if the event did not occur. Perhaps, in Punjab, they were not affected by it. The Punjabi authors who write in English have written most of the books on this subject. This is in sharp contrast to a plethora of books on the subject of Partition, which, in fact, has seen the largest amount of literature on any one particular topic. Even a writer like Amrita Pritam who was moved to write *Ajj ankha waris shah nu* in the aftermath of Partition, and who was in Delhi where the worst massacres happened in 1984, does not seem to have written anything about the genocide. The only exception is Ajeet Cour and some short stories featured in the anthologies. Recently, a new book *Unni Sau Chaurasi* (1984) by noted poet Harbhajan Singh has been released posthumously. The poems revolve around Operation Bluestar and the anti-Sikh pogrom. London-based Punjabi writer Amarjit Chandan has edited the book, and celebrated filmmaker Gurvinder Singh has designed the title. The book has 69 poems and also carries three essays.

The second omission is in regard to the lack of humour in most Punjabi works. Punjabis have a great zest for life and an ability to enjoy themselves despite terrible hardships, yet their literature is largely devoid of satire and humour. No attempt seems to have been made by our academicians and critics to find out a reason for this. However, it may reflect the dire straits in which the Punjabis have continued to exist. So alarming is the situation in Punjab that in the year 2012, a Punjabi Subaltern Summit was organized in Chandigarh. According to its stated agenda, the summit was:

> A bold attempt to reclaim the mantle of Punjabiyat. To break free from the parochial structures that have suppressed the social narrative on lesser-known issues like caste, religion, representation and federalism. By harnessing the spirit and dialect of new media, it strives to infuse the Punjabi intellectual

mainstream with a sense of purpose and direction, bringing back the long-lost ebullience into its ethos.

It goes on to add that:

> If one were to seek some refuge in humor then this modified quote – which was Clemenceau's take on America in its original form – seems apt to describe the situation, Punjab is the only society that went from barbarism to decadence without civilization in between. Overburdened with past and a misplaced sense of history, the parallel exposition of peoples' consciousness was tacitly overlooked under the post-traumatic stress of the partition, the green revolution and terrorism. Though this summit and its agenda were dealing with the pressing problems of the state yet it gives us a clue as to why our literature is devoid of humour.

Through this compilation then, I am joining the struggle to bring the works of our great Punjabi authors to the notice of fellow Punjabis who read in English, other readers in India, and, finally, the global readers. But that very struggle speaks to the hegemony of the English language. Why does English garner such a wide readership? Why is translation into English so necessary in order for a work to be recognized, or even read? The unequalled power that English enjoys in the global literary scene means that more and more people in India are losing touch with their mother tongues or with other regional languages they would have otherwise learned to read and speak. Not speaking one's mother tongue really cuts one off at the root; links must be re-established. The story is the same for almost all Indian languages – the global dominance of English has starved Indian regional languages of life. Translations then serve a dual purpose. For those who belong to a particular culture but don't speak the language, translations bring them closer to their roots; they make them proud of their culture and may one day even compel them to read in their mother tongue. For others, translations introduce them to the art, the culture and the stories of other regions. The importance of translation has been stated very well by various authors like Rana Nayar and Manjit Inder Singh. Furthermore, another article written by my daughter Anvita Budhraja for the magazine *Change* talks about this hegemony of English and the power dynamics of translation. All three pieces, extremely pertinent to my endeavour, have been included in the Appendix to the book.

Besides this, there are other reasons as to why Punjabi language has been languishing. Rupinder pal 'Roop' Dhillon's article addresses the need to modify the present art and craft of Punjabi Literature; while Mahmood Awan's article highlights how and why we have failed to make the issues of Punjabi as a language permeate to the common folk of Punjab and to it political parties, while also offering some solutions. I have included these articles at the end of the book too for the readers, with the authors' kind permission and consent.

Many authors have written books on the History of Punjabi Literature. I too have included a short journey of Punjabi Literature across all genres, which will give the readers a sense of how Punjabi Literature has grown and evolved over the years. Though the sources used in my research are mentioned in the bibliography, the major portion of it is sourced from the excellent work done by Rana Nayar on this subject. Similarly, the sub topics – New Trends in Punjabi Literature and Effect of Partition – are sourced from brilliant works on these by Nirupama Dutt and Mahmood Awan, respectively. Needless to say that these acclaimed writers have been very generous to permit me to do so.

A final word – a great deal of research has gone into compiling this book and it has been an extremely rewarding journey. I have personally acquired each of these books (some of the books were out of print and were very difficult to obtain) and have thoroughly enjoyed reading them and getting to know their authors. In writing about the books and the authors, I have used different sources like book covers, Wikipedia, Sikhiwiki, Sikhchic, websites of individual authors and websites of publishing companies. In the end, this work – like all others – is a work of collaboration by those who care deeply about appreciating and promoting Punjabi literature.

Some interesting facts about the books are included here:
1. There are some Punjabi writers writing in Urdu from East Punjab who appear in this book and have been translated into English are Rajinder Singh Bedi, Gian Singh Shatir, Balwant Singh and Krishan Chander (the last two also wrote in Hindi).
2. Punjabi authors writing in Hindi who have been translated into English and who are included in this book are Bhisham Sahni, Krishna Sobti and Yashpal. Amrita Pritam wrote in both Punjabi and Hindi.
3. Many Punjabi writers write with equal proficiency in English as well as in Punjabi. This book features their Punjabi works translated into English. They include Sant Singh Sekhon, Ajeet Cour, Niranjan Tasneem, Sadhu Binning, Fauzia Rafique, Amarjit Chandan and Swaran Chandan.
4. Every year, the Sahitya Akademi honours authors in all major Indian languages including Punjabi. Almost all the authors featured in this collection have, at some point, won this award for their seminal works. However, many Punjabi authors like Khushwant Singh and K. S. Duggal have been writing in English too but they never have won the Sahitya Akademi Award for English. Although both of them won the Sahitya Akademi Fellowship, which is the highest honour that it bestows on authors. The two Punjabi authors who won the Sahitya Akademi award in English are Mulk Raj Anand and Chaman Lal while the first Punjabi woman to win this award in English is Rupa Bajwa who received it for her debut work The Sari Shop at the young age of 26.
5. The other Punjabi authors to have won the Sahitya Akademi Fellowship are Gurbaksh Singh, Mulk Raj

Anand, Harbhajan Singh, Krishna Sobti, Bhisham Sahni, Amrita Pritam, Gopi Chand Narang and Gurdial Singh.
6. There are some father–son, father–grandson and father–daughter combination of authors/translators featured here. The children have not only continued the worthy work done by their fathers but have also translated them into English. Thus, we have Mohinder Singh Sarna and his illustrious writer son Navtej Singh Sarna; Nanak Singh and his grandson Navdeep Singh Suri; Harbans Singh and his daughter Nikky Guninder Kaur Singh. (She has translated a book by Dalip Kaur Tiwana amongst other works.)
7. The immortal love tales of Punjab like Heer-Ranjha (Waris Shah), Sohni–Mahiwal (Fazal Shah), Sassi-Punnu (Hashim Shah) and Mirza-Sahiban (Hafiz Barkhudar) do not have English translations (except Heer-Ranjha) available, although the stories are available in English. Sant Singh Sekhon, in his book A History of Punjabi Literature, Vol. 2, has provided translations of some parts of these stories.
8. Shilalekh Publishers, Delhi, has published a compilation of short stories of 101 female Punjabi authors, in two volumes. Most of them are not translated into English but it is heartening to see names of 101 female Punjabi authors.

Like most regional literature, Punjabi Literature faces problems like a lack of serious readership, an unsatisfactory distribution system, reduced sales and only an occasional upcoming young star. But this has not deterred some people from pursuing their love and carrying out the task of resurrecting the realm of Punjabi Literature. Special credit must go to diasporic writers who, despite living in countries like the United Kingdom, Canada and the United States, continue to write in their mother tongue and enrich it with their hard work and dedication. It seems that literature helps the community strengthen their identity; it is an aesthetic response to socio-cultural cries because it helps generate unconventional images of the community with regional variations.

Punjabis are brave, hard working, generous, compassionate and religious people who, nevertheless, like to live well. A reflection of the increasingly global outlook of the Punjabi community is that the translations actually sell better than the original Punjabi works, although one does fervently wish that more and more people learned to read Punjabi. I hope this book which showcases our rich literary tradition will inspire some to go back to read the original Punjabi classics.

Punjabi Literature: The Journey So Far

Punjabi Literature[1]

Punjabi is an Indo-Aryan language. It is the native language of about 130 million people and is the tenth most spoken language in the world. Most of the people who speak this language live in the Punjab region of Pakistan and India. It is also widely spoken in Haryana, Himachal Pradesh and Delhi. It is natively spoken by the majority of the population of Pakistan.

Punjabi literature refers to literary works written in the Punjabi language particularly by peoples from the historical Punjab of India and Pakistan including the Punjabi diaspora. The Punjabi language is written in several different scripts, of which the Shahmukhi and the Gurmukhi scripts are the most commonly used.

Emergence of Punjabi language in the Indo-Gangetic plain, strangely enough, coincided with the growth and development of English language in a far-off island inhabited by the Anglo-Saxons. However, English soon spread across several continents (thanks to colonialism), while Punjabi has had to stay confined rather diffidently to the plains of Punjab, place of its birth. It is

---

1 *Source:* With inputs from Rana Nayar's Introduction in his book *Slice of Life* and his other article *The Backdrop of Punjabi Literature*, which first appeared at cultivasian.org, which is now offline.

only in the past 50 years or so that the Punjabi people and their language have started making their presence felt across the globe.

The earliest Punjabi literature is found in the fragments of writings of the Nath yogis Gorakhnath and Charpatnah, which is primarily spiritual and mystical in tone. Notwithstanding this early yogic literature, the Punjabi literary tradition is popularly seen to commence with Fariduddin Ganjshakar (1173–1266) whose Sufi poetry was compiled after his death, in the *Adi Granth*.

For almost 300 years after Farid, until the advent of Guru Nanak Devji on the scene, Punjab went through an extended phase of foreign invasions, bringing its literary/cultural march to a sudden, temporary halt. This period was dominated by the community-based efforts such as *varaans* (heroic poetry). Some of the well-known *varaans* are *Var of Dulla Bhatti and Jaimal Fatta, Tunde Asraj di Var, Kahn Bhagwan di Var, Asa di Var* et al. Sung by professional singers (*mirassis*), these *varaans* were more like Western ballads. Often dealing with wars and conflicts, these *varaans* continued to surface in the Punjabi literature up until the middle of the 19th century. In a way, Shah Mohammed's *Jungnaama*, which presents a record of the Anglo-Sikh Wars, could be seen as one of the last surviving documents of this particular genre. Apart from sensitizing people to historical developments and the need to offer resistance to invaders and marauders, these *varaans* also served as significant documentary efforts at chronicling the people's view of history.

However, this literary/cultural inertia did not last very long. The birth of the great poet Guru Nanak Dev in 1469 A.D. heralded a new chapter in the cultural history of Punjab. His poetic effusions do not find very many parallels in the history of the Bhakti movement, either. Spiritualism may have been the main force of his poetic content but it always drew its ideological strength from a certain view of social reality he subscribed to.

Rejecting ritualism and superstition, Guru Nanak emphasized social equality and brotherhood as the essence of true religion. Being both philosophical and mystical in its thematic content, his *bani* ultimately found its rightful place in the Sikh scripture, the *Guru Granth Sahib,* a rare combination of the spiritual and secular heritage of Punjabis. Guru Angad, the second Guru, could be said to have contributed a great deal towards the growth and evolution of the Punjabi language, as he was the one who actively promoted *Gurmukhi* script by extensively using it for his teachings.

However, the ambitious project of compiling the *Bani* of the Sikh Gurus in the form of the holy *Guru Granth Sahib* was initiated by Guru Arjan Dev, the fifth Guru, a process completed by Guru Gobind Singh, the tenth Guru. The *Guru Granth Sahib* is truly a repository of the collective wisdom of the Sikh Gurus, a confluence of all faiths, Sikhism, Hinduism and Islam. Composed in 31 different *ragas,* the hymns of the *Guru Granth Sahib* correspond to different moods, times and seasons. Apart from the verses and teachings of the Sikh Gurus, *Guru Granth Sahib* gives a fair representation to the hymns and thoughts of Kabir, Namdev, Ravidas, Sheikh Farid and several others. In the context of the Punjabi literature, *Guru Granth Sahib* occupies the same pre-eminent, canonical position that is often conceded to *Bible* in the realm of English literature. Undoubtedly, it is one of the greatest works of poetry and/or literature in the history of the Punjabi culture and tradition.

The Janamsakhis or the life stories on the life and legend of Guru Nanak (1469–1539) are early examples of Punjabi prose literature. Guru Nanak himself composed Punjabi verse incorporating vocabulary from Sanskrit, Arabic, Persian and other South Asian languages as characteristic of the Gurbani tradition.

Between 1616 and 1666, a writer named Abdullah composed a major work called *Bara Anva* (Twelve Topics), which is a treatise on Islam in 9,000 couplets. Punjabi Sufi poetry developed under Shah Hussain (1538–1599), Sultan Bahu (1628–1691), Shah Sharaf (1640–1724), Ali Haider (1690–1785) and Bulleh Shah (1680–1757). In contrast to Persian poets, who had preferred the *ghazal* for poetic expression, Punjabi Sufi poets tended to compose in the *Kafi* (a poetic form).

Punjabi Sufi poetry also influenced other Punjabi literary traditions particularly the Punjabi *Qissa* (a narrative in verse), a genre of romantic tragedy, which also derived inspiration from Indic, Persian and Quranic sources. The Qissa of *Heer Ranjha* by Waris Shah (1706–1798) is among the most popular of Punjabi Qissa. Other popular stories include *Sohni Mahiwal* by Fazal Shah, *Mirza Sahiba* by Hafiz Barkhudar (1658–1707), *Sassi Punnun* by Hashim Shah (1735–1843) and *Qissa Puran Bhagat* by Qadaryar (1802–1892). Another form of poetic expression was *Masnavi*. Later, in the modern period, this strain of Sufi poetry reincarnated itself in the poetry of Bhai Mohan Singh, Shiv Kumar Batalavi, Surjit Patar and several others.

The Victorian novel, Elizabethan drama, free verse and Modernism entered Punjabi literature through the introduction of British education during the Raj. The first Punjabi printing press (using Gurmukhi font) was established through a Christian mission at Ludhiana in 1835, and the first Punjabi dictionary was published by Reverend J. Newton in 1854. Modern Punjabi literature began about 1860. A number of trends in modern poetry can be discerned. To the more traditional genres of narrative, poetry, mystic verse and love poems were added nationalist poetry in a humorous or satiric mood and experimental verse.

The Punjabi novel was developed through Nanak Singh and Vir Singh. Vir Singh wrote historical romance through such novels as *Sundari, Satwant Kaur* and *Baba Naudh Singh*, whereas Nanak Singh helped link the novel to the storytelling traditions of Qissa and oral tradition as well as to questions of social reform something that Sohan Singh Seetal and Jaswant Singh Kanwal, who were to come later, also tried to emulate, fairly successfully.

The novels, short stories and poetry of Amrita Pritam highlighted, among other themes, the experience of women and the Partition of India. Punjabi poetry during the British Raj moreover began to explore more the experiences of the common man and the poor through the work of Puran Singh. Other poets meanwhile, such as Dhani Ram Chatrik, Diwan Singh and Ustad Daman, explored and expressed nationalism in their poetry during and after the Indian freedom movement. Chatrik's poetry, steeped in Indian traditions of romance and classical poetry, often celebrated varied moods of nature in his verse as well as feelings of patriotism. Brought up on English and American poetry, Puran Singh was also influenced by Freudian psychology in his oftentimes unabashedly, sensuous poetry.

Modernism was also introduced into Punjabi poetry by Prof. Mohan Singh and Shareef Kunjahi. The Punjabi diaspora also began to emerge during the Raj and also produced poetry whose theme was revolt against British rule in *Ghadar di Gunj* (Echoes of Mutiny).

Najm Hosain Syed, Fakhar Zaman and Afzal Ahsan Randhawa are some of the more prominent names in West Punjabi literature produced in Pakistan since 1947. Literary criticism in Punjabi has also emerged through the efforts of West Punjabi scholars and poets, Shafqat Tanvir Mirza, Ahmad Salim and Najm Hosain Syed.

The work of Zaman and Randhawa often treats the rediscovery of Punjabi identity and language in Pakistan since 1947. Ali's short story collection *Kahani Praga* and Mansha Yaad's collection *Wagda Paani* and his novel *Tawan Tawan Tara* are quite celebrated. Another successful author has been Mir Tanha Yousafi, who has had his books transliterated into Gurmukhi for Indian Punjabi readers.

Urdu poets of the Punjab have also written Punjabi poetry including Munir Niazi. The poet who introduced new trends in Punjabi poetry is Pir Hadi Abdul Mannan. Though a Punjabi poet, he also wrote poetry in Urdu.

Punjabi fiction in modern times has explored various themes in modernist and post-modernist literature. Moving from the propagation of Sikh thought and ideology to the themes of the Progressive Movement, the short story in Punjabi was taken up by Nanak Singh, Charan Singh Shaheed, Joshua Fazal Deen and Heera Singh Dard. Women writers such as Ajeet Cour and Dalip Kaur Tiwana meanwhile have questioned cultural patriarchy and the subordination of women in their work. Hardev Grewal has introduced a new genre to Punjabi fiction called *Punjabi Murder Mystery* in 2012 with his Punjabi novel *Eh Khudkushi Nahin Janab!*

Qatl Hai (published by Lahore Books). Kulwant Singh Virk stories are gripping and provide deep insight into the rural and urban modern Punjab. He has been hailed as the 'emperor of Punjabi short stories.'

Modern Punjabi drama developed through Ishwar Nanda's Ibsen-infulenced *Suhag* in 1913, and Gursharan Singh who helped popularize the genre through live theatre in Punjabi villages. Sant Singh Sekhon, Kartar Singh Duggal, Balwant Gargi and Atamjit, amongst others, took Punjabi drama to a new level.

Punjabi diaspora literature has developed through writers in the United Kingdom, Canada, Australia and the United States, as well as writers in Africa such as Ajaib Kamal. Themes explored by diaspora writers include the cross-cultural experience of Punjabi migrants, racial discrimination, exclusion and assimilation as well as the experience of women in the diaspora and spirituality in the modern world. Second-generation writers of Punjabi ancestry such as Rupinderpal Singh Dhillon (writes under the name Roop Dhillon) have explored the relationship between British Punjabis and their immigrant parents as well as experiment with surrealism, science fiction and crime fiction. Other known writers include Mazhar Tirmazi, Sadhu Binning and Ajmer Rode, Amarjit Chandan, Harjeet Atwal, Shivcharan Jaggi Kussa and Surjit Kalsi.

Effect of Partition[2]

West Punjabis feel that they were the foremost losers of the script divide as almost all the Punjabi writers who migrated to East Punjab were well-versed in both Gurmukhi and Shahmukhi as Urdu and Farsi were compulsory subjects at primary level in public schools of the pre-partitioned Punjab. On the other hand, majority of the Pakistani Punjabi writers could only read and write in Shahmukhi.

One language, two scripts, many religions and divided land; this is how the Punjabis had been decisively divided by history.

---

2   *Source:* an abridged version of the article, *Scripted Wall of Punjab* by Mahmood Awan. Article used with permission of the author.

When the red clouds of partition cleared and Punjabis tried to make sense of all the blood and dust, literature became their only refuge. Laments were written and stories told, narrating a collective sense of grief and shame but partition of the scripts did not even let them cry together.

But as mentioned above, the language of Baba Farid, Guru Nanak and Damodar Das has something special about it. In the darkest of times and against all odds, it has had the resilience to survive. Soon after partition, this situation was realized and damage control was initiated. Darshan Singh Awara's *Baghavat* (Rebellion), Mohan Singh's *Savey Pattar* (Green Leaves), Amrita Pritam's *Navin Rutt* (The New Season) and Ahmad Rahi's *Trinjan* (The Joint) were the first few books to appear in both scripts and across borders.

In East Punjab, systematic transcription of 'Pakistani Punjabi Literature' (PPL) started in the mid 1970s with the publication of *Dukh Daryaon Par Dey* (With angst from across the river), an anthology of poems by 61 West Punjabi poets, edited by Attar Singh and Jagtar in 1975. Jagtar did the transliteration of this collection. He did transliterate a number of West Punjabi writers afterwards.

A decade later, Punjabi got another group of passionate workers in the shape of Jatinderpal Singh Jolly, Karnail Singh Thind, Prem Parkash and later Talwinder Singh and Jinder. Jolly transliterated many works of West Punjabi poetry and fiction with the help of his wife Jagjit Kaur. Prem Parkash also introduced Pakistani Punjabi Literature (PPL) on the pages of his prestigious magazine *Lakeer*. Balraj Sahni transliterated many poems of Faiz and Amarjit Chandan the Punjabi poetry of Habib Jalib. As Pakistani Punjabi Literature is part of post-graduate Punjabi syllabus in East Punjab and many dissertations are done on it, there is hardly any notable West Punjabi book, which is not published in the Gurmukhi script.

In West Punjab, these efforts were reciprocated by Sibtul Hasan Zaigham, Ahmad Salim and Afzal Ahsan Randhawa. Then came Ilyas Ghuman, Iqbal Qaiser, Maqsood Saqib, Afzal Saahir, Javed

Boota, Kitab Trinjan and APNA (Academy of the Punjab in North America). APNA continuously publishes transliterated books from Gurmukhi to Shahmukhi and vice versa, including works of Baba Nanak, Puran Singh, Balwant Gargi, Nanak Singh, Kartar Singh Duggal, Shiv Kumar, Pash, Surjit Patar, Mushtaq Soofi and Najm Hosain Syed. Fictional works of Santokh Singh Dhir, Kulwant Singh Virk, Waryam Sindhu, Gurdial Singh, Dalip Kaur Tiwana, Devender Satyarthi, selected poems of S.S. Misha and complete poetry of Pash were made available by Suchet Kitab Ghar.

Kitab Trinjan introduced us to Amarjit Chandan's essays and poetry and published selected poems of Lal Singh Dil. Akhtar Husain's monthly *Lehran* was the first to publish East Punjabi content and then Safir Rammah's *Sanjh* became the only magazine published in both scripts in separate volumes with identical content, from Lahore and Ludhiana.

I hope that these bridges stay intact, the friendship lives on, the publishers on both sides start respecting copyrights and we the bare-footed, meshed hair Punjabis keep rejoicing every message transmitted from across our five rivers in the name of Bulleh Shah *"Payron Nangi, Sirron Jhandoli, Aaya Saneha Paroun; Annhi Chunnhi Di Tikki Pakkay, Dayla Sandal Baroun."*

The Punjab is defined not by its political boundaries but by its linguistic geography, because political boundaries may be sublime but linguistic connections are permanent. This collective lingual unity of the Punjab has been nurtured by its selfless commoners for centuries and they are its real custodians. The people of Punjab belong to the land of Sapta Sindhu (ancient name of our land in Rig Ved proudly boasting of its seven rivers with Indus and Sarasvati included) and their culture and destinies are intertwined. Ours is an all-inclusive native phenomenon engraved in our souls by humanity and humility of Baba Farid, Guru Nanak and Damodar Das.

Punjabi Novel

According to author Prof Niranjan Tasneem, in his book, *Studies in Modern Punjabi Literature*, the Punjabi Novel, in the initial stages was occupied with presentation of the outer life of men and women. The story in a Punjabi novel was generally told from the omniscient point of view. It was supposed to have a conscious moral purpose also. It was usually thought of satisfying our curiosity, rather than our craving for beauty, meaning and significance. Initially, it had action and more action. Nanak Singh the father of Punjabi novel learnt his art from Munshi Premchand, Sarat Chandra and Leo Tolstoy. The emphasis in all his novels was on the outer life and not the inner life. He was of course conscious of inner tensions in human beings, but he never allowed his readers to peep in the minds of his characters. He wanted his readers to feel satisfied with the description of the outward manifestations of inner strains and stresses.

Like a colossus, Nanak Singh walked across half a century of intense creative activity. He influenced almost all the Punjabi novelists, one way or the other. However, Gurdial Singh makes a break from this tradition. Though his primary concern is also to tell a story, but he takes pain to delineate his characters, not in broad strokes but with small strokes. His characters reveal their mind through conversations and at times through introspection.

Nanak Singh, Jaswant Singh Kanwal and Gurdial Singh are 'materialists' and regard fiction more as a criticism of life than as a re-creation of the complexities of experience. However, writers like Surinder Singh Narula, Amrita Pritam, Narendrapal Singh, Kartar Singh Duggal and Surjit Singh Sethi are mostly concerned with re-creation of the complexities of experience, the registering of the minutest details of modern sensibility and capturing of the very atmosphere of the mind of their characters. Kartar Singh Duggal's *Andraan*, a novel written in the Pothoari dialect and steeped in the localism of the same region, its geography, economy, ecology, customs and conventions, was published as far back as 1948. In a way, emergence of this particular form of novel did help in foregrounding hardcore social realism in the Punjabi novel, which was to acquire its ideological underpinnings from a curious blend of Marxist thought and Gandhian socialism. Sant Singh Sekhon, Surinder Singh Narula, Amrita Pritam and Narinderpal

Singh, among several others, made a consistent and significant contribution towards this paradigm shift. By enabling the fiction to shed its obsessive, maudlin sentimentality, even quasi-romantic character, these luminaries slowly but surely paved the way for the advent of a truly modernist novel in Punjabi, with a distinctive psychological/sociological thrust.

This can be seen especially in S. S. Narula's *Peo Putter* (Father and Son), Narendrapal Singh's *Tapu* (The Island), Duggal's *Ik Dil Vikau Hai* and his trilogy *Hall Mureedan Da* and Surjit Singh Sethi's *Ik Khali Payala*. In Amrita Pritam's novels, an attempt has been made to see into the life of things. She is seized with the ultimate reality and not the immediate one. Her efforts have been to catch the tone, the light and shade of experience, especially in her works like *Jalawatan* and *Ik Si Anita*. Realism takes a deeper hue in Sant Singh Sekhon's novel *Lahu Mitti*. The tradition is further carried on by writers like Dalip Kaur Tiwana, Ajeet Kaur, Om Prakash Gasso, Ram Sarup Ankhi and Mohan Kahlon amongst others.

If Gurdial Singh radicalized the Punjabi novel by infusing into it a new consciousness about the oppressed/underprivileged, Ajeet Cour and Dalip Kaur Tiwana opened up newer possibilities by interrogating the marginalized status/position of Punjabi women in a heavily accented, feudal and patriarchal, societal regime. Niranjan Tasneem, Mohan Kahlon, Surjit Sethi and several others, in their distinctive ways, have continued to push the frontiers of the Punjabi fiction.

The contemporary Punjabi Novel is now a maelstrom of various trends and has taken firm roots. A new social-political consciousness has crept in the writers of today who want to project their point of view forcefully, their theme, in the main being, the conflict between haves and have-nots. These writers belong to rural areas and have first-hand knowledge of both the exploiters and of the exploited. Story-telling has given way to character delineation. Well-made novel is yielding place to the point of view novel. The element of story is still very important in the Punjabi novel, but generally speaking, it is no more told from the omniscient point of view. The novelist now identifies more with his/her characters. The modern Punjabi novel has not escaped the impact of changing concepts of morality. The age-old conceptions of right and wrong in moral behaviour have given place to new ones. As a result, the treatment of sex is finding a predominant place in the creative efforts of some of the modern Punjabi writers. Writers like Rajinder Singh Bedi in *Ik Chaddar Adhorani*; Amrita Pritam in *Chak Number Chhatti*; Surjit Hans in *Mitti di Dheri*; Manjit Rana in *Angrez Kurian*; Jagjit Chhabra in *Lahu Mass*, Mohan Kahlon in *Beri te Bareta* and very recently Fauzia Rafique in *Skeena* are examples of modern Punjabi novelists who are fully conscious of their role in fast-changing society. They are grappling with the basic issues of life, intimately connected with new morality.

All this does not mean that the old has completely yielded. The old and the new are existing side by side. This co-existence is undoubtedly enriching the Punjabi novel.

Punjabi Poetry

Poetic works of Muslim fakirs who were called Sufis makes a major portion of Punjabi poetry of the middle period, i.e. sixteenth and seventeenth century A.D., Sheikh Farid being one of the major figures, followed by Shah Husain, Bulleh Shah, Ali Haidar, Damodar Gulati, Pilu, Hafiz Barkhurdar, Hashim Shah, Muqbil, Waris Shah and Fazal Shah.

Fazal Shah wrote five kissas, *Sohni-Mahiwal, Sassi-Punnu, Laila-Majnu, Heer-Ranjha* and *Yusuf-Zuleikha*, according to the convention of Khamsa (five) or Panj Ganj (Five Treasures) set by Persian poet Nizami; Mohammad Baksh is best known for his romance of *Saif-ul Maluk*, though he has written some other kissas also like *Sohni-Mahiwal, Shirin-Farhad, Mirza-Sahiban* and *Badi'ul Jamal*; Kishan Singh Arif (1836–1900) inherited his love of kissas from his father Narain Singh and was a disciple of Sant Gulab Das or Gulab Singh Nirmala and wrote 26 works some of which are kissas, like *Heer-Ranjha, Shirin-Farhad, Puran-Bhagat, Bharthari-Hari, Raja Rasalu* and *Dulla*

Bhatti. Mohammad Buta Gujarati wrote about 20 compositions including Khamsa (five) of romances, *Sohni-Mahiwal, Sassi-Punnu, Mirza-Sahiban* and *Chander Badan*. The last is a story of two lovers Chander Badan and Mayyar. Ahmad Yar and Qadaryar wrote both Kissas and Vaars.

Punjabi Poetry in the Modern Context

Apart from Bhai Vir Singh, Dhani Ram 'Chatrik,' Puran Singh, Mohan Singh, Amrita Pritam are among the prominent poets of the first generation, who sought to re-inscribe the ideology and aesthetics of Punjabi poetry in the modern context. Though in some form or the other, their poetry bore the scars of the trauma of Partition, each one of them wrote in as varied an idiom and as distinct a voice as anyone could. Steeped in the Indian tradition of romance and conforming to the classical rigour, Chatrik used poetry to celebrate varied moods of nature, or occasionally evoke an undying sense of patriotism through his nationalist verses. Brought up on a heavy dose of English and American poetry, Puran Singh was definitely more liberal and direct than most of his predecessors, and his poetic expression always bristled with naked sensuousness and primal celebration of human body. Mohan Singh could be described as a 'progressive modern' for it was he who liberated Punjabi poetry from the constraints of mysticism and/or revivalism. He was a very versatile poet who wrote on a wide range of subjects, from the romantic felicities of *Saave Pattar* to the political consciousness of *Adhvate*, from the Freudian flights of *Kasumbhara* to the socialist fancies of *Vadda Vela*. If there is anything that defines Amrita Pritam's poetry, it is the boldness of her expression, pungency of her social criticism and relentless critique of defunct morality that often works to the detriment of women.

After Mohan Singh and Amrita Pritam came the soul-stirring lyricism of Shiv Batalvi and the thought content of Harbhajan Singh that infused new possibilities into Punjabi poetry scene. Shiv Batalvi created such haunting melodies of pain and suffering that they continue to resound in our hearts, even today. To this day, his poetic drama *Luna* remains one of the best works ever produced in contemporary Punjabi literature. Among the second generation of poets, we may mention Pritam Singh 'Safeer,' Santokh Singh Dheer, Prabhjot Kaur and Jaswant Singh Neki, who, through their varied contributions, enriched the ever-growing corpus of modern Punjabi poetry.

In the 1960s, Punjab suddenly found itself in the vortex of the Naxalite movement, much in the manner of other states of India, where the failure to implement land reforms had backfired. So extensive was the influence of this movement that it threatened to swallow up all the major gains Punjab was poised to make on account of the Green Revolution. Such were the conditions that led the progressive movement into its militant phase, with Bawa Balwant, Pash, Ravinder Ravi, Ajaib Kamal, Harbhajan Halwarvi, Amarjit Chandan and several others emerging as its major votaries. Their poetry is political and has revolutionary fervour, showing solidarity with the oppressed.

Though this phase did not last very long, it seems to have left a lasting impact on the growth of the contemporary Punjabi poetry. Surjit Patar and Dr. Jagtar are among those who were influenced by it, but have, over the years, softened a great deal and now integrate their lyrical aestheticism with social criticism truly well. Among others, some of the younger poets are Mohanjit, Jaswant Deed, Swrajbir, Joga Singh, Sati Kumar and Dev.

Another feature of modern Punjabi poetry is the presence of an overwhelmingly large number of women poets, who have impressed their readers not only by virtue of their prolific output but also by the quality of their contributions. Manjit Tiwana, Pal Kaur, Surjit Kalsi, Nirupama Dutt, Gagan Gill, Amar Jyoti and Vineeta are some of the younger women poets who have charted new paths in the Punjabi poetic tradition.

Punjabi Poetry Across the Border

It has its own distinct tone, tint and flavour. Its language is one commonly spoken by the people and its themes are down to earth. Some of it is still akin to Punjabi folklore and in the main it exudes warmth and vitality, inherent in the poetry of the soil. Some is nostalgic too with an intense longing for remedying the wrongs committed by the all-too-enthusiastic people in the past. For example, Anked Saleem's poem *Main Gondal da Dhola*.

Fakhar Zaman is perhaps the most talked about poet on this side of the border along with Munir Niazi. Fakhar is an ultra modern poet using Western terms and phrases to bring home his point. In his collection of poems *Vangaar*, he has touched on many new aspects of modern civilization.

Love of course dominates over most of the poems, but in some of them, the treatment given is pleasantly novel, for example in Munir Niazi's poem *Tareeya Chalittar*.

Further many of the poets like Faiz Ahmad Faiz, Ahmed Saleem, Abbas Athar, Shareef Kunjahi, Mohmammad Safdar, Munir Niazi, Laeeq Babri, Safi Safdar and a host of others wrote both in Urdu and in Punjabi.

Punjabi Short Story

Punjabi short story writers have developed their own unique way of portraying love, longing and malice. Spanning a century, this collection of stories deal with life in the village and the town, and every story is redolent of the fragrance of Punjabi soil. Building upon the oral tradition of immortal kissas like Heer–Ranjha and Sohni–Mahiwal, the Punjabi short story began its journey a century ago. The subjects extend from love and longing in both village and town, Dalits, the other side of Punjab, extremism and the emigration of Punjabis to foreign lands.

The Punjabi language and literature, which dates back to the 9th or 10th century, certainly has a long, established tradition of storytelling. According to the literary historians, the earliest forms of short story in the Punjabi language could be traced back to the medieval forms of Sakhi literature and heroic legends such as Varaans. Interestingly, the Punjabi short story never went through its mythical stage as, quite simply, there is nothing mythical about the Punjabi language and culture; history being its constant companion right from the very beginning. Among other things, this also explains, to an extent, the preponderance of different varieties of realism in the Punjabi short story. Later, the storytelling assumed another guise in form of quissas (versified forms of popular legends), essentially based upon the extraordinary love legends of the ordinary human beings, inspired by the Sufi tradition that resonated in the land of Punjab, all through the medieval period.

In the Punjabi language, however, Charan Singh Shaheed, Joshua Fazal Deen, Heera Singh Dard and Nanak Singh were among the early practitioners of the short story. Some of the factors that helped in popularizing this form in its early days were the proliferation of printing presses across Punjab, the mushrooming of literary magazines, journals and newspapers, as well as the spread of literary education. In its initial stages, at least, the Punjabi short story was used as a tool for propagating Sikh ideology and thought, as most of the story-tellers also happened to be strong votaries of the Singh Sabha Movement.

With the emergence of Gurbaksh Singh Preetlari, Sant Singh Sekhon, Kulwant Singh Virk, Kartar Singh Duggal and Sujan Singh, the Punjabi short story anchored itself firmly into the progressive, Marxist ideology. This is also the time when attempts were made to harmonize the conflicting claims of ideology and aesthetics. More than others, it was Kulwant Singh Virk who understood and responded rather well to the multiple challenges that the story, as a modern form, often poses.

In a manner of speaking, most of his successors, especially Mohan Bhandari, Gurbachan Bhullar, Prem Parkash and Gulzar Sandhu *et al* owe their understanding of the art and craft of story writing to him. This tradition is being ably supported and enriched through the efforts of some of the promising storytellers on the scene today, like Chandan Negi, Jasbir Bhullar, Prem Gorky, Waryam Sandhu, Swaran Chandan,

Harjeet Atwal and Veena Verma. The contemporary Punjabi short story, being an extremely vibrant and innovative form, has a fairly bright future and even the potential to compete with the best anywhere in the world.

Punjabi Drama

Unlike the short story, drama as a form in Punjabi has not had a very eventful or a consistent track record of growth and evolution, as it has been somewhat sporadic. Interestingly, the beginnings of the Punjabi drama/theatre are often traced back to the efforts of Norah Richards, the Irish wife of a Unitarian minister preaching in Punjab. An amateur actor, she had also been associated with the Irish National Theatre Dublin once. Around 1913–14, Norah started drama competitions among her students of Dyal Singh College, Lahore, where she was teaching then. It was in one of these competitions that Ishwar Nanda, then a student and now widely recognized as one of the pioneers of Punjabi drama, discovered his talent for playwriting. His one-act play *Suhag* (1913) was adjudged the best and that marked the beginning of the indigenous theatre movement in Punjabi. Ishwar Nanda went on to write over 21 act plays, all of which show a definite influence of Ibsen, fired as he was by an unsparing zeal for social reform and change.

Among others, this tradition of playwriting found able and worthy legatees in Sant Singh Sekhon, Gurdial Singh Phul and Harcharan Singh, who not only strengthened but also nurtured the dramatic tradition founded by Ishwar Nanda. From time to time, Kartar Singh Duggal, Surjit Sethi, Harsharan Singh and Balwant Gargi contributed very significantly towards the incremental growth of this tradition. Of course, Gursharan Singh stands apart by virtue of his formidable contribution to the popularity and growth of street theatre in the far-off villages of Punjab.

Over a period of time, Punjabi drama has not only acquired a distinctive identity of its own but also managed to get overwhelming support from the public as well as the much-needed official recognition. That for two successive years, Sahitya

Akademi chose to confer its prestigious literary award upon two eminent playwrights in Punjabi, Charan Das Sidhu and Ajmer Aulakh, is an ample proof of the kind of popularity Punjabi drama is beginning to enjoy now.

Atamjit, who invariably writes and directs his own plays, has, in fact, crossed the narrow, geographical barriers of Punjab and staged his plays in Canada as well as the United States. Another person, who is responsible for giving international exposure to Punjabi theatre, is Neelam Man Singh Chaudhury, though she is primarily a director, not a playwright. Fusing together elements of Punjabi folk and classical forms such as the dhadhi (a form of recital), kavishar (ad lib performance) and gatha (martial arts), she has – under the banner of her production house, The Company – staged plays in France, England, Germany, Japan, the United States and elsewhere.

New Trends in Punjabi Literature[3]

At present, Dalit writing is occupying center stage in the world of Punjabi letters, motivated as it is by the struggle against oppression.

When Sikhism came into being during the 15th century, it was primarily as a protest against the caste system, in the same manner that leftist and other progressive movements came into being in reaction to the same malaise in modern times. In this context, the road to the Dalit identity has been a long one in Punjab, largely because such identification was submerged in the Sikh identity, with much pride and celebration in the earliest known Dalit writings of the 17th century – Bhai Jaito. The celebratory mood was one of overcoming the ills of caste-ridden society. In time, however, the tone saddened, as a religion that had started out to reform Hinduism, it fell prey to the same ills of caste-ridden social hierarchy.

Thereafter, the second-known Dalit writer of Punjab was Peero Preman (1830–72). Peero had earlier been a Muslim

---

3   *Source:* Abridged version of Nirupama Dutt's article "Waiting for Spring" in *Himal Southasian.* Article used with permission of the author.

courtesan named Ayesha and later joined the Gulabdasia sect and inherited sainthood from her mentor, Gulab Das. Ditt Singh Giani (1852–1901), another Dalit writer, also made significant contributions to Punjabi literature, particularly in terms of defining Sikh thought. He was also founder-editor of a newspaper, *Khalsa Akhbar*, in Lahore. Similarly, Sadhu Daya Singh Arif, also a Dalit, (1894–1946) was a theologian and writer who enjoyed great popularity.

Punjab has a higher percentage of Dalits than any other state in modern-day India, making up almost 30 percent of the population. However, this community owns just 2.3 percent of the cultivated agricultural land in the state. Some 70 percent of Sikhs live in rural Punjab, as did a major chunk of the Dalits who worked as labourers in the fields before they moved to other jobs, making way for migrant labour to take their place. The relationship between the Jat landlords and their landless labourers was a complex one. The lower castes worked with the upper-caste Jats and, although the 'otherness' was the accepted order, there were instances of close bonding and even addressing elders as uncle (chacha or taya) or aunt (bhua, masi). The experience and skills of the elders were respected; tilling of the land was a shared task, and the relative well-being of everyone depended on it. The lower castes took on the caste name of their masters, and it was natural that there were amorous ties. Yet the clear-cut caste divide was always there – as were separate wells for drinking water and separate cremation grounds.

In the customary scheme of working relationships, outcastes such as Mazhabi (chura or sweeper Sikhs), Ramdasi (chamar or leatherworker Sikhs), Balmiki, Ravidasi, Musalli, Teli, Mochi and others were not allowed to own land but were allowed to build temporary structures on the shamlat, or village common land.

It is against this backdrop that contemporary Dalit writing emerged. The early Dalit writers of modern times were distinctly leftwing in their approach, with a strong belief in an equal social order. The first poet to voice these concerns was Gurdas Ram

Alam (1912–89). Direct descendants of Alam's creed were Sant Ram Udasi (1939–86) and Lal Singh Dil (1943–2007), revolutionary poets whose work served as inspiration for the Naxalite uprisings of the 1960s.

In this context, the past decade has also seen the emergence of the autobiography, including those of Dil, Madhopuri, Prem Gorkhi and Attarjit. The latter two are accomplished short-fiction writers and have explored the Dalit consciousness through their reality. In addition, Des Raj Kali, Bhagwant Rasoolpuri, Mohal Lal Phillauria and Nachhatar are among other contemporary fiction writers exploring the Dalit consciousness.

Across the border, in East Punjab, also the Hindu malaise of the caste system was sadly transferred even to Islam, and caste stratification can today be found in Pakistan. Indeed, the titles used in the two Punjabs for Dalits who were taken into the folds of Sikhism and Islam – Mazhabi (one who has a religion) is used for the Dalit who embraced Sikhism and Musalli (one who offers prayers) for those who have embraced Islam – are technically positive, but are generally used offensively. This implies that a change of name need not necessarily be accompanied with a change of attitude.

In contrast to the situation in Indian Punjab, Pakistan does not have Dalit writing as such, unlike the voluminous writing on the Dalits in India, especially from the left. In East Punjab, in his classic novel *Marhi da Diva*, Gurdial Singh immortalized Jagseer – the landless protagonist who toils and dies unsung but for the wife of the upper-caste Jat, who goes and lights a lamp on his humble tomb, as they shared unexpressed love for each other; and in West Punjab, meanwhile, Major Ishaq Mohammad, founding president of the Mazdoor Kissan Party (MKP) and a revolutionary thinker, poet, playwright, told the unhappy tale in his very popular play called *Musalli*.

The journey of Punjabi Literature would comprise of many more things like growth of Punjabi criticism, literature of the Punjabi diaspora, etc. However, attempt has been made here to just give a bird's eye view of Punjabi literature and to sum up some of the major trends, movements and developments that swept through the Punjabi literature and/or literary forms in course of its long march over a thousand years or so. This is not a comprehensive guide but an introduction of sorts, which it is hoped, may motivate readers to delve deeper and to know more.

AUTOBIOGRAPHIES

Ajeet Cour

- *Pebbles in a Tin Drum* by Ajeet Cour; Translated by Masooma Ali; Published by Harper Collins.

Author, activist and social worker Ajeet Cour (1934–), one of the best-known writers in the Punjabi language, believes that the arts and literature can help build bridges across cultures. She set up the Foundation of SAARC Writers and Literature, a unique track II (people-to-people contact) initiative to establish peace on the subcontinent.

Ajeet Cour began her career as a romance writer, but soon matured into a realist. Women's issues and peace have always been the overriding concerns in her works. Her columns and writing have established her role as a crusader for women's issues. Known for having pioneered the art of writing novelettes in Punjabi, she has authored 17 books of fiction and two volumes of autobiographies. Cour also set up the Academy of Fine Arts and Literature, which aims to create an atmosphere of greater understanding through the arts. She has also initiated a process of translation of literary works in different languages of the region, believing that this will help the people of South Asia develop a broader and more genuine understanding of one another.

Her memoir, *Pebbles in a Tin Drum* was published in Hindi and Punjabi as *Khanabadosh* (which means 'nomad' or 'vagabond'). It is a very personal, candid and touching account of her life although it is just the first volume. The second volume, published in Punjabi and Hindi as *Koorha Kabara*, has not yet been translated into English.

Cour was born in Lahore. From a very early age, she was aware of the prevalent discrimination against girls. Although she had a warm and enchanting childhood, her grandparents and even her Darji (father) would prohibit her from doing many things. After Partition, they moved to Shimla, Jalandhar and finally settled in Delhi. Despite restrictions, she attended college and met Baldev, her English teacher, who introduced her to a life of writing and with whom she had a failed romance filled with trivial misunderstandings and conflicts of egos. Baldev went on to join the IAS, but Cour continued loving him even though she did not ever contact him again.

Her eventual marriage was a disaster; her husband, Rajinder Singh was a doctor and, by all accounts, a sadist. She suffered 12 long, nightmarish years with him while he detested her for producing two daughters. Finally, unable to bear the trauma, she walked out on him and started life afresh. As a single mother in Delhi, she struggled to support herself and her daughters while working as a writer. She started her career in the 1960s as a teacher and the editor of the business journal *Rupee Trade*, which she ran for 32 years. Those were the days of extreme poverty but she savoured her independence and managed to put life back on track. She also educated the girls at good schools. Delhi is unkind to most people, especially to women, and Cour had many enocunters with powerful, scheming landlords. In 1974, she lost her younger daughter, Candy (just 19 years old), to a fire accident in France. *Pebbles in a Tin Drum* starts with a very moving account of this tragedy; heartbroken, Cour writes, 'She has spent her childhood sharing her mother's poverty and how she had to face her father's temper and hatred. Things have just started getting a little better.'

In her memoir, she also gives an account of her experience as a Sikh woman in Delhi during the Sikh genocide in 1984. In fact, one of her short stories, *Navambar Chaurasi* (November 1984), is about the pioneering work she did in providing relief to the victims while her landlord, a lawyer and an M.P., was harassing her to vacate the house. The books ends with her love affair with a person called Oma, a married man. She, 'the other woman' (she has also written a short story of this name and about this), carries on with him for seven years in the vain hope that he would leave his wife and come to her (a promise which he had made). The sheer honesty with she describes those days is overwhelming. Many people feel that the dividing line between fact and fiction is difficult to detect, especially when she expatiates on her love affairs. The first volume ends on the breakup with Oma.

Even though Cour's life has been pretty unconventional, she remains, in many ways, a traditional Punjabi Sikh woman. For instance, when her daughter is dying in a French hospital, she takes frequent recourse in prayer. This autobiography amazes the reader with the honesty and the simplicity with which the most searing and tumultuous events in a person's life are described. It is a tribute to her spirit – a spirit that was not overcome by such events. Instead, Cour rose above and went on to write beautiful literature and do pioneering work in the field of arts and social service.

Amrita Pritam

- *The Revenue Stamp (Raseedi Ticket): An Autobiography* by Amrita Pritam; Translated by Krishna Gorowara; Published by Wide Canvas, an imprint of Vikas Publishing House Pvt. Ltd.

Amrita Pritam (1919–2005) was the first prominent woman writer who was loved on both sides of the India–Pakistan border. With a career spanning over six decades, she produced over 100 books of poetry, fiction, biography, essays, a collection of Punjabi folk songs, and an autobiography that was translated into several Indian and foreign languages.

Khushwant Singh, the acclaimed writer, once told Pritam that the story of her life was so inconsequential and tiny that it could be written on the back of a revenue stamp. Keeping this jest in mind, when Pritam penned her autobiography, she gave it the title *Raseedi Ticket*, or *The Revenue Stamp*. As it turned out, this inconsequential and tiny memoir went on to become one of the most translated books of Punjabi Literature.

This book is about her friendships and relationships, interspersed with her verses and thoughts on some characters. The book is a delightful assembly of snippets from her life. She keeps, more or less, to the chronology of events. Her story is laid out in a series of episodes that she feels were significant in her life. So, we hear, among other things, about how her mother married her father, the genesis of her name, her mother's death, her disillusionment with God at that moment and why she took to writing.

Although it does not read like a cohesive story, we do get an idea of what her life was like. She speaks about her relationship with Sahir, her relationship with the Pakistani writer Sajjad

Haider, and, of course, with her dream companion, Imroz. She recounts numerous episodes in her life featuring these men. She is completely honest about how she feels about them and, just as it should be, spares us the indignity of voyeurism by leaving out intimate details.

There are chapters devoted to her dreams and how she believes they are omens and often solutions to the problems she faced at the time. Her spirituality is eclectic; she believes in Sikhism, Sufis of various types, and Sadhus and Sants rumoured to have special powers.

She is true to herself as a woman and believes in telling the truth, as she knows it. The few poems and nazms that she showcases in the book are breathtaking. She writes about what inspired her to create her famous poem, *Ajj Akhan Waris Shah Noon* (Today I invoke Waris Shah – "Ode to Waris Shah" – an elegy to the 18th century Punjabi poet), an expression of her anguish over massacres during the Partition of India. She also recounts the acclaim the poem received all over. In Pakistan, where a special festival takes place on the theme of Waris Shah, her poem is recited and enacted to this day.

When it was first published, her other famous poem, *Mata Tripta Da Sapna*, ran afoul of the Sikh clergy. They were mortified that anyone could write so naturally and intimately about the mother of Guru Nanak. Pritam tells us of how one winter night when her son calls her on the phone. She slips hurriedly out of a warm quilt to receive the call. Exchanging a few words with her son fills her with tender warmth all over. She is reminded of what it is like to carry a child in her womb, but she was just an ordinary woman bearing an ordinary child. She wonders what Mata Tripta felt when carrying a divine child like Guru Nanak.

She also pens a heartfelt ode to her constant companion, Imroz, who gave her emotional space and continuously supported her. Pritam's prose is extremely poetic and full of metaphors and delightful imagery.

Many describe Pritam as the goddess of defiance – a rebel and a revolutionary who lived her life intensely. She had an admirable influence on Punjabi literature and is known as the most important voice for women in Punjabi literature. In 1956, she became the first woman to win the Sahitya Akademi Award for her long poem, *Sunehe* (Messages). Later, she would become a recipient of the Bhartiya Jnanpith for *Kagaz Te Canvas* (The Paper and the Canvas), the Padma Shri, the Padma Vibhushan, and India's highest literary award, the Sahitya Akademi Fellowship given to the 'immortals of literature' for lifetime achievements in the field of literature. She would also go on to receive the International Vaptsarov Award from Bulgaria and Ordre des Arts et des Lettres (Officier) from France. She was nominated as a member of the Rajya Sabha (1986–92) and she received honorary degrees from many universities including Delhi University, Jabalpur University and Vishwa Bharati.

Towards the end of her life, she was awarded by Pakistan's Punjabi Academy – Punjabi poets of Pakistan sent her a *chaddar* (quilt) from the tombs of Waris Shah, Bulle Shah and Sultan Bahu.

Pritam worked until 1961 with All India Radio, Delhi. She edited *Nagmani*, a monthly literary magazine in Punjabi for several years, which she published with Imroz. After Partition, she wrote prolifically in Hindi as well.

Bachint Kaur

- *Tracks and Trails (Pagdanddian): An Autobiography* by Bachint Kaur; Translated by Ranjit Singh; Published by Unistar Books Pvt. Ltd.

I have included six autobiographies in my collection and all six are heart-rending. All these authors had had a very difficult life, yet they managed to complete their education somehow and fulfilled their desire to write. These books are a life lesson to all of us, and we salute their indomitable spirit. It doesn't mean that the other writers featured here had an easy life, but since we are not privy to their autobiographies we can comment only on what we have.

The author, Bachint Kaur, had a modest upbringing in Village Bharo and then in the city of Patiala. She was the third daughter born to her parents, and her grandmother berated both the mother and the little girl on her birth. However, three brothers succeeded her and only then was she was treated as a lucky charm – one who brought happy tidings thereafter.

Circumstances in the family resulted in her getting married at the young age of 11 to a wayward boy. The boy's family hoped that marriage would force him to be responsible, which he eventually never did. She became a mother at the age of 14 or 15, but her elder brother-in-law threw her family and her husband's parents out of their house. Her father-in-law was a tailor but her husband did not work and so, after she had another child, she decided to study up to matriculation (Grade 10) so that she could get a job. Her sister-in-law was also with them. Ultimately, she enrolled in grade 8, her sister-in-law enrolled in grade 7 and her daughter started nursery – all in the same school.

She and her sister-in-law got a job to distribute milk in the morning for Rs. 50 per month before going to school. Then, she would come back to do housework, take care of the kids and only after dinner, try to finish her homework. She did all this when she was only 16 years old. The house they lived in had no electricity, because they could not afford it. For 17 years, they lived without electricity, studying under a kerosene lamp.

Kaur wanted to study but she was required to work and earn to bring food to the table. She joined as a sales girl in a store where she had to work for 10 hours a day along with her morning milk distribution work. But she continued relentlessly taking various examinations privately as she could ill-afford to join regular classes. She learnt type writing, learnt the job of telephone operator, and graduated grade 10 in the hope of getting a government job, but she was rejected everywhere because she had no recommendations. She then did her Gyani (Honours in Punjabi), applied for FA (Intermediate Class equivalent to Class 10 & 11) (could clear after three attempts) and then B.A., all the time working, bringing up the kids and battling an indifferent husband. Her difficult experiences at the store resulted in her writing her first story, *Deevian wali Raat*, which she sent to an almost unknown magazine but it got published.

Her success at graduation motivated her to study for an M.A. in Punjabi, and she joined evening classes at Delhi University where she would go after her job ended at 6 pm, only returning home at 11 pm. She finally managed to apply for an M. Phil after she got her first daughter married – at the age of 35. Such was her zest for studying.

But behind each of these steps there were multiple challenges and the harrowing tales of difficulties faced by her at each step. She would face unruly and lecherous customers at stops as girls staffing shops was a new thing at that time; she would be harassed by equally lecherous men on her return from college at night and face open suggestions for sexual favours to get jobs. Along the line, she lost her only and constant support at home (her father-in law) and soon their landlord threw them out of house. Her family had nowhere to go and resorted to building a hut on an open plot. With no water supply, they had to get water from the common municipal tap, often waiting for long in the queue; her mother-in-law suffered from paralysis and had to be attended to; soon the corporation razed their hut and they had to rebuild it.

Finally, in 1965, at the age of 25, after battling so much at such a young age, she landed her first government job as a keypunch operator for a salary of Rs. 200. She continued her education, taught her children, successfully raised them and continued to write. She now has a great body of work, having written numerous short stories, travelogues, novels, poems, children's literature, stories for TV and films, and a literary biography too.

This autobiography ends on a very poignant note – Kaur led a life without much love but she fondly remembers one man, Krishna Raj, who was a producer at All India Radio and who also translated many of her stories. They started liking each other but her husband mistreated him and this relationship ended even before it began. Though they never met after that, she writes that she could never forget her selfless love for Raj.

After reading this book, one is stunned at Kaur's endurance and her indomitable spirit to continue writing and inspiring others. What makes a person go on, despite everything? Perhaps she herself does not know, as she writes,

> What I craved, I lived not
> What I lived, I craved not
> Who prompted me to move
> And go this far I know not.

Read on:

- The other book of Bachint Kaur, translated into English is *The Rider of The Spotted Horse* (a collection of short stories); Translated by Dr. Rajinder Singh; Published by Shilalekh, Delhi

Dalip Kaur Tiwana

- *A Journey on Bare Feet* by Dr. Dalip Kaur Tiwana; Translated by Jai Ratan; Published by Disha Books.

In the pantheon of Punjabi literature, Dr. Dalip Kaur Tiwana occupies a special place. She is a renowned novelist and short-story writer who has bagged regional and national awards and is a widely translated author. She retired as Professor of Punjabi, and Dean, Faculty of Languages, Punjabi University, Patiala.

Tiwana was born in 1935 in village Rabbon in a well-to-do land-owning family. She was educated in Patiala where her uncle, Sardar Sahib Tara Singh Sidhu, was Inspector General of Prisons. She had a distinguished academic career. She got first class first in M.A., and was the first woman in the region to get a Ph.D. degree from the Panjab University, Chandigarh. She received the Padma Shri in 2004 for her contribution to literature and education but returned it in 2015 against increasing communal tension and intolerance in the country.

Tiwana studied in the Singh Sabha School up to the fifth grade and then at Victoria School. She learned to appreciate poetry from a tuition teacher. Her father made her leave school but she got readmitted. She writes nostalgically of her years in Mohindra College in Patiala where she studied for B.A. Honours. She stood first in the Gyani examination in Punjabi. She did her M.A in both History and Punjabi. Her first job was at the Government College in Dharmsala.

She has received several awards such as Sahitya Akademi Award for her novel Eho Hamara Zeehna, Best Novelist of the Decade (1980–1990) from the Punjab Academy, Govt. of Punjab Award for *Sadhana* as the best book of short stories, 1960–61, and

Gurmukh Singh Musafir Award (Languages Department, Govt. of Punjab) for *A Journey on Bare Feet*.

She has written about different stages of her life in five autobiographical books – Nange Pairaan da Safar (A Journey on Bare Feet), Poochte Ho To Suno, Tere Mere Sarokaar, Jeeun Joge and Turdyaan Turdyaan. Only the first one of these appears to have been translated into English.

This autobiographical novel is an intensely moving account of the tough struggle of a woman to realize herself both emotionally and intellectually despite open hostility. The struggle acquires poignancy when it is placed against the backdrop of a Punjab dominated by Zamindars with strong negative values. Tiwana's grandmother mourned the fact that her daughter-in-law delivered only daughters (Tiwana was the third girl in a row). Tiwana's grandmother never spoke gently to her daughter-in-law and, in fact, rebukes her in the worst manner, 'What good are you if you cannot give us a son?' Similarly, Tiwana recalls the time her marriage was arranged. With only a few months left for the wedding, boy's parents broke off the engagement. The social stigma attached to a rejected daughter was uppermost in the minds of all at home. The rejection of a daughter for marriage would also affect the prospects of Tiwana's two sisters.

Tiwana's autobiography articulates a quintessentially Indian social scenario and the associated social issues. Her account is personal, yet her struggle is universal to all women. Tiwana focuses on several concerns of women such as dowry, women's education, the general preference for sons, and the status of women. It is creditable that despite this background and the hardships she faced, she could prevail and become the most productive and most popular Punjabi novelist of our age. Dr. Tiwana has to her credit 27 novels, seven collections of short stories, her autobiography, and one literary biography. Her language, in particular, is spontaneous, lyrical and a marvel of economy and elegance.

Gian Singh 'Shatir'

- *Gian Singh 'Shatir'* by Gian Singh 'Shatir'; Translated by Azad Gulati; Published by Sahitya Akademi.

This is an autobiographical account of the author Gain Singh 'Shatir' – of the first 18–20 years of his life. Singh is an Urdu writer and won the Sahitya Akademi Award for this book. Born in 1936 at Dudiana Kalan, Hoshiarpur, Punjab, Singh did his Certificate in Mechanical Engineering from Delhi Polytechnic and worked with WHO from where he retired and settled in Hyderabad. He writes in Urdu and has published a collection of Urdu poetry called *Chand Aur Roti*.

Born into a family of carpenters who also practiced agriculture, Singh writes a touching account of his life in this book. His book is one of the most candid books in this collection. While many authors have had an extremely difficult life and tyrannical fathers, few have disclosed the full details of all that they were subjected to while growing up. Autobiographies such as that of Gurdial Singh, Dalip Kaur Tiwana, Ajeet Cour and Bachint Kaur give details of their extremely tough upbringing but the brutally honest personal details Singh provides are unparalleled.

Because of his extremely good looks as a child and young man, Singh was subjected to molestation and sodomy many a times and was even labeled as a calamite. These instances scarred him deeply. Also, his father was a complete tyrant who mercilessly abused and beat Singh and Singh's mother at every available opportunity.

The author is merciless to his younger self in this book. He does not say a single good thing about himself and berates himself for being a coward and a wayward man. For instance, his sister was born immediately after him and he was quickly weaned off from his mother's breast, although he longed to continue to be breast-fed. He resented his sister and finally found his Taiji (aunt) who breast-fed him. He mentions that this act of Taima saved him from atrophy and malnutrition, but very soon he had a thankless attitude towards her. Such an incident may not be something extraordinary but such critical and at times harsh self-appraisal by the author continues throughout the book.

He gives details of his various dalliances, his thefts and his loathing for hard work. But if all this fails to surprise, he writes the book in such great detail that one is unable to suspend one's disbelief in the author's ability to recount all the instances of his life in such particulars. Even the instances of his very early childhood are given with intricate details. He has described the flora and fauna of the village, its various houses, the people living nearby and what they said at various occasions. Similarly, each and every detail of his school, his childhood friends, escapades with them, sexual encounters and brother's marriage are mentioned. At the age of 17, following a disagreement, his father asks him to leave the house and again he describes in great detail his journey to Delhi, his first sightings there and even each and every item that was placed at the house of his relative Labh Singh where he lands.

The author had an extremely tough and difficult life in the village and, after being thrown out by his father, the tough times continue at Delhi where he is forced to work as a mason and a carpenter. His only solace in life that saw him through all these times was the saintly advice from his Taiji who was always there to help and soothe him. Second was his love for literature, which, from his childhood, drew him to poetry and songs and later in Delhi to Sahir's and Iqbal's sahyri. While he drudged along, he always harboured a wish to study and the book ends when he has just been admitted to an engineering college although he has no means of paying for that course, and his father again ruthlessly rejects any help to him.

Because of his traumatic experiences with relationships, Singh thought of never marrying. But, as he mentions in the book, due to his lust and endless craving for women (and with no way to permanently gratify it) he surrendered to marriage but told his wife that they would not have any children. He did not want his children to suffer the physical and spiritual shocks that he had endured. But even here he helplessly went astray due to the entreaties of his wife and finally agreed to have one child and then underwent vasectomy.

This autobiographical novel has been translated into Hindi, Punjabi and English. The English translation published in 2009 by Sahitya Akademi did not win his approval, and in protest, he returned the Sahitya Akademi Award. He is, at present, re-translating the book into English himself.

Gurdial Singh

- *Two Lives of a Man: An Autobiography* by Gurdial Singh; Translated by Paramjit Singh Ramana; Published by National Book Trust, New Delhi.

Gurdial Singh is undoubtedly the best and the most respected fiction writer of our times. However, his has been an arduous journey through life. Singh was born to Jagat Singh (a carpenter) and Nihal Kaur on 10 January 1933 at Bhaini Fateh, a village near Jaito. Though poor, his life was full of childish delights till the time his father was working jointly with his *Taya* (father's elder brother), both of whom worked for more than 16 hours a day. But when they separated, Singh was made to leave school at the age of 12 and join his father. Singh worked hard as a carpenter with his father from 1945 to 1953. Everything about manual labour revolted him – long hours of work, his own bent of mind and his frail constitution. Meanwhile, he got married to Balwant Kaur when he was only 13 years old.

Soon there were differences between him and his father, and they too separated. To support himself and his wife, he had to set up his own carpentry unit, a tough and challenging task. His whole body ached at night and he had blisters on his hand. He wanted to study further and soon left work and opted to study and teach on the side (at Rs. 20–30 a month).

The initial three to four years when he started reading and writing were the most difficult. There was hardly any money at home, and they had two children to support. He was doing Gyani and at the same time teaching junior classes. He also accepted two big carpentry assignments to have some back up money to enable him to study. He even had to sell his wife's jewelry. Had it not been for the constant guidance and inspiration of Madan Mohan

Sharma, the headmaster of a middle school in Jaito, Singh would not have been able to improve his qualifications. Masterji goaded him into doing Gyani and Matric.

It was Master Madan Mohan, again, who took him to a colleague, an inspector of schools, for a job. In Nandpur Kotra, he got his first job as a schoolteacher at a salary of Rs. 60. To be able to get a running grade, it was imperative for him to go through formal training, which meant taking leave without pay. In 1962, he became a teacher of Punjabi in a village. Masterji continued to goad him to study further and so it was B.A by parts, first English, then history.

Along with familial responsibilities and economic hardships, Singh completed his graduation in 1964 and postgraduation in 1967. He started teaching Punjabi in the Middle and High schools in 1963. In 1971, he joined Government Barjindra College, Faridkot, as a lecturer in Punjabi and retired as a professor from Punjabi University, Patiala. After his retirement, he settled at his native place, Jaito Mandi.

It was in 1957 that he published his first ever story called *Bhaganwale* in *Panj Darya*, a magazine edited by Prof. Mohan Singh. Most of his stories were published in *Preetlari*, edited by the redoubtable Gurbaksh Singh.

Singh writes that with the constant and unwavering support of his Masterji and his wife, he was able to make his living as a teacher and a writer; yet his financial conditions were never rosy. Further, throughout his teaching career, he travelled 50–60 miles daily and soon had to shoulder the responsibility of educating of his children and getting them married. He took up translation work from Navyug Press and National Book Trust to earn some extra money to support his family.

The two parts that make up this autobiography were originally published in Punjabi as two separate books: *Niyan Matian* (1999) and *Duji Dehi* (2000). When they were being translated into Hindi, they became two parts of one book with a new title. The English translation is a combined book too.

Singh's books are widely translated and all of them are masterpieces. In fact, *Marhi Da Diva* was a trailblazer in Punjabi Literature that rejected the traditional concept of a hero being a high-ranking and influential man. Singh shifted his focus from upperclass peasantry to ordinary men. With his entry into the world of Punjabi literature (especially in novels), the focus in literature was shifted dramatically from idealism to realism and further from realism to hyperrealism.

Yet, his autobiography is the book chosen for this collection. The kind of turbulent life that Singh led is an inspiration. Despite the hardships, he managed to reach such dizzying heights and that is why, though one must read all of his literature, one must first read this autobiography. Like the other autobiographies included here, his story is a tribute to the indomitable human spirit and an enduring inspiration to writers of the future.

Read on:
- Gurdial Singh's book *Anhe Ghore da Daan* (Alms for a Blind Horse) has been translated into English by Hardilbagh Singh Gill and recently by Rana Nayar.
- The noted director Gurvinder Singh has also made it into a movie. The film won three awards at the 59th National Film Awards (2011) – best direction, best cinematography and the best feature film in Punjabi. It also became the first Punjabi film to be showcased at Venice Film Festival.
- Earlier, his other book *Marhi da deeva* (The Lamp of the Tomb) was made into a film by director Surinder Singh. This film too had won the National Film Award for Best Feature Film in Punjabi (1989). The book has been translated into English as *The Last Flicker* by Ajmer S. Rode and published by National Book Trust.
- Another novel *Unhoye* has been translated as *The Survivors* by Rana Nayar; Published by Katha.
- Similarly *Parsa* (Punjabi) has been translated into English as *Parsa* by Rana Nayar; Published by National Book Trust.

- A collection of his best short stories has also been translated and published in an anthology, *Earthy Tones* by Rana Nayar; Published by Ajanta Books International.
- *Gurdial Singh: A Reader* by Rana Nayar; Published by Sahitya Akademi is a comprehensive compendium of Gurdial Singh's writings.
- *Night of the Half Moon* is the English Translation of *Adh channi Raat* published by Palgrave Macmillan.
- *A Handful of Sand* translated into English from Hindi by Ravi Nandan Sinha, National Book Trust. Earlier it was translated from the Punjabi *Rete di Ek Muthi* into Hindi.

NOVELS

Amrita Pritam

- *Pinjar: The Skeleton and Other Stories* by Amrita Pritam; Translated by Khushwant Singh; Published by Tara.

The story of Amrita Pritam's life shows that Partition was a crucial moment that defined her worldview. Her vivid childhood memory, as evoked in her autobiography, *Raseedi Ticket*, is from her mother's village in Gujranwala, where she notices *pani* (water) being hawked at the railway platform as Hindu *pani* and Muslim *pani*. She questions her mother, 'Is water also Hindu/Mussalman?'

This book contains a double treat. Along with one of her most famous and well-known works, *Pinjar*, we have another novella, *The Man*, which is an equally griping and profound story. Her novel, *Pinjar* **(Skeleton)**, is a compelling account of her deeply personal experience of Partition and Independence. Pritam writes with courage, passion and devotion. She was an eyewitness to the Partition of India and portrays the pathetic and falling standard of humanity in this novel.

Pinjar tells the story of Puro, a young woman of Hindu background, who lives a charmed life with her family during the time of the Partition of 1947. She is betrothed to a wealthy and sweet young man, Ramchand, from a promising family akin to her own background. However, Puro's bliss is shattered one day as a leisurely trip to the fields beyond her home turns traumatic as she is kidnapped by a mysterious man, Rashid – a Muslim.

Puro's family once scorned Rashid's – a few generations before theirs and one of Puro's uncles had kidnapped Rashid's aunt. Puro's kidnap marks the triumph of Rashid's family over hers. It is, however, clear that Rashid is attracted to Puro and would do anything for her. He had not wanted to kidnap Puro but was forced to do so for family honour. Puro manages to break free from Rashid's home and runs back to her parents. In an extremely emotional scene, her parents woefully turn away their daughter, explaining that if Puro were to stay, Rashid's family would slaughter theirs. Left with no support at home, Puro returns to Rashid who is well aware of Puro's escape. Though she lives with him, she cannot bring herself to like him.

Puro, now Hamida, gets pregnant. While Rashid and his aunts rejoice, Puro finds herself horribly depressed and deliberately strains herself in housework in order to miscarry. Meanwhile, chaos ensues for Puro's family. As India attains freedom from the British, warfare occurs between the Hindus and Muslims who flee from opposing sides for safety. Puro, aware that Hindus from Ramchand's village are passing by her places, decides to visit the night camp where locals go to give food. There she meets Ramchand who tells her of his sister Lajjo's situation – she, too, has been kidnapped. Puro begs Rashid to help her find Lajjo and rescue her.

Racing from home to home under the alias of a saleswoman, Puro finally finds Lajjo and, with Rashid's assistance, manages to set her free and unite her with Ramchand. Puro's brother and Ramchand ask her to come along but she, indebted to Rashid, reconciled to her fate, and won over by his care and affection, refuses to go with them. *Pinjar* remains a very realistic and sensitive account of Partition and of the pain that people, especially women, had to undergo during that time.

That Man: Pritam, extremely knowledgeable about Sikh scriptures, was also very interested in Hindu mythology and had studied all the ancient Hindu texts. This story is set in a village that has a Shiv–Parvati temple and its head-priest, Mahant Kripa Sagar. The protagonist of *That Man* is a young man who realizes that when he was merely a year old, his mother left him in the service of a temple. He harbours an immense hatred for his parents and grudgingly carries on duties assigned by the Mahant. However, on his deathbed, the Mahant makes a confession that further shatters his world. His mother, unable to bear children for years, had been visited by the Lord in her dreams who commanded her to have the child born out of a union with the Mahant. The Mahant, his father, anoints him as the next Mahant and dies. The new Mahant Kripa Pattar lives an anguished life, hating all those responsible for his wretched existence, until one day the truth is further refined and revealed to him.

Mixed with references from Puranas and mythology, the story is touching and contemplative. It also has accounts of all types of Sadhus visiting the temple and the special and secret herbal formulas that they have.

Read on:

- Films made on Pritam's books:
  1. *Dharti Sagar te Sippiyan*, was made as *Kadambar* (1965).
  2. *Unah Di Kahani*, was made as *Daaku* (Dacoit, 1976), directed by Basu Bhattacharya.
  3. *Pinjar* was made into an award-winning Hindi movie (2003) by Chandra Prakash Dwivedi
- In 2007, an audio album titled *Amrita recited by Gulzar* was released by noted lyricist Gulzar, with poems of Amrita Pritam recited by him.
- Play by M. S. Sathyu based on *Raseedi Ticket*.
- World Punjabi Congress at Lahore, Pakistan, organized an International Conference on Amrita Pritam in 2007. They decided to produce a special book on Pritam. It was later published (~1100 pages) by the Pakistan Academy of Letters under the Chairmanship of Fakhar Zaman.
- Most of her books have been translated into English – both prose and poetry.
- Many books have been written about her. Some of the ones in English are:
  - *Amrita Pritam A Living Legend* – This book was published by India International Cultural Association, Chandigarh, in the year 1996 and commemorates

50 years of her writing. It contains articles and interviews by many contributors.
- *Inner Dimensions of Amrita Pritam* by Dr. Chaman Lal Raina; Published by Dynamic Publications.

Amrita and Imroz

- *In the Times of Love and Longing* by Amrita and Imroz; Translated by Arvinder; Edited by Uma Trilok; Published by Full Circle.

There have been various legendary Punjabi lovers – Mirza – Sahiban, Heer–Ranjha, Sohni–Mahiwal, Sassi–Punnu…and then there are Amrita and Imroz.

The love and the unique relationship that they shared have been the subject of several books, plays and essays. The two of them have never shied from speaking about it and so most people (especially those associated with literature) are quite familiar with their story. This book – a compilation of their letters written when they were apart from 1959 to 1975 – offers an insight into their true emotions. The letters have earlier been published in their original in Punjabi as well as in a Hindi translation. Now, they have been translated into English by Punjabi poet, Arvinder, who has done a wonderful job.

The letters portray their intense love for each other and the fact they never shied from expressing their true feelings. The names that they gave to each other also demonstrate the depth of this unique relationship. His endearments for her range from my love, mistress of my soul, Aashi, Maja, Zorbi, all of which have a story behind them, and I leave it to the reader to discover them by reading the book. And she called out to him with names like Jeeti, Ranjha, Mirza, Imma.

The letters also tell us about their temporary estrangement – his desire to settle in Mumbai while she was reluctant to leave Delhi. In her letters, she pines for him and, although she never wanted to be a hurdle in his career, she kept urging him to come back to Delhi. And so he returned and they shared a house for nearly five decades, even though they weren't married. Such a living arrangement was not heard of in India at that time but they kept at it, sharing expenses and the uprbringing of Amrita's two children, till Amrita's death in 2005.

Amrita, in her letter, writes of the loneliness she felt before she met Imroz, in whom she found the perfect soulmate – the kind she had always been writing about in her poems and other writings…her Rajan. Similarly, for Imroz, Amrita was a muse and an inspiration. He loved her deeply and the sense that one gets from reading these letters is that he gave more to this relationship, although he is too humble, self-evasive and big-hearted to ever admit it. In any case, their relationship went beyond such petty calculations and was a pure, divine and selfless one. That is the reason their story continues to be told and retold and continues to inspire generations of readers.

Besides providing a glimpse into their deep and unparalleled love, the letters also reflect on their work – details of Amrita's travel to Russia and other European countries for poetry meets, her observations about writers and poets there and how those societies treat them. For instance, she writes about Romania where a library publishes books every week, first editions usually have 75,000 copies, and every book runs into several editions. She contrasts this with state of affairs in Punjab and a lack of similar zeal for books. She also talks about how she would be happy just reading and writing and that she hates the attendant work of paying taxes, getting licenses renewed, paying for insurance police and other mundane tasks.

We also get closer to Imroz's beliefs. Commenting on the horrific happenings all over the world as reported in newspapers he writes, 'If one word talks of love and takes the shape of Amrita Pritam and the poetry of love, millions of others spread hatred through books of hatred that they call scriptures.' It is a strong condemnation of all that is being done in the name of organized religions all over the world.

For Imroz, Amrita continues to live on. All his work, paintings and poems continue to talk about her and all around him there is a fragrance of their beautiful love. Their story will endure, as have the other Punjabi love legends. As Rana Siddqui Zaman wrote in *The Hindu*, If Amrita wrote a poem "Main tumhe phir milungi" before her death for him, Imroz, who turned poet soon after her death in 2005, has just completed another love poem on her: "Usne jism chhoda hai, saath nahi."

Baldev Singh

- *Anndatta: The Hand That Feeds* by Baldev Singh; Translated By Narinder Jit Kaur; Published by Punjabi University, Patiala.

Anndatta is about the plight of farmers from the Malwa region of Punjab and is a part of the Punjabi literature curriculum at the Guru Nanak Dev University and Punjabi University. *Anndatta* adds to the wonderful narratives on this subject, which has attracted numerous writers of this region to write about it. As the translator informs us, 'Baldev Singh has a very authentic grip over the Punjabi dialect of the rural Malwa region, which provides a background and a depth to the tragic saga of shattered and devastated farming community of Punjab.' *Anndatta* means the God that provides us with food. The author mentions in the book that at one time the farmers had adequate land holdings and could easily sell crops, so much so that the visiting *mirassis* and acrobats to the village would bless people with words 'May God bless the Anndatta, may there be prosperity and may you have heaps of grains…'

But the story in the book shows that the peasantry in Punjab is broken. It deals with the various problems of the farmers like the Jat families dividing and sub-dividing their lands and their inability to work together; the decrease of agricultural productivity; the proclivity to take loans for showmanship and spending beyond the means; the loan sharks taking advantage of the lack of education of the farmers by charging exorbitant rates of interest and then cheating them with forged documents; the farmers' dependence on Sadhus and babas as well as on liquor and drugs; the corruption and harassment of revenue officials and the police; and the militancy problem. All of these make a powerful cocktail that submerges the decent farmer who is working hard to make ends meet. Only the crooked and crafty farmers indulge in all kinds of subterfuge, and in connivance with the officials and police, to survive and make some profit out of agriculture. The others can barely survive and are forced to sell parts of their land every year to keep their head above water.

The author traces the story of a Dhillon family who, at one time, used to own almost 80 acres of land but within three to four generations have lost almost the entire land. Tragedy befalls the family at every step. The grandfather is old and biding his time in the cattle shed. The father is weak after a serious injury resulting from a fall while repairing the roof of the house.

Out of four children, the eldest wants a tractor or wants to go abroad. Meanwhile, he hobnobs with robbers and takes advantage of the name of militants to loot money and then finally become a sadhu, at last gaining respectability and wealth but neglects his family. Militants abduct the daughter, and the meager resources of the family are depleted in finding her, bribing the police and fighting court cases but she simply disappears. The other son is fond of music and has nothing to do with the family. In fact, he demands his share of land, which he sells to have a cassette released. The fourth is the only one who wants to farm but is crushed under the weight of all these demands and pressures, village politics and a meager land holding.

The novel is a sort of a magnum opus, touching on all aspects that ail the peasantry today. One is reminded of Ram Sarup Ankhi's *Partapi* and *Kothe Kharak Singh*, which too deal in detail with the day-to-day life and hardship of the farmers of Punjab. What is amazing is that though the plight of farmers has been so well-documented and highlighted by these writers and many others, the government or the civil society has not done much to correct it. Even after being reduced to destitution, the farmers have not rectified their way of life and are continuing the sad practices. More so, in the present times, the focus has shifted to the drug menace while the real reforms in the agricultural sector have been forgotten. Maybe drugs are the last resort of these impoverished and thoroughly beaten farmers. Earlier it was home-brewed liquor.

While India and the world eulogized the Green Revolution, after reading these books and those of Gurdial Singh we realize that despite those bountiful crops, the life of an average farmer has always been bad, burdened by caste and class wars, traditions and illiteracy. Worse yet, it has been going downhill ever since. The response – earlier during the Naxalite movement and later during militancy – has been violent.

Author

Baldev Singh (b. 1942, also known as Baldev Singh Sadaknaama) is a Punjabi novelist and storywriter of Punjab, India. He has written 55 novels and various short stories and plays. Singh was born in the village Chand Nawaan, in the Moga district of Punjab. He started his career as a teacher in the Muktsar area and spent some time in Himachal Pradesh as a teacher as well. Later he moved to Kolkatta and worked as a truck cleaner, taxi driver and truck operator.

Singh is known for his novels *Sadaknaama* and *Laal Batti*. His novel *Sadaknaama* was a road narrative of truck drivers from Punjab. It started as a column in Amrita Pritam's magazine *Nagmani* and was later published as a three-volume novel. The stories in the novel are based on Singh's real experiences as a truck driver for 10 years. The book became very popular in Punjabi literature and 'Sadaknaama' became part of his name for his fans.

Laal Batti deals with the red-light area of Kolkatta, for which he studied the subject for over a decade. It was also adapted for the stage; in fact, and many of his plays (like *Mitti Rudan Kare)* have been performed over 400 times by the Punjabi University, Patiala. His work *Dhahwan Dilli De Kingre*, about the legendary rebel Dulla Bhatti won him a Sahitya Akademi Award for Punjabi in 2011.

Noted columnist Nonika Singh in an article in *The Tribune* (22/1/2012) wrote, 'In a way his life's story reads like a novel. For how often do you come across a teacher-turned-driver blossom into a Sahitya Akademi Award-winning writer?'

Bhai Vir Singh

- *Sundri* by Bhai Sahib Bhai Vir Singh; Translated by Bimal Kaur; Published by Bhai Vir Singh Sahitya Sadan.

Unlike most of the popular religions, Sikhism stresses the equality between men and women and asserts that it is sinful to consider either sex above the other. Singh reflected this belief in his novels and featured in them a number of strong female characters. In fact, his very first novel was *Sundri*, which featured Sunder Kaur, a woman who converted from Hinduism to Sikhism and then proceeded to lead a life of adventure in the jungles with a band of Sikh warriors. It was the first novel penned in the Punjabi language. Through Sunder, Singh hoped to embody all the ideals of Guru Nanak's lessons. The book was well received by the community and gained popularity almost immediately. Other important female characters he wrote were Rani Raj Kaur, Satvant Kaur, Subhagji and Sushil Kaur. Even by modern standards, these female characters are considered to be well-rounded and an inspiration to both men and women. Bhai Vir Singh went even as far as often portraying the women in his novels as more prone to spiritual enlightenment than their male counterparts.

Sundri is a symbolic representative of the period that it is set in and is based on a folk song. The Mughal leadership was bent upon annihilating the Sikhs. The rulers were corrupt and engaged in the systematic forced conversion of the non-Muslim people. The management of the government was in the hands of Nawabs and bandits who were grossly unfair, discriminatory, lustful and tyrannical. The story in the novel depicts incidents and events that encouraged universal brotherhood and love for humanity.

Sundri depicts the story of the Sikh women during those hard times, where they remained steadfast and composed, facing ordeals and hardships but still smiling in the name of the Guru. *Sundri* is about a brave woman who did not lament her helplessness nor did she think herself as pitiable. She was a meek and vulnerable girl but discovered her innate strength to fight against tyranny and injustice with the help of the glorious Sikh history, principled Sikh values and ethos, and her valiant brother, Balwant Singh, who adopted the Sikh way of life to fight the cruel rulers of the times. The novel was first published in 1898 and over the past 118 years has become the most widely read piece of Punjabi literature with 40 editions of the novel gone into print.

Author

Bhai Vir Singh (1872–1957), born in Amritsar, was a poet, scholar and theologian. His identification with all the important concerns of modern Sikhism was so complete that he came to be canonized as Bhai, an honorific often given to those who could be considered a saint of the Sikh faith. For his pioneering work in several different genres, he is acknowledged as the father of modern Punjabi literature and he is also honourably known as the 'Sixth river of Punjab.'

Bhai Vir Singh wrote many books, prose, novels, poetry, plays, historical research and articles pertaining to the Sikh history, Gurbani and understanding of the Sikh principles. Through his writings, Bhai Vir Singh succeeded not only in restoring the morals of the people of his time but also in providing Punjabi – his mother tongue – the honour and glory long denied to it as a result of political and cultural slavery. A colossus of modern Punjabi Literature, Bhai Vir Singh alone wrote more than all his contemporaries put together. There is no aspect of Punjabi culture that Bhai Vir Singh has not illumined and enlarged. Through his dedicated and inspiring works, he put the Punjabi language on the same pedestal as other modern Indian languages.

Panjab University conferred on him a doctorate in Oriental Learning, and the Sahitya Akademi awarded him its first annual award for outstanding contribution to Punjabi literature. He was also awarded the Padma Bhushan and was nominated as a member of the Punjab Legislative Council in 1952.

Bhai Vir Singh took an active interest in the affairs of the Singh Sabha movement, launched the Khalsa Tract Society, started a Punjabi weekly, the *Khalsa Samachar* and was among the principal promoters of several institutions, such as Chief Khalsa Diwan, Sikh Educational Society, and the Punjab and Sind Bank.

In literature, Bhai Vir Singh started as a writer of romances, which proved to be the forerunners of the Punjabi novel. In 1919, he published *Rana Surat Singh*, the first Punjabi epic, a long narrative of over 14,000 lines followed by the first play written in Punjabi, *Raja Lakhdata Singh*.

Read on:
- *Sundri: The Brave Kaur* is the third animated movie from Vismaad – the producers of the highly successful *Sahibzadey* and *The Rise of Khalsa* movies. The movie has received rave reviews and been successfully screened in Toronto, Vancouver, British Columbia, Calgary, Detroit, Fremont, Los Angeles, Chicago, London, Scotland and many other cities.
- Dr. G. S. Mansukhani has done another English translation of *Sundri*.
- *Khalsa Samachar*, the weekly newspaper started by Bhai Vir Singh in 1899, is still being published and has completed 116 years. Earlier, it was published from Amritsar, but in December 1990, it was shifted to Delhi from where it is now published by Bhai Vir Singh Sahitya Sadan (BVSSS).
- Bhai Vir Singh Sahitya Sadan, a premier literary and cultural organization in Delhi, was established in 1958 in the memory of the father of modern Punjabi literature and Saint-Poet of India, Bhai Vir Singh. Shri V.V. Giri, the President of India at the time laid the foundation stone of the building in March 1972. President N. Sanjeeva Reddy inaugurated the memorial in 1978.

- Bhai Vir Singh Study Circles: To promote the writings and the message of Bhai Vir Singh, study circles are functioning in New Delhi, Kanpur, New York and Toronto. The Study Circles are the autonomous sister institution of the Sadan, and they regularly arrange monthly Kirtan durbars where, apart from regular kirtan, Bhai Vir Singh's poems are sung and his 'message' is read.
- Panjab Literary Forum (PLF) is a Book Club of BVSSS. The main event of the PLF is organized once in a month where one author presents his or her work – fiction, non-fiction, poetry, drama, films as text; the focus is Punjab's literature, culture and history.
- Bhai Vir Singh Niwas Asthan at 60, Lawrence Road, Amritsar, which has since been renamed as Bhai Vir Singh Marg, has been converted into a Museum/Library.
- Most of his books have been translated from Punjabi into Hindi, English, Urdu and Bengali. Many of his works are also available as audio books.
- In a survey conducted by the leading daily, *Hindustan Times*, to find out who is the most influential Sikh of the 20th century, Bhai Vir Singh emerged as the clear favourite. As part of the tercentenary celebration of the Khalsa, the Government of Punjab honoured Bhai Vir Singh with the Nishan-i-Khalsa.

Bhisham Sahni

- *Tamas* by Bhisham Sahni; Translated by him from Hindi; Published by Penguin.

Tamas is based in a small-town frontier province in 1947, just before Partition. Sahni recounts the years leading to India's Independence by a plain narration of events springing from the tortuous relationship between Hindus and Muslims with the background of the villainous British ruler who intensified the hatred.

The book begins with the slaughter of a pig by an innocent low-caste tanner (Nathu) who is intentionally not told about the real reason by a Muslim fundamentalist who hires him. We are introduced to a singing party getting assembled to do community work. But they get a warning of an on-coming storm. The news of the dead pig spreads like wildfire and, within hours, a cow is slaughtered and thrown in front of the temple in the same village. A series of one or two such incidents puts a dense cloud over the whole district, making the environment chilling. Riots follow and the Muslim League intensifies its demand for a Muslim majority State – Pakistan. The Congress, on the other hand, is itself divided, as the party workers cannot decide how to follow the Gandhian policy of non-violence when attacked by those who want to kill them.

On a hilltop lives the British Deputy Commissioner Richard who is at the helm of affairs. He does not want to control the situation. The Britishers aim solely to prove their superiority in administration. The veil of darkness that spreads over the village is enough of a warning signal for the politicians and fundamentalists to hold meetings and form peace committees. But their attempts are soon thwarted as the situation grows beyond control. All villagers are transformed into revolutionaries. The riots flare up and become widespread. Sahni delineates poignant stories of estranged Sikh parents separated from their families, broken relationships, true stories of agony and pain eventually leading to intense fear and deep hatred. The later portions of the book deal with how the characters respond to the traumatic developments.

The focus shifts swiftly in the book. This continuous shifting of focus is quite unique, and *Tamas* tells you the incidents from the viewpoint of almost every kind of family in the village. The introduction of new characters provides much-needed relief and at no time is the book strenuous to read. After the characters have been introduced, the story runs parallel, describing in exhaustive detail the trauma each character goes through, as they all have a common background of Partition.

The book teems with a variety of characters that are sucked up by circumstances beyond control. The reader is left as troubled as Nathu who bears the guilt of the crime he committed unknowingly. The book evokes haunting memories of the disastrous effects of communalism, and the lessons from the book are as valid today as they were in that period.

Author

Bhisham Sahni (1915–2003), writer, teacher, translator, playwright, polyglot, was born in Rawalpindi. *Tamas* (Darkness), his magnum opus, which won him the Sahitya Akademi Award in 1976, gained worldwide acclaim for its powerful and passionate account of the communal riots and carnage that accompanied the Partition. *Tamas* was translated into English in 1988.

Sahni's works reflect his unflinching commitment to India's pluralist ethos and secular foundations. They expose the divide and rule policy of the British and the rank opportunism of the upper classes of both Hindu and Muslim communities. They show how the real victims of all sectarian violence are always common people, irrespective of their faith, caste or class. He bagged the Padma Bhushan for literature in 1998.

In 1948, Sahni started working with the Indian People's Theatre Association (IPTA). From 1956 to 1963 he worked as a translator at the Foreign Languages Publishing House in Moscow and translated some important works into Hindi, including Tolstoy's novel *Resurrection*. On his return to India, Sahni resumed teaching at the Delhi College. He also edited the reputed literary magazine *Nai Kahaniyan*. Sahni has published seven novels, nine collection of short stories, six plays and a biography of his brother Balraj Sahni.

Read On:
- *Tamas* was very ably transformed into a five-hour show on India Television directed by Shyam Benegal.
- Bhisham Sahni wrote *Balraj My Brother* on his famous film and theatre actor brother, Balraj Sahni.
- His collection of short stories titled *We Have Arrived in Amritsar and Other Stories* was translated by Jai Ratan; Published by Sangam Books.

Dalip Kaur Tiwana

- *Twilight and Mark of the Nose Ring* By Dalip Kaur Tiwana; Translated by Narinder Jit Kaur and Jai Ratan; Published by National Book Trust.

Delightful Double Treat of Compelling Storytelling
This book consists of two delightful novellas written straight from the heart, each with an endearing woman protagonist whom the reader will like, relate to and feel deeply about.

The Mark of the Nose Ring
This is the shorter of the two stories. It opens with an introduction to Kiranjit – the young widow of a war-hero. Contrary to what most people would want to believe, life is not over for this charming, naïve girl. She has eyes that like to dream and see beyond the tragic reality that life has made her lot. However, society is blind to her wishes for her future. She is expected to conform to norms that she chooses to defy. Even when ornaments are not allowed to adorn her, the mark of her favourite diamond nose ring (that she used to wear) holds the promise of an unknown tomorrow. The story is powerful and appealing. The reader keeps wondering if Kiranjit's desire to breathe free will be able to inch towards fulfillment. There are poignant poems and phrases weaved beautifully into the story. The delicate original story written in Punjabi has been handled with the utmost sensitivity in this translated version.

Twilight
This is an intense story of love, desire, misunderstandings and despair. The protagonist, Harjit, is a young, middle-class Punjabi

girl from a conservative family who gets married after becoming economically independent. Harjit harbours a soft corner for her colleague, Amrik. What is extremely interesting is the way Tiwana portrays the guilt in Harjit's mind. Every time her heart skips a beat for Amrik, she fears how her husband might react if he could read her mind.

Harjit is an independent lady brought up in a middle-class family. Nevertheless, her ideas of love and marriage are traditional. Even though her heart is captivated by the thought of perfect love, her mind is chained. That is why she is unable to relate to the liberal views of her friend Sonal whose free-spirited life disturbs Harjit instead of comforting her. The book conveys an important social message through Harjit – that despite being honest and independent, she fears being rebuked and blamed for a mistake she didn't commit.

The characterizations are fascinating and real. Rajinder, Harjit's husband, comes across as the typical dominating man who stalks his wife and deserts her due to his own baseless insecurities. The portrayal of the mental battles that tear Harjit apart are beautifully expressed in this story. While, on the one hand, Harjit feels jealous at the thought of her husband being with another woman, on the other, she displays self-restraint and puts her self-respect above her emotional dilemmas.

The story is a masterpiece and readers would surely want to devour the original Punjabi version after reading this book. The extraordinary life of ordinary people is key to the narrative. Overall, this is a memorable story to be cherished and recommended to others.

Read on:
Other books of Dr. Dalip Kaur Tiwana translated into English:
- *The Tale Of The Phoenix* – translation of *Katha Kuknoos Di* by Nikky-Guninder Kaur Singh; Revised & edited by Bhupinder Singh & Elizabeth A. Siler; Published by Unistar Books Pvt. Ltd.

- *And Such Is Her Fate* – translation of *Eho Hamara Jiwana* by Jai Ratan; Published by Punjabi University, Patiala.
- *Who Am I* – translated by Dr. Rajinder Singh; Published by Diamond Pocket Books Pvt. Ltd.
- *Tell the Tale, Urvashi* – translation of *Katha Kaho Urvashi* By Bhupinder Singh; Published by Orient BlackSwan Pvt. Ltd.
- *Gone are the Rivers* – translation of *Langh Gaye Darya* by Bhupinder Singh & S. C. Narula; Published by Macmillan.

Fakhar Zaman

- *Bewatna and Other Novels* By Fakhar Zaman; Translated by various translators; Published by Unistar Books Pvt. Ltd.

This book consists of five of his Punjabi novels. Unistar Publishers deserve credit for publishing these five heart-wrenching novels in a single volume. The novels included are: *Ik Mare Bande Di Kahani (The Dead Man's Tale), Satt Guache Lok (The Lost Seven), Bandiwan (The Prisoner), Bewatna (The Alien)* and *Kamzat (The Low Born)*. Not all of them were part of the five books banned by the government, however. The translation from Punjabi has been done with utmost care so as to not disturb the essence of the original stories. Many poems are part of the stories, which makes for an interesting combination of prose and poetry.

Followers of Punjabi literature, wherever they are situated, are all exposed to Fakhar Zaman's luminous work. Readers are aware of the abundant creativity he possesses, which is so apparent in his writings. As with the novels *Ik Mare Bande Di Kahani* or *Satt Guache Lok* (both translated from Punjabi by Khalid Hasan), once a reader begins reading Zaman's work, he/she will not be able to leave the book midway. The power to hold a reader's attention by sheer simplicity and brilliance is noteworthy.

Malik M Zamurrad, in his foreword to *Satt Guache Lok*, says that it is Pakistan's first surrealistic novel. Although it is a novel of modern sensibilities and is a story of any nation, any religion and any race that has lost its bearings, yet it is laced with quintessential Punjabi flavour and Ranjha, Heer, Sahiban, Farid, Kharal and Bhagat Singh move in front of our eyes like a colourful pageant.

A special note must be made of *Bandiwan*, the longest story in this collection. Translated into English by Khalid Hasan, this story is an enticing blend of the real and the abstract. A prisoner's ordeal has been delicately portrayed and the narration has quotes from literary greats like Shakespeare, Kafka, Gibson and others, making the passages more appealing and engaging. The judicious use of dialogue done enhances the overall essence of the story.

When we read about the protagonists in each story, we cannot help but admire the connection, the dissimilarities and the conflicts. Each character has a voice that is distinct and unique.

While reading the story *Bewatna*, one will wonder what in essence is a 'homeland' and how its connotations vary from person to person across generations. This intense story, translated by Asif Javeed Mir, is strong yet subtle, disturbing yet touching, real yet alluring.

The story titled *Kamzat*, translated by Gilani Kamran, begins with the news of death. From thereon, the twists in the tale and the absolute brilliance in narration are bound to move the reader. The verses complement the storyline beautifully making the read enjoyable and memorable.

The creative genius of Zaman is evident in every paragraph. The poetic approach and the romantic flavour add freshness to the stories, regardless of the time they had been penned. Rebellious times, love buried in pain, struggle sagas – it seems that all have found refuge in this beautiful collection. Whatever a reader's preference in genre, this book is sure to tug at the heartstrings. To sum up, this mixed bag is a treasure trove of literature.

Author

Fakhar Zaman was the chairman of the Pakistan Academy of Letters. A leader of the Pakistan Peoples Party (PPP) and the chairman of the World Punjabi Congress, he has also been playing a notable role in politics to achieve his sociopolitical ideals. He is a celebrated Pakistani writer who is the author of 40 books in Punjabi, Urdu and English. Almost all his writings fall into the category of resistance writing or protest literature and have been part of his political struggle for the restoration of democracy and establishment of a just society in Pakistan.

His most celebrated works have been in his mother tongue, Punjabi. His Punjabi novels and poetry have been translated into several major languages of the world and are taught at the graduate level in different countries for students seeking PhD and M.Phil degrees. Plays based on his novels have been staged and televised in Pakistan and India.

Five of his Punjabi books, including his modern classic novel *Bandiwan* (The Prisoner), were proscribed, forcibly lifted from book stores and burned publicly by the military government in 1978. After lengthy litigation, the ban was lifted – making him perhaps the only writer in the world whose five books were simultaneously banned and then released 18 years later.

He has received several international and national awards including the Hilal-e-Imtiaz and Sitara-e-Imtiaz awards from the Pakistan government, Shiromani Sahitak award from the Indian government and Millennium Award for Best Punjabi Novelist of the 20th century.

He has been editing and publishing an English monthly *Voice*, an Urdu monthly *Bazgasht*, a Punjabi weekly *Wangaar*, all of which were banned by the military regime in Pakistan.

Fauzia Rafiq

- *Skeena* by Fauzia Rafiq; Published by Libros Libertad, Surrey[4].

Every so often an important novel is written, enriching the canon of Punjabi literature. *Skeena* is one of those. Sadhu Binning has said that, 'Skeena is a prideful addition to Punjabi literature.' Rafiq began writing it in 1991 and completed it in 2004. It was initially released in Pakistan in only the Shahmukhi script and was a resounding success. This is, of course, very encouraging for Punjabi, a language neglected in both the Punjabs. The book was then released in Canada, both in the Gurmukhi transcript and as translated into English.

Skeena is the journey of an intelligent girl who questions everything. She questions the treatment of servants. Skeena is taught to say please, but scolded when she applies this to the household help. Skeena does not shy away from questioning the illogical nature of Wahabbi Islam as imposed in Pakistani society from Bhutto's time right up to now, especially on the treatment of women. We meet Skeena at the age of seven and the story then takes us to her young adulthood, to the Pakistan of General Zia, to Canada, to a forced marriage with a complete stranger and to finally finding love with the last person she expected, amongst the blueberry fields of British Columbia.

In Canada, life becomes worse rather than better. She finds herself married to a doctor who does not love her, has her as one of many wives and keeps her housebound for a whole decade.

---

[4] This review of *Skeena has* been adopted from one done by noted author Rupinderpal Singh Dhillon for the magazine *Sikhchic.com* and is reproduced here with his express permission.

Life becomes even more unbearable as she is barren and has the worst mother-in-law one can imagine. Do her family in Pakistan help? No, as behzti and izzat are higher values than her daily life.

And so the scene is set for how an educated Punjabi Muslim girl must face the world, until one violent night circumstances lead her to be able to break the yoke and find herself in the arms of a Sikh lover who, unlike all the other men in her life, treats women with respect and kindness. However, soon the attack on the twin towers in the United States brings fresh trouble for both of them.

Skeena is the stark and true experience of many a Punjabi woman, in this case one bought up in Islamic Culture, but it can so easily apply to those women bought up in Sikh or Hindu cultures as well. What is the common factor? Punjabi attitudes.

Rafiq's writing is brave and fresh. *Skeena* at one point depicts two lesbian couples, one of them Pakistani. *Skeena* does not shy away from masturbation, contains swearing and deals with reality. This is grown-up stuff and much needed. The new generation of Punjabi readers is savvier and wants to read about more than just village life and bickering over land.

Author

Fauzia Rafiq is a South Asian–Canadian writer of fiction and poetry. Her English and Punjabi writings have been published in Canada, Pakistan and on the Web.

Rafiq worked as a Screenwriter for Pakistan Television and adapted Fyodor Dostoevsky's first novel, *Poor Folk* in Punjabi as *Apay Ranjha Hoi,* and Altaf Fatima's Urdu novel *Dastak Na Do*. She also wrote an original play on the profile of a ragpicker. She was recognized in 2012 by peer group WIN Canada as 'Distinguished Poet and Novelist' for her first novel *Skeena* and the first chapbook of English and Punjabi poems *Passion Fruit/Tahnget Phal*. Her eBook of poems *Holier Than Life* was published in 2013. Earlier, she edited an anthology of writings of women of South Asian origin *Aurat Durbar: The Court of Women*. Her second novel *The Adventures of Saheban: Biography of a Relentless Warrior* has been published in November 2016 while her third novel *Triple* is in pipeline.

Through creative writing, blogging and community development work, Rafiq supports freedom of expression and equality. She publishes blogs on Punjabi literature, blasphemy and honour killings. She is a co-founder and the coordinator of Surrey Muse, an interdisciplinary art and literature presentation group that meets every month in Surrey since 2011. She runs a blog called Uddari Weblog for Punjabi literature, authors and publishers.

Read on:

- Punjabi Gurumukhi Edition of Skeena has been published by Uddari Books, Surrey 2011.
- Punjabi Shahmukhi Edition of Skeena has been published by Sanjh Publications, Lahore 2007.

Gurdial Singh

- *Marhi Da Deeva* (The Lamp of the Tomb) by Gurdial Singh; Translated into English as *The Last Flicker* by Ajmer S. Rode; Published by National Book Trust.

Sukhdev Singh Sirsa, President of Punjabi Sahitya Akademi, said of Gurdial Singh, 'He was one of the last ones in the Munshi Prem Chand tradition of writing about the downtrodden. He brought alive the struggle of the working classes of rural Punjab.' Well-known Hindi critic Vishnu Khare, in an appraisal of Singh's work said, 'His essential sensibility and locale are rural and his medium is not the urban, middle-class Punjabi but a language liberally, even belligerently, laced with his native Malwi vernacular.' This novel has been considered as the best piece of writing done in Punjab since 1947.

Singh was a path-breaker and made impressive contributions to Punjabi literature. He wrote the novel, *Marhi da Deeva* when he was only 30. It is a remarkable combination of personal and impersonal emotions, and Singh's writing and experience make the book more interesting to read. *The Last Flicker* demonstrates that beneath the façade of idyllic joy in rural areas there lie monstrous social evils bred by caste and backwardness. The novel narrates the story of 40-year-old Jagseer Singh who suffers the cruelty of caste system, social hierarchy and economic exploitation in Indian society. The plot is masterfully constructed and portrays the ravages of feudal traditions still prevalent in Punjabi society. Singh's intimate contact with rural reality and his engagement with village life are palpable in the character of Jagseer Singh.

The protagonist, Jagseer, is the first Dalit hero in Punjabi fiction. Loving and polite, he shares good relationships with his parents, friends and other villagers. However, tragic times soon break his soul, and his life is marked with stark poverty, unfulfilled love and deep passivity. The narrative provides a realistic depiction of a typical village story, with the familiar ingredients of love, courtesy, jealousy and friendship.

At the forefront are Dharam Singh and Jagseer Singh whose fathers are as good as brothers. But as generations pass, relationships run sour and Dharam Singh's son refuses to uphold this bond between the families. At stake here is a piece of land that Dharam Singh's father has gifted to Jagseer Singh's father. It could not be transferred legally but morally there was no question about it. This single incident triggers a whole host of developments and conflicts. This conflict over a small piece of land structures the novel.

Jagseer Singh's tale is simultaneously personal and political. It reveals how the social fabric tears into an individual's soul and ravages him beyond belief. Adding to his troubles is Jagseer's love for Bhani, the wife of his friend Nikka. He resorts to opium to alleviate his agony; his existence becomes the true definition of chaos.

Singh's summary of the village and its houses is informative and highly evocative. This book represents Singh's attempt to portray the complexities of his cultural memory and encapsulate them into one long fictional work. *Marhi Da Deeva* is a modern classic that gave a new turn to Punjabi fiction after its publication in 1964. The title *Marhi Da Deeva* has a cultural significance that soon acquires a suggestive power far beyond its immediate context.

Gulzar Singh Sandhu

- *Pole Stars* by Gulzar Singh Sandhu; Translated by D. R. Goyal; Published by Publication Bureau, Punjabi University, Patiala.

There are very few Punjabi authors – especially those writing in Punjabi – who base their stories outside the typical Punjabi milieu. Most stories are based on the peasantry, the problems faced by them, the nostalgia for west Punjab, historical figures and so on. These themes, as many authors note, interest the majority of readers who are largely based in Punjab. However, there is also a need to go beyond traditional subjects, especially when the Punjabi reader is also reading Gorky, Tolstoy, Shakespeare and even Paul Coelho in recent times (all translated into Punjabi). In recent times Roop Dhillon, an author based in the United Kingdom, has been stretching the boundaries of subjects by writing on various atypical subjects like science fiction and producing diverse books like *Gunde, Samurai, O, Bharind*. (Unfortunately, none of his books have been translated into English yet and hence are not included in this collection). It is to be noted that Punjabi authors writing in Hindi and English have written on many diverse subjects.

Pole Star, thus, is a different book. It was first published in 1985 as *Kandhin Jaye (Born Behind Walls)*. It is the story of orphaned children, abandoned by their parents near a dilapidated wall, the rail track or a gutter. The book is based on the real story of one such orphanage based in South India (Coimbatore and Dindigul in Tamil Nadu). Gulzar Singh Sandhu heard about the lives of these orphans, met the principal characters of this story on a train journey and then traveled to the orphanage himself. Touched by their story, Sandhu wrote this novel to depict the grit and determination of these orphans and to recognize the admirable work done by the orphanage. Sandhu, in the preface to this English translation, writes, 'The Novel, in fact, is an essay in understanding the essence of children in adversity. So its new title *Pole Stars (Dhru Taare)*. I hope the new title helps in comprehension of its true significance.'

In this novel, a young man named Victor travels from the United States to India to find a wife for himself. He just wants to marry a dark, young and moderately educated girl from the east. After travelling to Bangladesh, Nepal and West Bengal he travels through UP to Kerala to finally reach Coimbatore. At an orphanage there he finds a girl Krishna. Krishna, happy in her surroundings, is suddenly jolted by his proposal. Before she commits herself to marriage, she needs to find answer to the question plaguing her – did her parents leave her as an unwanted child? She is relieved to find that her parents were swept away by a flooded river, and this revelation prepares her for a journey to a foreign shore, away from the cocooned environment of her orphanage. Meanwhile, the orphanage authorities make meticulous enquiries about Victor through the American embassy and make all kinds of arrangements to ensure her well-being.

The novel is an endearing story about her life in the United States, about her friends from the orphanage who also find lives for themselves and their unwavering connection to the orphanage and its children.

Author

Gulzar Singh Sandhu (1935–) was born at Kotia Badia, district Ludhiana. Sandhu after doing his M.A. in English Literature migrated to Delhi and secured an editorial job in the well-known Punjabi monthly, *Pritam*. Later, he switched over to a sub-editors job in the Punjabi section of the Publications Division of the Indian Council of Agricultural Research. He taught in Punjabi University as a professor of journalism and mass communication. He was also the chief-editor of prominent newspapers and the founding editor of *The Punjabi Tribune* published from Chandigarh.

He has four collections of short stories to his credit, out of which *Amar Katha* (Immortal Story), won the Sahitya Akademi Award for the year 1982. His stories give an insight into the social and economic conditions prevailing in the villages of Punjab. Though he is famous as a short story writer, his novel *Pole Stars* has been considered a very successful new experiment in Punjabi novels.

He is also the recipient of an award from the International Association of Authors, Playwrights and Artists of Canada in 1992 and Shiromani Punjabi Sahityakar Puraskar from the Education Department of Punjab in 2001. His columns are published regularly in noted Punjabi magazines and newspapers in India and abroad.

Gurmukh Singh Sehgal

- *Hijrat* by Gurmukh Singh Sehgal; Translated by Parvesh; Published by Unistar Books Pvt. Ltd.

After the Partition of India in 1947, the people of Luarhgi (Landikotal) in NWFP (now in Pakistan) migrated in two different directions. Most of the people reached India, but there were some people who had relatives in the Afghan cities of Jalalabad and Kabul. They preferred moving to Afghanistan where they kept living peacefully for about 35 years. But the turbulent change in the political climate of Afghanistan, developing for nearly two decades, forced them to migrate once again. *Hijrat* portrays this historical period of Afghanistan (1947–1997).

Sehgal himself, along with his family, went through this harrowing experience, and this book is a rare first-hand documentary of the horrors they experienced. We have had many books and stories on the theme of Partition from writers who were witness to it in India or who witnessed the mayhem while migrating from Pakistan to India. But this is the first book to give an account of the experience of Sikhs migrating from Pakistan to Afghanistan.

In the story, a joint family of frontier Sikhs safely crosses the Afghan border with the help of Malik Annat Khan, a powerful Pathan chief. The family's elder, Manak Singh, has a sister-in-law, Pritam Kaur, married to Kartar Singh, a powerful Sikh businessman of Jalalabad. So the entire family of four brothers and two cousins, along with their wives and children, arrive at the house of Kartar Singh, affectionately called Bhajaan.

The new arrivals soon rent a separate place and start their own business. After having surmounted the initial hurdles, they strike roots in the new soil, though a kind of insecurity persists. Two incidents are indicative of this.

First is the incident with Balwant Singh (a Sikh boy) whose bride, Pasho, is forcefully carried off by a Pathan boy, Aslam, to his home in the distant hills. When a group of Sikhs led by Bhajaan go to the hills to retrieve her with the help of some local middlemen, the girl refuses to come with them as she fears that, having been abducted, she may not be fully accepted back by her husband who would mistreat her anyway. The law does not help the Sikhs.

Another incident relates to Sakina, the beautiful wife of an Afghan. Sakina is a nymphomaniac and tries to entice Sikh boys. Two Sikh boys, Jasbir and Dharam, fall victim to her advances but they are caught and severely thrashed by the Afghans before being handed over to the police. Death is the punishment for such acts. Sakina also turns against them, imputing them of sexual molestation. The Sikh community in Jalalabad and Kabul is perturbed. They decide to save the boys and so bribe the Kazi who is to try them. But the Kazi accepts a fat bribe and still sentences the boys to be hanged. The Sikhs are crestfallen. Undoubtedly, if both the parties had been Afghans, there would have been a different verdict. Though the Sikhs are financially well off in Afghanistan, yet they have to live lives as second-rate citizens. The Afghans dominate both physically and politically and live without any regard for the rule of law.

Finally, in the nineties of the last century, the Taliban sweep the country and Islamic fundamentalism becomes the dominant state ideology. The Sikhs can barely survive in the dogmatic environment. Ultimately, as a submissive minority, they are forced to migrate to India and those who stay behind lead a life of servile non-entities. After nearly half a century, the terror, fear and psychosis of the Partition days revisit them.

Sehgal has first-hand knowledge of the life patterns and cultural mores of the people in these regions. In the Punjabi text, the characters speak their local dialect (Hindco) and, at times, Pashto and Persian. This adds to the verisimilitude of the narrative.

Author

Gurmukh Singh Sehgal (1940–) born in Landikotal (Pakistan) is presently living in Patiala. He is M.A. in English, Punjabi and Music and by profession a teacher and a writer. He worked at Modi College, Patiala, as a lecturer in Punjabi language and Literature for 30 years. He has been a Ghazal Singer for All India Radio. For his literary achievements he was awarded Bhai Vir Singh Galp Puraskar by Guru Nanak Dev University, Amritsar for his novel *Nadion Vichhre Neer*; his novel *Sargam* was awarded Nanak Singh Puraskar by the Department of Languages, Government of Punjab. Besides Punjabi, Hindi and English, he also knows Urdu, Persian, Pashto and Gujarati.

In Punjabi, Sehgal has emerged as a significant novelist writing about life in a particular region – the North West Frontier Province (NWFP) of Pakistan, as it existed before Partition. His two early novels *Nadion Vichhre Neer* and *Luarhgi* are vivid narratives of the Pathan way of life in that region – their customs and traditions, their entertainments and eating habits, friendships and hostility, revulsion at civil society and faith in natural justice. His third novel *Hijrat* (migration), as the title indicates, is about the migration of Sikhs.

Inder Singh Khamosh

- *On the Trails of Fire* by Inder Singh Khamosh; Translated by NarinderJit Kaur; Published by Punjabi University, Patiala.

On the Trails of Fire (Karzai Supne) is a novel in which Inder Singh Khamosh has successfully depicted the socio-economic conditions and human relations in the society of Punjab, which is struggling to overcome manifold problems. The novel expresses his maturity as a writer as well as his understanding of human nature, the travails of human life, and man's helplessness in giving practical shape to his dreams.

The two major characters, Kultar Singh and Gurdev Kaur, are ordinary people with simple dreams for their lives. But these dreams are repeatedly thwarted by the social system and, in order to survive, they have to adjust and fine-tune their dreams. Gurdev, daughter and daughter-in-law of very rich and affluent families, has her simple dream of a happy marital life shattered when she finds herself surrounded by an impotent husband, licentious father-in-law and a rapist brother-in-law. She ends up working as a schoolteacher in a small village, struggling to stand on her own feet.

Kultar, a hard-working recluse, wants to become a government officer but has to compromise by being a schoolteacher. And his dream of marrying the girl of his choice is shattered twice as he ends up marrying a woman whom he has never seen or met. It is a tale of the alienation of man from society and of his struggle for survival. Both the characters are misfits. Gurdev finds herself alienated in her in-law's family, and even in the house of her sister-in-law and stepmother. Kultar is estranged wherever he goes – his pastoral village, his maternal village and his Mama (uncle)'s urban home. Yet these characters create a world of their own where they support each other to lead a respectable life.

Kultar worked hard to overcome all obstacles and passed his B.A in Economics and proceeded to acquire a B.Ed. He fell in love with a girl called Shakuntala with whom he exchanged poems. She was a brilliant girl who stood first in the B.A Exam. Fate intervened and his marriage with Shakuntala was thwarted. Despite his high qualifications, Kultar had to accept a job as a teacher. Another chance for a wedding was also thwarted. His third ladylove was a girl who was ready to marry him but was not willing to obtain the consent of her parents. The village Sarpanch rushes to his help and the marriage is conducted without pomp and drama.

Khamosh has given a new status to Punjabi realism and has successfully placed Punjabi fiction in line with the fiction of other prominent Indian languages. NarinderJit Kaur has translated this Punjabi novel into English with great excellence and proficiency.

Author

Inder Singh Khamosh has made significant contributions to Punjabi Literature by writing three books of poetry, one book of short stories and six novels. He has translated Leo Tolstoy, Anton Chekhov and others into Punjabi. His novel *Kafar Messiah*, based on the life of Tolstoy, has been widely read and acclaimed.

Jaswant Singh Kanwal

- *Dawn of the Blood* by Jaswant Singh Kanwal; Translated by Sant Singh Sekhon; Published by Ajanta Publications.

Dawn of the Blood is considered Kanwal's most notable as well as most controversial novel. In it, he writes about the Naxalite Movement that became a fearsome political factor in Punjab in 1966–67. The novel became so controversial during the Emergency of 1970s that no publisher was ready to publish it. Kanwal had it published in Singapore and smuggled its copies to India. It was only after the Emergency that it was published in Punjab. In this novel, Kanwal has given – in fictional form – an account of the few years of Naxalite activities in Punjab, which were opposed by the government and suppressed with an iron hand.

The Naxalite movement had its roots in Bengal where it endeavoured to bring about a socialist society while also fighting for the rights of agricultural labour versus the feudal class. In his novel, Kanwal talks of armed struggle, invoking Bhagat Singh, yet he has not been able to detach himself from the paradigm of romantic idealism, which pervades Punjabi life and literature.

"Whatever one's political and moral inclinations, there is no denying the fact that the Naxalite revolutionaries evinced a tragic dimension which compels sympathy in the manner of Greek and Elizabethan tragedy. So, it is hoped, too, that this novel will put across the basic trait of the Punjabi peasantry which has throughout history made it fight tyranny with a desperate heroic suffering," says Sant Singh Sekhon, the translator of the book.

Dawn of the Blood is quite different from Kanwal's earlier novels where he presented a socialist and progressive worldview based on social idealism aiming at public welfare. But in this novel, Kanwal is distancing himself from social romanticism and takes up politics as his genre as he deals with the socio-political conditions of Punjab in a given period of history, i.e. the Naxalite movement. Though a writer of a political novel looks at the historical events and incidents through the prism of his imagination, he is expected to give shape to a futuristic society. In *Dawn of the Blood*, Kanwal looks at all the social conditions of Punjab from a political standpoint and raises his voice against human exploitation.

Sekhon's affiliation to Marxism in the 1930 gives him an edge as the translator of *Dawn of the Blood*, as he could understand Kanwal's perception and treatment of Naxalite philosophy. Also, the fact that Sekhon was a teacher of English, but preferred to write in Punjabi, came as an added qualification for him as he could relate to the literary idiom and culture of both the languages. There is no doubt that Sekhon has produced an excellent English version of a great literary work by keeping intact the sanctity and integrity of the original thought process presented by Kanwal in the Punjabi version.

Author

Jaswant Singh Kanwal, the septuagenarian Punjabi novelist, short-story writer and essayist, was born in village Dhudike, Distt. Moga, Punjab, in 1919. A writer with left leanings, Kanwal stands against social norms and the beliefs of his times in most of his writings. He is known for his descriptions of realistic, rural and rustic life in Punjab, particularly the Malwa region. He took tough political stands in his newspaper essays and, at one stage, supported the Naxalite movement and later the Khalistan movement.

Kanwal has written around 32 books including novels, short stories, poetry and essays, though he is prominently known for his novels. His works include *Puranmashi (Full Moon Night), Raat Baaki Hai (The Night is Unfinished), Civil Lines, Roop Dhara (Layers of Beauty), Haani (Soul-mate), Mittar Pyare Nu (To friend Beloved), Lahoo Di Loe (Dawn of the Blood), Gwachi Pug (Lost Turban), Punjabio*

Marna Hai Ke Jeena (O Punjabi! Do you wish to die or live?), *Mukti Maarag (Freedom Way)*, *Khoon Ke Sohile Gavee-aih Nanak (Nanak! Sing Sonnets of Blood)*, *Aniaan Chon Utthey Surma (From the Masses Will Rise the Valorous)* and *Rooh Da Haan (Friendship with the Soul)*.

He was conferred with the Sahitya Akademi Award for his novel *Taushali di Hanso* in 1998, the Punjab Sahit Shromani Award in 2007 and degree of Doctor of Literature (Honoris Causa) by Guru Nanak Dev University, Amritsar, in 2008 for his contribution to Punjabi literature.

Read on:

- Kanwal's book, *Gawachi Pug (The Lost Turban)* has been made into a movie by Navtej Sandhu.

Kartar Singh Duggal

- *Alien Heart* by K.S. Duggal; Translated by Jai Ratan; Published by Disha Books.

Alien Heart is the English translation of Duggal's classic Punjabi novel *Man Pardesi* and is about a family of nationalist Muslims in the years following Partition. Events are seen through the eyes of Zeba, the daughter of Sheikh Haseeb.

The Partition was a trying time for Muslims living in India, as they had to choose between living in India and migrating to Pakistan. It was natural for Muslims staying in West Punjab and other areas that fell in Pakistan to stay there, but for the Muslims spread all over India, it was a Hobson's choice. The Muslim League and some other communal forces portrayed that, after independence, India would be a Hindu country where the Muslims would not be given equal rights, or worse, would be prosecuted. Many, however, had faith in the utterings of Mahatma Gandhi and Nehru that the minorities would be well protected and hence were convinced to continue living in India. And an equal number, if not more, were fence sitters who were watching how the newly independent India and Pakistan would behave before deciding.

This story is set in Meerut, Uttar Pradesh, and, as the blurb on the book says, 'we see how Zeba moves from a position of belief in the separateness of Muslims to a firm conviction that her own after and that of her community lies in India. She realizes that her roots are in India and that her future too is linked with that of India. To deny this would be to make hers an alien heart, one that belongs nowhere and knows no peace.'

The book is also a semi-historical account of that period as people were trying to make sense of the circumstances. Many have relatives on both sides of border and could not decide whether they should call Pakistan an enemy country, especially during the war when Pakistani planes start dropping bombs on India. The author, very candidly, discusses issues that were disturbing the minds of many Muslims at that time.

Duggal's short stories are very powerful, especially those related to Partition and Hindu–Muslim–Sikh relations, and many of his anthologies have been translated into English. He also wrote a trilogy, which covers an eventful period for Punjab, starting with the struggle for freedom and ending with the announcement of general elections by Mrs. Indira Gandhi after the Emergency.

The first novel in the trilogy is entitled *Haal Mureedm Da (The Plight of the Devotees)*. It describes life in a typical Punjab village, with Hindus and Muslims living in complete harmony. There are glimpses of the struggle for freedom. However, Hindu–Muslim amity is maintained. This is shattered with the Muslim demand for Pakistan. The novel ends with the Partition. The second novel of the trilogy, first published as *Maa Pio Jaaye (Born of the Same Parents)* and later renamed as *Ab Na Bason Eh Gaon (No More Will I Live in This Village)*, is the story of the blood-soaked Partition. The third part of the trilogy is the novel *Jal Ki Piyas Na Jaaye (Water Remains Thirsty)* when the characters are engulfed in the Emergency declared by Indira Gandhi and the ensuing high-handedness of the administration.

Duggal is unique in Punjabi literature for having fictionalized important events in the contemporary history of India. The way he has interwoven the personal relationships of these unforgettable characters with the historical events between 1918 and 1979 shows his superb literary craftsmanship.

Author

Kartar Singh Duggal (1917–2012) was a writer who wrote with equal felicity in Punjabi, Urdu, Hindi and English. His works have been translated into many Indian and foreign languages. He was born in Dhamal, Rawalpindi (now in Pakistan), and received his M.A. Honours in English at Forman Christian College, Lahore. Duggal started his professional career with All India Radio (AIR). He was then the Secretary/Director, National Book Trust and finally served as an Information Advisor at the Ministry of Information and Broadcasting (Planning Commission).

He founded many institutions, including Raja Rammohun Roy Library Foundation, Institute of Social and Economic Change, Bangalore and Zakir Husain Educational Foundation. Duggal was the President of Punjabi Sahitya Sabha, Delhi, nominated Fellow of the Punjabi University and was also honoured with a nomination to the Rajya Sabha in 1997.

Duggal won many awards throughout his career including the Padma Bhushan, the Sahitya Akademi Fellowship, Ghalib Award, Soviet Land Award, Bharatiya Bhasha Parishad Award, Bhai Mohan Singh Vaid Award, Bhartiya Bhasa Parishad Award, Punjabi Writer of the Millennium Award of Government of Punjab and Bhai Vir Singh Award.

Duggal is a master storyteller and he wrote 24 collections of short stories and 10 novels interweaving the historical strands of the Partition saga and the intricacies of human relationships in modern society. He also penned seven plays, seven works of literary criticism, two collections of poems and an autobiography. Duggal rendered a fine translation of the Holy Guru Granth Sahib in poetic English in tune with the spirit of the scripture. Various universities for graduate studies have adopted many of his books into their curriculum.

It was his exploration of a woman's psyche that gave him a distinct identity and made him a powerful voice for the other gender in a patriarchal society. His tone is restrained and urbane and his portrayals of the north Indian upper-middle-class families, especially those of Muslim descent, are deft as well as authentic. The environs of Pothohar, especially its dialect, became an integral part of his works, which were filled with nostalgia and intimacy.

Read on:

- *K.S. Duggal: A Reader* by Paramjeet Singh Ramana; Published by Sahitya Akademi is a comprehensive compendium of Duggal's writings.
- *Twice Born Twice Dead*, a novel on the issue of Partition by Duggal has been translated from Punjabi (*Nahuntey Mas*) by Jamal Ara with the author; Published by Vikas Publishing House Pvt. Ltd. It has also been translated in Urdu, Hindi, Sindhi and Malayalam.

Krishna Sobti

- *Zindaginama* by Krishna Sobti; Translated by Neer Kanwal Mani with Moyna Mazumdar; Published by Harper Perennial.

Hailed as an unparalleled classic of Indian literature, Krishna Sobti's much-acclaimed novel *Zindaginama* was published in 2016 in English translation. The translation comes nearly 40 years after it was first published in Hindi in 1979. The novel is set in pre-Partition Punjab and celebrates the composite culture of Punjab that came to a sad end.

The story is set sometime in the first decade of the 20th century. The British have been in India for over 150 years. However, life in the small village of Shahpur in undivided Punjab has remained largely unchanged. There are no protagonists or antagonists in this story. Through the everyday life of people of that village, the story of India of that period is told. Hindus, Muslims and Sikhs live side-by-side and celebrate their sorrows and happiness together. The character that binds the village is the wealthy and worldly wise Shahji, his wife Shahni and his benevolent younger brother Kashi to whom all the villagers look for support and advice, even though Shahji charges exorbitant interest rates on loans and has almost the entire village land mortgaged to him.

Soon the winds of change start blowing, as incidents and movements like the Jallianwala Bagh massacre, World War 1, Ghadar Movement, Arya Samaj Movement suck the village into their vortex and the village can no longer remain unaffected. The youth are recruited to the British Army and that brings further changes to the idyllic life of the villagers.

Sobti's magnum opus, *Zindaginama*, through the intricately woven personal histories of a wide set of characters, brings alive the story of the undivided Punjab in that particular idiom, and there are enough people on both sides of border who would look at that wistfully and with nostalgia. The people then lived with a grace although there were occasional tiffs, robberies, murders and the ubiquitous police corruption and its excesses. The translation retains the earthy Punjabi flavour of those times with terms like *Balihari Jaoon, Ni ri, chup ri, Hain ri, Ari, Lo ji, oye, Badshaho, Kairon se, Haiyyi shabash, Bhraji*.

There is a little trivia associated with this book. *Zindaginama* won the Sahitya Akademi Award in 1980. Four years later, when noted Punjabi author and poet Amrita Pritam published a biography of a minor revolutionary called *Hardatt ka Zindaginama*, the word 'Zindaginama' created problems and Sobti demanded that the word be deleted from Pritam's book as it amounted to plagiarism. Pritam insisted that it was no plagiarism. Sobti filed a case in court. The copyright fight over the title evoked much interest because it involved two literary legends. Interestingly, both of them came from the same region of Gujarat in Pakistan–Punjab and were witness to the tragedy of the Partition. The case lingered for over a quarter of a century and was finally decided in favour of Pritam in 2011, six years after her death.

Author

Krishna Sobti (1925–) is a Hindi fiction writer and essayist, who won the Sahitya Akademi Award for her novel *Zindaginama* and in 1996, was awarded the Sahitya Akademi Fellowship, the highest award of the Akademi. She was also the recipient of the first Katha Chudamani Award, the Shiromani Award, Hindi Academy Award,and Vyas Samman. Her works include *Channa, Dar Se Bichchuri, Mitro Marjani, Yaron Ke Yar, Tin Pahar, Suraj Mukhi Andhere Ke*, etc.

Sobti is an iconoclast, if there is one. Her major selected works are available in *Sobti Eka Sohabata*. Each work has the advantage of being written in Hindi and also steeped in the flavours of the region the story is set in. Her innovative use of language, technique and delineation of strong women characters have opened new vistas in Hindi literature. Her writings cover issues dealing with Partition, upheaval and turmoil in Indian society, man–woman relationship, feudalism and dissolution of human values.

Considered the *grande dame* of Hindi literature, Sobti also writes under the name 'Hashmat' and has published *Hum Hashmat*, a compilation of pen portraits of writers and friends. A number of her works are now available in English and Urdu.

She was offered the Padma Bhushan by the Government of India in 2010, which she declined, stating that as a writer, she had to keep a distance from the establishment.

Krishna Sobti

- *To Hell With You Mitro* by Krishna Sobti; Translated by Gita Rajan and Raji Narasimhan; Published by Katha.

The novel revolves round the dynamics of a joint family in a typically Indian rural setup. 'Mitro' or 'Sumitravanti' is married to the middle son of the Gurudas family. She is a woman who is honest about her emotions – not worried or concerned about comments about her and her behaviour. Her paramount quality is that she ruthlessly satiates her intensified libido.

Mitro Marjani created quite a commotion when it was initially released as it depicted a wedded woman and her unrequited sexual appetite against the backdrop of a typical joint family in Punjab bound by tradition. Fiercely independent and courageous beyond belief, Mitro flaunts her sexuality, which is not usually displayed in a closed society. She encounters the anger of her husband and tantrums of a recalcitrant mother-in-law with equanimity. The novel does not tie itself into knots of a psychological hue but is a surprisingly acceptable recount of developments.

Her courage is apparent not only in the audacity with which she taunts a closed society but also in her ability to change her own attitude when she feels it necessary. Or perhaps it is the basic honesty of her nature that allows her to face herself and all she has believed in as unflinchingly as she faces her husband's violent wrath and mother-in-law's tantrums.

Sobti's choice of characters is certainly unique – she has picked them up from a raw rural background. The setting is so typically Indian that an average Indian readily relates with every aspect of it. The perennial quarrels between mother-in-law and daughter-in-law, the wars between avaricious brothers, the games of power politics between brothers, the helpless father and the covetous daughters-in-law.

Mitro is an embodiment of the 'Free Woman' and overcomes all obstructions. She is not hesitant to aim at any man that takes her fancy, even her brother-in-law. The heroine declares with warmth, 'Strange are the ways of the body. A drop leaves it as unquenched as a sea.' Sobti analyses Mitro as if she is on a psychiatrist's couch. The heroine is a good and acceptable daughter-in-law and at the same time meets her sexual needs; hence, Mitro gave utterance to things not contemplated then in society. Both the author and her heroine refused to be confined into boxes of exemplary behaviour, and Sobti stands out as a crusader for woman's freedom for the last 50 years. Sobti's fiery novel is candid, honest, vivid and simply bold.

The translators: Gita Rajan is a professional Editor and Raji Narasimhan, a novelist with five books to her credit. The duo has marvelously translated this novel.

Read on:
- Krishna Sobti's other novel *Samay Sargam* has been translated from Hindi into English as *The Music of Solitude* by Vasudha Dalmia; Published by Harper Perennial.
- *Ai Ladki* translated by Shivanath as *Listen Girl* (English); Published by Katha.
- *Dil-o-Danish*, translated into *The Heart Has Its Reasons* into English.

Nanak Singh

- *A Life Incomplete* by Nanak Singh; Translated by Navdeep Suri; Published by Harper Perennial.

A Life Incomplete is the first-ever English translation of *Adh Khidiya Phul*, a classic from an author regarded as the Father of Punjabi Literature. Singh draws on personal experiences to create this compelling portrait of Punjab in the 1920s. It is an intense meditation on the choices people make and the consequences these may have. The author's engagement with social issues like superstition and blind faith, religious bigotry, casteism and the emancipation of women seems as fresh and relevant today as it was when he wrote this book.

Written as a draft by Singh in jail, it was redrafted 18 years later as a novel. Suri calls the book a 'tragedy.' Present in the book are several incidents and characters that are drawn from the first 25–30 years of the writer's life.

The narrative begins with political prisoner Kuldeep Singh's days in Lahore jail, where the only thoughts that sustain him are those of his beautiful wife, Satwant. Kuldeep is desperate to go home to Peshawar and mend fences with his wife who suspected him of cheating on her. The lovesick Punjabi prisoner sporting a 'brown beard' strikes an unusual friendship with a Pathan jail guard, Ahmed Khan. The friendship is a testament to inter-faith tolerance at a time when hostility between the Hindus and the Muslims was on the rise. Kuldeep returns home to find that his wife had died, leaving behind an infant child. Kuldeep's world collapses, and he is pulled in different directions and finds himself drawn to Prakash, his child's maid.

Kuldeep negotiates the divergent pulls exerted by people around him: a holy man who advocates renunciation, his childhood friend Saroj who has always loved him and the tempestuous Prakash who hides an unsavoury past. The character of Saroj stands for women empowerment. She is a strong, talented and educated woman who has suffered the social ignominy of being a child widow but she rides over this and contributes to society through her idealism.

It now falls upon Ahmed Khan to redeem the star-crossed love and reunite the lovers. Kuldeep Singh decides to hand over his son to his Muslim friend Ahmad Khan and his wife Zubeida. The beauty of the story lies in Ahmad's admonition to Zubeida to mind the Sikh taboos of beef and tobacco. He says these items must never enter their home now.

Nanak Singh was more than a writer; he was a part of the reform movement. The characters in his novels gave a social message, which is still relevant and universal. The work recreates the magic of Singh through a poignant story set in Peshawar of pre-Partition days. The last few paragraphs of the translation bring out the work's relevance in today's times when communalism is straining the country's secular fabric. A high point of the book is that it challenges superstition, bigotry and godmen.

Author

Nanak Singh (1897–1971), born poor, did not receive a formal education but went on to become one of the most revered and prolific writers in Punjabi. He started his writing career at an early age, writing verses on historical events and even devotional songs. In 1918, he published his first book, *Satguru Mehma* (containing hymns in praise of the Sikh Gurus).

The Jallianwala Bagh Massacre impelled Singh to write *Khooni Visakhi*, an epic poem that targeted colonial rule. The British Government banned the book. Singh also participated in India's independence struggle by joining the Akali movement. He was charged with participation in unlawful political activities and was sent to the Borstal Jail, Lahore. His second book, *Zakhmi Dil*, which described the savagery and oppression of the British on peaceful Sikhs during the Guru ka Bagh Morcha demonstration, was also banned.

Singh wrote novels while in jail. He wrote over 40,000 pages in long-hand Gurmukhi script. He wrote 59 books, including 38 novels. He was undisputedly the best-selling Punjabi author in India during the pre-Independence years. Singh's writings are widely available in Punjabi and he addressed almost all the social issues that made the headlines in the early 20th century. His works have been translated into Hindi and many other Indian languages. Natasha Tolstoy, granddaughter of novelist Leo Tolstoy, translated Nanak Singh's novel *Chitta Lahu* into Russian.

Singh was recognized with many awards, including Punjab's highest literary award in 1960. His great historical novel, *Ik Mian Do Talwaran* (*One Sheath and Two Swords*, 1959) won him India's highest literary honour, the Sahitya Akademi Award in 1962.

Nanak Singh

- *The Watchmaker* by Nanak Singh; Translated by Navdeep Suri; Published by Penguin.

Nanak Singh's novel, *Pavitar Paapi* became immensely popular and won him literary acclaim. It was translated into Hindi and several other Indian languages and was adapted into a successful motion picture *(Pavitra Paapi)* in 1968 by his ardent admirer, Balraj Sahni. Currently, the novel is in its 28th reprint in Punjabi.

The novel, now titled *The Watchmaker*, was originally written in Punjabi by Nanak Singh in the 1940s and has become a classic. Navdeep Suri, the translator (and the author's grandson) has clarified that the book was earlier published as *Saintly Sinner* but due to issues with the original publisher, Suri (with their consent) worked with Penguin and republished it as *The Watchmaker*. It included a few modifications and tighter editing.

The tale is set somewhere between Amritsar and Rawalpindi during the time between the Wars. Panna Lal, burdened by business losses and unpaid debts unknown to his wife, finds himself working for the watchmaker, Attar Singh. But he works as an accountant because his poor eyesight – though he is only in his late thirties – prevents him from learning how to repair watches. Panna Lal's wife, Maya is a few years younger, they have four children, and although Panna Lal's small income keeps the family going, and Maya is a brave, honest homemaker, they face other financial responsibilities. The most pressing of these is a marriage for their 15-year-old daughter, Veena. A wealthy family has made a proposal, Veena is eager, and Panna Lal believes he can do something good and right.

Now the first blow falls. The boy's family breaks off the arrangements; Panna Lal and Maya think the other family considers them too poor. Maya, undaunted, says they can sell her jewelry and ask Attar Singh for a loan of some kind.

Then the second blow falls. Panna Lal arrives at work to find himself sacked. A much younger man, Kedar Nath, who has overcome the early death of his watchmaker father and his mother by getting a B.A. and learning the watchmaker's craft as well, has walked into Attar Singh's shop and has been instantly employed to replace Panna Lal. With a silent look Kedar never forgets, Panna Lal walks away and disappears.

Panna Lal's anguished family sends Veena and one of her brothers to look for their missing father. Kedar, guilty and unable to tell the truth, invents a story to help the distraught family. He tells them that Attar Singh has sent Panna Lal to Bombay on business. Kedar promises to visit the family next day. He ends up, at their suggestion, renting a room next door. He eats with them and starts tutoring both the little son, Basant and the daughter, Veena before he leaves for work in the morning, all the time hoping that Panna Lal would return soon.

As all the family comes to adore him, Kedar's lie presses ever harder upon him. He writes the family a weekly letter purportedly from Panna Lal and reads it out to them, but he cannot let Veena see it because she will know it is not in her father's hand. Somehow, he manages to convince Maya that he is missing his own mother, and he fends off Veena's insistent questioning about his unhappiness. Yet he is drawn deeper and deeper into the family, and it is at his suggestion – and on his promise to raise money for the wedding — that Maya bravely goes and gets the wedding arrangements restored. Meanwhile, he falls in love with Veena but cannot muster up the strength to ask for her hand due to the circumstances and the guilt that he was carrying.

Kedar is forced into lie after lie in a tale unsentimentally clear about the inevitability of fate. Finally, to help the family, he is forced to use the money of Attar Singh without his knowledge. He then leaves the town after confessing about his crime to Attar

Singh in a letter and with a promise to repay the amount. He settles in a different town and works hard to keep his promise and regularly sends money to Attar Singh. He spends his remaining life in memories of his love for Veena.

Niranjan S. Tasneem

- *The Lost Meaning* by Niranjan S. Tasneem; Translated by him from Punjabi; Published by Sahitya Akademi.

This book is an English translation of his Punjabi novel, *Gwache Arth*, which bagged the Sahitya Akademi Award and is an odyssey in search of the lost meaning of life during the turbulent period of the 1980s in Punjab. The protagonist is a forlorn figure caught in the complex web of rampant social prejudices and political manipulations. He realizes the utter futility of barriers created by society and becomes aware that the two communities in Punjab are inextricably intertwined and inter-dependent.

The author has depicted the interior monologue of characters in his novels, which was considered something new in Punjabi fiction at that time. The novel begins in a village where a Hindu political leader has been shot dead resulting in tension between Hindus and Sikhs. We get harrowing descriptions of the scenes following the desecration of the Akal Takht and of Harmandar Sahib being infiltrated and vandalized by the Indian Army. 'Operation Bluestar' was simply outrageous and shook the faith of an entire community. It inevitably led to more outrageous acts like the assassination of Indira Gandhi and its painful aftermath – the genocide of Sikhs.

Fear is key and spreads like a miasma over the entire narration. Roopinder (a character) asks, 'For what crime are we punished? […] They wanted to kill me simply because I had a turban on my head, beard and moustaches on my face and belonged to the Sikh faith.' A section of the people was highly traumatized and their honour violated. The punishment had been meted out to none others than the devotees and that too on the martyrdom day of Sri Guru Arjan Dev.

Tasneem writes with astonishing fidelity, 'I depicted the loss as people were living very cordially, but Partition in 1947 divided the communities and caused suffering at both sides... Now I have started feeling as if we were residing in an alien land. Everyone looks at us with distrustful eyes. I am not talking about the places outside Punjab, where we have no standing at all. Even in Punjab, our own brothers and sisters distrust us.'

Tasneem considers the novel an 'art form' and, as such, narrative purity has been of prime importance to him. He depicts the plight of the modern man as a victim of existential dichotomy. *Lost Meaning* is a true down-to-earth narration of Man 'red in tooth and claw' as a poet puts it.

Author

Tasneem taught undergraduate and postgraduate classes in English for more than three decades and was Professor Emeritus from 1987–1993 at GHG Khalsa College. He has also been Fellow at the Indian Institute of Advanced Study, Shimla. He has won the Punjabi Sahit Ratan Award and the Shiromani Sahitkar Puraskar of the State's Languages Department. He started writing in Punjabi at the age of 35 and has been contributing to Punjabi literature for the past 51 years. He has written 12 books in English, two Urdu novels, and 10 novels and 10 literary books in Punjabi.

Professor Tasneem dabbled briefly in Urdu ghazals and then switched over to Urdu fiction. Later, he immersed himself in Punjabi novel and criticism.

The Indian Institute of Advanced Study, Shimla, published his book *Narrative Modes in Punjabi Novel*. This, as the critics say, has cut new ground as far as Punjabi literary criticism is concerned. The other book in Punjabi, *Aaeene de Rubru*, is his literary autobiography. Professor Tasneem has also written scores of middles in *The Tribune*. These are being compiled into two books, *The Corridors of Time* and *The Golden Mists*. Now, a publisher in Delhi has planned to publish his 100 middles in a book entitled *Moods and Moments*. According to the prolific Tasneem, these articles, in their totality, can be termed as his spiritual autobiography.

Om Prakash Gasso

- *The Hot Wave (Tatti Hawa)* by Om Prakash Gasso; Translated by J. S. Anand; Published by Punjabi University, Patiala.

Tatti Hawa covers a wide canvas of issues. The story is set in an unnamed village in Punjab where the protagonist Narinder (Nindi) is a hardworking, conscientious young man. His father, a hotheaded man, goes to jail after hitting a man for a dispute on water sharing in the fields. But Nindi works hard, is fond of reading books, keeps away from organized religion and is a great humanist who is always ready to help others. He has a good knowledge of agriculture, and the villagers turn to him for expert advice on all issues relating to farming.

He appears to be the author's alter ego as Gasso uses this idealistic young man to voice his opinions on all matters that plague Punjabi society and the nation. Issues like Partition of the country, the Khalistan movement, the role of religion and their mahants/granthis in fooling people, the Hindu–Sikh relations on the language issue as well as during the militancy phase, the attack on Harmander Sahib and Akal Takht are all dealt with in a candid manner. Some issues are, of course, tackled subtly in the story; for instance, when Nindi gets his friend's sister, Kulwant married to Sardara Singh, an educated and austere man who is totally against dowry and the rituals of marriage and who takes her in a simple ceremony devoid of any pompous arrangements (the likes of which have plagued Punjabi society), Gasso takes a stand against the expenditure on weddings which leaves Punjabi fathers, especially Jats, in debt and hence reluctant to have daughters. But this man who is an idol for Nindi, goes further and gives due importance to his newly wed wife and on 1st of every month, hands over his salary to her. The author makes his point clear regarding the equality of gender and the need to respect women.

Nandi grasps with bewilderment how people and their allegiances alter with the change in fortune of the political establishment. When, for example, the Congress Party is defeated, its supporters discard white khadi and start sporting blue turbans favoured by the Akali Party. Some even carry two sets of flags in their cars. From politics, the story moves to talking about using natural fertilizers like dung heap and doing efficient farming. The author is also much disturbed by the misuse of religion in the country especially its detrimental impact on the poor. The rich, he says, have no religion. He is equally critical of the West hailing India for its democracy but at the same time not qualifying it by saying that it is was an imperfect and dirty democracy. The State continues to deny many major rights to a vast majority of its citizens. It does not empower its citizens but makes them grovel before it for things that are basic rights. At the same time, those who protest or try to reform are hounded and, as the writer very succinctly points out, we have not accepted that somebody who is anti-government is not anti-nation. In fact, one who challenges the wrong policies of government is the real well-wisher of the country.

Punjabi University, Patiala, has done a yeoman's job in translating several Punjabi masterpieces like this one.

Author

Om Prakash Gasso is a legend of Punjabi literature. He is a realist who portrays, with immense artistic skill, the superstitions, customs and rites of society. Known as the literary tree-man of Malwa, he has written more than 50 books and has planted around 50,000 trees; of these 40,000 are now fully grown. He has been doing this for the last 40–50 years. A Shiromani Sahitkar Award winner, he cycles his way through villages with a jute bag containing books to popularize reading. At all gatherings, he never fails to plant trees.

However, his love for trees does not stop there. He treats the trees as his children and uses the proceeds from them to repair leaking roofs in schools. His love for trees started well before Partition and has continued throughout his teaching career. So much so that he has even used his pension fund to buy saplings.

Gasso has written a number of novels on the dregs of rural society. He has observed these neglected persons from close quarters and this lends special credence to what he writes about their hopes and fears. His most famous novel *Mitti da Mull* (1972) carries a message of strife and struggle. This novel has been widely presented as plays, and a Punjabi film has been made on it too.

His works include novels and poetry anthologies in Punjabi and Hindi. A serial based on his novel *Bujh Rahi Batti Da Chanan* has been produced and directed by Ravi Deep for Doordarshan under the title *Parchhaven*.

Gasso, like Ram Sarup Ankhi, writes very poignantly about the rural life of Punjab. However, the difference is that while Ankhi's thoughts are conveyed through the life and deeds of characters and woven into the story, Gasso does not leave anything to chance and so, wherever possible, his thoughts on most subjects are delivered unambiguously in the book by the protagonist and by some other characters too.

Rajinder Singh Bedi

- *I Take This Woman* by Rajinder Singh Bedi; Translated by Khushwant Singh; Published by Orient Paperbacks.

Ek Chadar Maili Si is Bedi's most enduring novel. Khushwant Singh, an expert in Punjabi and Urdu, has translated this novel with great charm into English as *I Take This Woman*. His translation has limpid prose that combines power with grace.

Poverty is the backdrop of this novel about rural Punjab with its special social mores. The story is set in Kotla village, a place of pilgrimage nestling under the benevolent gaze of Vaishno Devi.

Rano, the daughter of poor parents, is married to a Tonga driver named Tiloka. Typically, she is beaten by Tiloka when he gets drunk, which is often; her mother-in-law keeps on harassing her on a daily basis; and her parents maintain a distance after the marriage. The mother-in-law is even prepared to sell her granddaughter. Rano hates Chaudhry Meherban Das who had initiated her husband into evil ways, such as procuring young girls.

Rano starts worrying about her growing daughter, Waddi and her marriage. Another member of the household is Mangal, her husband's younger brother. She brings him up just like her son. She prays to God, 'O God, do not burden even an enemy with the curse of a daughter! She is hardly grown up when her parents throw her out to live among strangers; and if the parents-in-law don't like her, they kick her back to her parents' home. She's like a ball made of cast-off rags. Only when she becomes heavy with her own tears is she incapable of being bounced to and fro.'

One day she sees Chaudhry Meherban Das in handcuffs being led through the bazaar along with a young man whose clothes were stained with blood. The young man's sister, 13 years of age, had been sent by Tiloka to satiate the lust of the headman. The brother had killed Tiloka.

Tiloka's sudden and devastating death means that Rano becomes a widow with no one to support her and she faces constant hostility from her mother-in-law. The plight of a widow is quite miserable; in fact, society viewed widows as a threat. After long deliberations by the village heads and seniors, a solution was arrived at – to get Rano married to her deceased husband's younger brother (which was not frowned upon by custom). Both Rano and Mangal, her brother-in-law, looked upon this proposal with utter horror as they share a mother–son relationship. Meanwhile, Mangal falls for a Muslim girl, Salamat.

Since it is ordained that the good of the community must be placed above that of an individual, they decide to proceed with the alliance. As per custom, Mangal places a sheet over Rano as a sign of protection. A slightly soiled, somewhat tattered three-yard cambric sheet (*a maili si chadar*) symbolizing safety and security, which is transferred from the dead husband to his younger brother for affording the woman to remain under his roof, deliver his children and perform all wifely duties.

With the efflux of time, the couple comes to terms with their forced marriage, consummate it and commence a voyage of passion. The union may be questionable but it is sanctioned by social custom. What springs out of the novel is the victory of the human spirit. Rano emerges as a symbol of strength and unbounded courage.

Soon, her courage is again tested when, to cap the horror, the elders bring Waddi to wed the same young man who had killed Tiloka, her father. The young man, feeling guilty for killing Tiloka, is seeking repentance. Although his good character and the highly moral act impress everybody, it is a difficult choice for Rano. Can she forgive her husband's murderer?

Author

Rajinder Singh Bedi (1915–1984) was an Urdu writer and a playwright, who later became a Hindi film director, screenwriter and dialogue writer. Bedi is considered one of the leading 20th century progressive writers of Urdu and one of the most prominent Urdu fiction writers, known most for his tales on Partition of India.

Bedi was born in Sialkot district, Punjab, now in Pakistan. He spent his early years in Lahore, where he received his education in Urdu, as it was common to most Punjabi families, though he never graduated from a college.

His collection of short stories include, *Daan-O-Daam* (The Catch), featuring his prominent story *Garam Coat* (Warm Coat), *Grehan* (The Eclipse), *Kokh Jali* and *Apne Dukh Mujhe Dedo*. He also wrote a collection of plays, *Saat Khel*. Bedi's stories are memorable because of his depiction of the plight of the heroines: women who are victimized by caste, feudalism, lust and patriarchy, but who also harbor sexual desire in their myriad roles as lovers, mothers, wifes, daughters and sisters.

In 1943, he joined Maheshwari Films, a small Lahore film studio, but then went on to work at All India Radio, Jammu until 1947. By the time of Partition, Bedi had published numerous more short stories and had made a name for himself as a prolific writer. After the partition of India in 1947, he moved to Bombay and started working for films and wrote dialogues for films like *Badi Bahen, Daag, Mirza Ghalib, Devdas, Madhumati, Anuradha, Anupama, Satyakam* and *Abhimaan*. He then directed movies like *Dastak, Phagun, Nawab Sahib* and *Aankhin Dekhi*.

His Novel *Ek Chadar Maili Si* bagged the Sahitya Akademi Award in 1961. Bedi was honoured with the Padma Shri in 1972 and the Ghalib Award in 1978. 'The Rajinder Singh Bedi Award' was created by the Punjab Government to honour his memory.

Read on:

- His novel *Ek Chadar Maili Si* was made into a film in Pakistan, as *Mutthi Bhar Chawal* (1978) and later in India, as *Ek Chadar Maili Si* (1986).
- *Ek Chadar Maili Si* was also translated in English as *Ordained by Fate* by Avtar Singh Judge; Published by Sahitya

Akademi. It has been translated in Hindi, Kashmiri and Bengali.
- His Story *Garam Coat* was made in a film directed by Aman Kumar and featured Balraj Sahni.
- Neena Gupta in 2006 made his short story *Lajwanti* into a telefilm.

Rajinder Singh

- *The Ganges in Her Platter: Dauntless Courage of a Teenage Widow* **by Dr. Rajinder Singh; Published by Dynamic Publications.**

As regards this book, though Rajinder Singh had made jottings of its story in English, the Punjabi version based on those jottings was published first. It is called *Pratrai 'ch Ganga* and then its Hindi version *Nari Ka Sach* followed. Finally, the English version has been published in 2015, although it is not an exact translation of the Punjabi or Hindi version.

As the title suggests, the novel is about a young woman who was married at the young age of 14, as was the custom then, and who, within five years of her marriage, becomes a widow (at the age of 19). The couple had had two children but they didn't survive and finally the young husband dies due to tuberculosis, leaving the widow childless. The writer explains in his introduction that the novel is greatly inspired by his late mother 'whose miserable but defiant life as young widow always inspired me to write about the problems faced by a widow in our society.' He further adds that a widow is not regarded as a human being in the real sense, and they suffer exploitation by lusty insiders and voluptuary advances by outsiders in the male-dominated society. Draconian laws of chastity forbid her to live a life, suppressing her natural instincts and aspirations.

Thus, Jeevi – born to a relatively well-off family in the town of Jalalpur and known for her great beauty – is married to Lehna Singh, son of Pritam Singh. Lehna also has a sister, Melo. Pritam Singh has a brother Satnam Singh who has a son, Sant Singh. Both families live nearby. Jeevi is renamed as Apachhar Kaur and simply called Achhari at her new home.

After the son's death, the family loses another son and all this takes a toll on Pritam Singh who is heartbroken and loses all his business. The young widow resolutely takes up all the housework and even starts some tailoring work to support the family income. Sant Singh also loses his wife, but he had always liked his cousin's wife for her beauty and good nature and so wants to marry her. A ray of hope is born for Achhari. But Pritam Singh on one side and Sant Singh's mother on the other side bitterly oppose the marriage. Sant Singh marries elsewhere, and Achhari is left bitter by his lack of courage.

Pritam Singh's family continues its slide into poverty while that of Sant Singh prospers and his new wife begets one child after another. Sant is guilt ridden and finally, to atone, he convinces his wife to give one son to Achhari who he thinks will be the support for her in her old age. This good deed does bring some respite to Achhari who had been told by Pritam Singh to observe extreme chastity. Achhari focuses on bringing up the child but with no income they live in extreme poverty. She undertakes all sorts of work and undergoes extreme hardships to make ends meet and to educate him.

The novel is quite a bold attempt and provides graphic and realistic details. Very few Punjabi authors dare to write about such things openly. Out of the books included here, *Skeena* by Fauzia Rafiqe is the only novel that comes close in this respect. The author talks of how the young couple consummates its marriage, the mother's advice to daughters on their periods, the young son being given herbs to make him strong as sex makes him weak and others. When Achhari is bringing her son up, they live in a small shed where they sleep, cook, attend nature's call, have baths and even keep a buffalo. The young son is exposed to his mother's anatomy as there is no privacy and he, being inquisitive, asks questions which she has to answer. A young relative, who is also a doctor and is smitten by Achhari, keeps on visiting them and kindles some sort of physical attraction. There are various scenes where he is trying to cure her ailment and again the author describes their encounter vividly although they never seem to bring themselves to go the whole way. All this makes it a unique novel and very realistic. As it is semi-autobiographical in nature, the author could provide such realistic details although it requires quite a lot of courage to pen them and present them to the world. The author needs to be complimented for this honesty.

Author

Dr. Rajinder Singh (1934–) is a retired central government officer and writes in Punjabi, English and Hindi. He has 17 original writings to his credit besides being one of the most prolific translators of leading Punjabi, Hindi and Urdu writers, among both Indians and Pakistanis, into English. He has written five novels in Punjabi, one in Hindi and three in English. He has also re-written Bhai Santokh Singh's magnum opus in simple Punjabi (*Sri Nanak Prakash Saral Vyakhya*) from Brajbhasa, with explanatory notes. Based on this *Saral Vyakhya*, he has written an English version, *Nanak the Divine Light*. He has also translated 85 books, which include authors like Bachint Kaur, Nanak Singh, Sutinder Singh Noor, Pritam Singh Kambo, Dalip Kaur Tiwana, Kulbir Kang and others. He wrote numerous tracts, articles, book reviews and even edited *Khushkhabari*, a Punjabi–Hindi–English monthly of Jalandhar for four years.

Ram Sarup Ankhi

- *Kothe Kharak Singh* by Ram Sarup Ankhi; Translated by Avtar Singh Judge; Published by Sahitya Akademi.

Known as a mesmerizing storyteller, Ankhi chronicled rural life in the Malwa region of Punjab in the latter half of the 20th century. The Malwa landscape comes alive in his writing. His Sahitya Academy Award winner novel *Kothe Kharak Singh*, named after a fictitious but typical Malwa village, is a novel of epic dimensions spanning three generations. It covers the period starting from 1940–42, moving to the Janata Party's rule after the Emergency in the 1970s and then to Indira Gandhi's return to power in the early 1980s. It has 60-odd characters and portrays a realistic picture of the socio-economic backwardness of the region.

The story interweaves the life of villagers with the history of the time, from World War II, the death of Hitler, the coming of Clement Attlee, Bhagat Singh, the Independence of the country, formation of Congress and then Akali governments, to rise of Naxalism and so on. The writer speaks of the concerns of the villagers, be it the problems created by moneylenders, the prevalent superstitions, the scheming village officials such as Patwaris and Sarpanches, the inhuman behaviour of the police force, the Jat's fascination with land and liquor, the rise of deras (religious cults) of Babas and more. Since the canvas available with the author is so huge, he is able to weave almost all events of those times as well as all concerns that plague the Punjab villages. Covering the importance of education, the influence of Russian books, the presence of class and caste distinctions, the coming of roads, buses, electricity, tractors, Ankhi's is a fascinating account of the life and times of that period in Punjab. He also depicts the change in society being wrought by education and new political awakening.

The novel ends on a positive note for that village in Punjab as Indira Gandhi comes back to power after the defeat of Janata Party. However, as Gurbachan Singh Bhullar observes in the preface to the book in 1985, though the novel ends here, the tragedy for Punjab continues – the rise of militancy, Operation Blue Star and the gruesome and heart-wrenching genocide of Sikhs after Indira Gandhi's murder. But he hopes that Punjab will move on and so does Ankhi's novel. Sadly, the hope of Bhullar Sahab has not been fulfilled as Punjab continues to wallow in new tragedies even today.

Author

Ram Sarup Ankhi was a prolific Punjabi writer with 15 novels, eight storybooks and five collections of poems to his credit. Ankhi was Brahmin by caste but Sikh in appearance. He kept the Hindu name, as is the custom in the Malwa region of East Punjab. Only a tiny minority of Brahmins converted to Sikhism and changed their names – Bhai Bhagwan Singh of Ghadar Party, Gyani Hira Singh Dard, SS Amol and Vidhata Singh Tir being the four most famous names amongst them.

Ankhi (1932–2010), born in the village of Dhaula in Barnala district of Punjab, started as a poet but ended up writing fiction. He abandoned his college education midway to work in agriculture. He then got a job as a schoolteacher from which he retired in 1990. His well-known works include *Kothe Kharhak Singh* and *Partapi* while *Malhe Jharhian* and *Apni Mitti De Rukh* are his autobiographies.

In his later novels, self-evidently titled *Salphas* (a chemical used by debt-ridden Malwai Jatts to commit suicide), *Jamināñ Wāley* (The Landed Gentry), *Kaṇak da Qatalām* (Slaughter of the Wheat) and *Bhima* (a Purbia farm worker), etc., he portrayed the post-Green Revolution Malwa with all its acute socio-economic problems such as the onslaught of corporate capitalism, pauperization of small peasantry, mass drug addiction, influx of *Purbia* migrant labour and, in consequence of all this, the disintegration of village communities.

Ankhi also edited a Punjabi short fiction quarterly *Kahāni Punjab* assisted by his son Krantipal. Ankhi received many awards, including the Sahitya Akademi Award and the Kartar Singh Dhaliwal Sarb Shresht Sahitkaar Award.

Ram Sarup Ankhi

- *Partapi* by Ram Sarup Ankhi; Translated by Avtar Singh Judge; Published by Punjabi University, Patiala.

Content with his life in his native village Dhaula, its surrounding areas and later on in the town of Barnala, Ankhi has always sought his themes, locales and characters from within this region. He explains how, with the passage of time, the same landscape has seen a sea change and this transformation is depicted in his novels.

About his choice of subjects, which deal primarily with the plight of villages of Malwa, Ankhi remarked, 'These 50 villages that fall in three districts of Mansa, Bathinda and Sangrur are closest to my heart. I know them very well and can talk about them with authority. Beyond these 50 villages, I have never tried to even step out. I have written about farmer suicides, farmer indebtedness, drug addiction and other issues that can be seen in this area.'

Partapi was the only daughter of her parents; she had four brothers and they were residents of Merllan. As Partapi attained the age of 20, her parents began the search for a suitable groom for her. Her mother, Dyalo started in earnest and accumulated a lot of things for her. While still in the process of making up their minds, two or three years passed. Dyalo asks her husband to finalize Partapi's wedding with a boy, Gajjan, from Jogipur. She favoured him, as his mother had passed away and he owned lot of land and property. However, the girl had fallen in love and decided to marry Jewnna who was also from the same village and belonged to a higher caste. Generally such alliances were frowned upon.

Partapi's mother was engaged in delivering milk to the villagers. On one occasion, Partapi was asked to deliver milk to the highly respected holy man of the village, Dharam Dass. He was a short-statured and thick-skinned man who was the religious head of the village after the death of his Guru. That holy man, as soon as Partapi had entered and delivered milk, closed the doors and raped her. His behaviour changed from that of a holy man to that of a wild bull, endowed with immense strength. Partapi becomes pregnant. Utterly humiliated, she decides to punish him – she takes a sharp sickle and accosts Dharam Dass during his morning walk and summarily beheads him. Jewnna's mother, who knows of his love for Partapi, then influences her son to flee from the village, and he settles down in Malikpur.

Arrangements are made for the marriage of Partapi with Gajjan. In six month's time, she delivers a son who is passed off as premature delivery. Later she presents Gajjan with two daughters. One is named Bibi and as she grows up, Partapi seeks the help of Nek Dass for a suitable match. Dass selects a boy from Malikpur, the place where Jewnna lived. This causes a flutter in Partapi's mind. As she feared, the boy Chand Soon happens to be a relative of Jewnna.

Partapi prepares to go to Malikpur to meet the boy's parents, She discovers that Jewnna had married and had three sons. When she meets him, he is seriously sick and succumbs to the ailment. Her husband, Gajjan loses his life in a stampede in Hari-ki-Pouri, Hardwar. Partapi returns to her village and by the close of the novel, passes away. She is a character that has endured severe trials and tribulations.

The novel is a heartwarming tale told with great realism and complete simplicity. The vagaries of rural life in Punjab are presented very vividly.

Read on:
- A film titled *Sutta Naag* (2014) was made based on Ram Sarup Ankhi's short story of same name. The narrative portrays 50 years old Punjab and addresses serious subjects like infidelity and the suppression of women.

- It was premiered at Punjabi International Film Festival, Toronto.
- Ankhi's selected Punjabi Short Stories have been translated by Suresh Kumar Singla in a collection called *Wrinkles*; Published by National Book Shop.

Read on (Themes)

Movies made on Punjabi books not translated in English and hence not included in this book:
- *Nooran* (2014) – based on famous Punjabi author, Balwant Gargi's story *Rabbo Marasan*, which represents a woman's emotions, was sent for Cannes Film Festival, Short Film Corner.
- *Khoon* (2015) – a film based on Gurbachan Singh Bhullar's Short story was shown at the Punjabi International Film Festival, Toronto.

Sant Singh Sekhon

- *Blood and Soil* by Sant Singh Sekhon; Published by National Book Trust of India.

Blood and Soil is a novel by Sant Singh Sekhon written in English in 1930s. At that juncture, he had resolved to engage English as the medium of writing. Around that time, he wrote plays and poems, some of which were published in publications like *New Verse* and *Adelphi* amongst others. From the 1940s onward, Sekhon was determined to write primarily in Punjabi. Impelled by the national struggle for freedom from the colonial rule and the urge to see the country progress in the socialist direction, he resolved to enrich a language that was, until then, lagging behind due to social, political, communal and historical reasons. In the six decades to follow, he established himself as a celebrated storywriter, playwright, novelist, translator, literary critic and historian of Punjabi language and literature. So overwhelming was his engagement as a multifaceted writer of Punjabi that he did not bother to publish earlier writing in English in book format.

Since then, the English version of *Blood and Soil* remained in manuscript form though its Punjabi translation *Lahu Mitti* appeared in several editions. This novel has been hailed as the first realistic novel in Punjabi. Posthumously, The National Book Trust, in 2014, finally published the English version, almost three quarters of a century after it was written.

Blood and Soil is set in rural Punjab during the first quarter of the 20th century. It unravels the cultural ethos through social, political and religious intricacies. The narrative begins in 1901. A newly wedded couple, Baij Singh and Daya Kaur migrate from their village in the eastern Punjab to the western Punjab, now part of Pakistan. The village is Chak 22 where the Britishers had allotted land to peasants. Even though Jagat Singh did not get any land, he had cordial relations with the owner Hari Singh who had been allotted land. They try to make the newly dug canal system a success in this hamlet. How did this family live for this time interval? Did they prosper as they had hoped to? How did this move affect them? The story revolves around complex emotions of the characters who, faced with the difficult life of peasantry, struggle to ensure the future of their offspring.

The book starts in the year 1901 and the story continues for the next 30 years. During this period, the country is going through change but we are only shown that change with respect to the characters of the story. The older generation is in awe of the British rulers and it is the younger generation that displays the spirit of nationalism.

Author

Sekhon (1908–1997) was one of the pioneering Punjabi writers of the 20th century. As a novelist, short story writer and playwright, his contribution is unparalleled. Recipient of Sahitya Akademi Award for *Mittarpiara* and the Padma Shri, Sekhon is hailed as the major trendsetter in Punjabi for his analytical literary criticism, histories of Punjabi literature and language, and a prolific translations of classics from Punjabi to English and vice versa. His autobiography is also considered a classic in itself. He graduated with Masters Degrees in Economics and in English. His first collections called *Samachar* (Tidings) and *Chhe Ghar* (Six Abodes), a short story and one-act play, respectively, had their beginnings in the Punjabi language. He altogether authored five collections of short stories, four one-act dramas, two novels, 10 full-length plays, five books of literary criticism and two volumes of historical evaluations of Punjabi literature.

He also wrote five books of literary criticism. His scholarly works include *Sahityarth*, a theory of literature, and the pioneering work, *Punjabi Boli Da Itihas* (History of the Punjabi language).

His translations are accompanied by his deep understanding of the literary processes and feelings for the Punjabi language and literature. He offers a profound commentary on the romances of Heer–Ranjha and Mirza–Sahiban, Hindu–Sikh didactic literature, Mythical Wars, etc.

In recognition of his works, Punjabi University at Patiala made him Professor of Eminence and set up a Chair in his honour.

Read on:
- *Sant Singh Sekhon: A Reader* by Tejwant Singh Gill; Published by Sahitya Akademi is a comprehensive compendium of Sekhon's writings.

Satnam

- *Jangalnama: Travels in a Maoist Guerilla Zone* by Satnam; Translated by Vishav Bharti; Published by Penguin Books.

The Punjabi writer and leftist activist, Gurmeet Singh, popularly known as Satnam, spent two months with Maoist guerrillas and adivasis in Bastar in the year 2001. Three years later, he published a remarkable travelogue called *Jangalnama* based on this experience, which is a unique and humane portrait of some of the most misunderstood people in one of the most backward parts of the country – the 'liberated zone' of Bastar. It is an insightful first person account of the Maoists and the tribals and their complex relationships. The Maoists are outlawed, demonized and hunted by the State.

In *Jangalnama*, Satnam wrote, 'People in the jungle don't know who Nehru was, or what happened in 1947. Nor do they know about the change of rule from the Whites to the Browns. For them, "Dilli" (Delhi) is only a word associated with the government, and to them, the government means greedy contractors, repressive police, displacement and harassment.'

About *Jangalnama*, Bharti, the translator, writes, 'People were for the first time reading accounts from the jungles of Bastar that the Maoist movement was not only about Improvised Explosive Devices (IEDs) or killing security personnel, but it was also about how people were struggling to change their fate when the state is absent.'

The book, a translation from Punjabi to English, makes for an effortless reading. It is written lucidly and undoubtedly keeps the reader glued with brilliant judgements that Satnam arrives at about the life of the Maoist guerrillas and the tribals among whom they work. The descriptions are dignified and not alarmist.

Satnam spent two months in remarkable intimacy with the guerrillas: travelling with them, sharing their food and shelter, experiencing their lives first hand. Through his up-close and personal account of their daily lives, we register them as human, made of flesh and bone. We are convinced that the guerillas are totally dedicated to root out oppression. *Jangalnama* is not only a piece of travel writing but a social document concerned with the human situation. It is a compelling argument to recognize the humanity of those in conflict with the mainstream of Indian society and to acknowledge their dream of a world free of exploitation.

The book, like *The Motor Cycle Diaries* of Che Guevara, is an eye-opener to the travails of the Adivasis of Bastar and the service rendered to them by the Guerillas.

There are observations on how the guerrillas work with the tribals – how they have accorded medical care their topmost priority, next only to resistance against plunder and governmental repression. Pisiculture and even simple things that one takes for granted, like the use of vegetables and fruits that are rich in nutritional or medicinal properties, are beyond the ken of the tribal people and educating them on their uses is a challenge for the Maoists.

The campaign for education – literacy as well as political education – is described as a lived experience. There are snippets, too, of the writer's conversations with some of the guerrillas – young Gond men and women whose personal stories point to the fact that behind the tribal upsurge there are also as many stories of personal rebellions as there are guerrillas.

Author

Satnam, who was born in Amritsar, joined the Naxalite movement and dedicated the rest of his life to radical leftist politics. He worked with marginalized communities, including religious minorities and dalits. He was involved in the work of various

Muslim democratic organizations following the Gujarat riots. He was a member of the People's Democratic Front of India and the Mumbai Resistance. He spoke out against human rights abuses in Kashmir and was one of the leaders of the movement against Operation Green Hunt, which was launched in 2009. The first book written by him was a translation of Spartacus. He had studied humanities at the Jawaharlal Nehru University in New Delhi.

Satnam played several roles. He is an underground Maoist guerrilla, often a democratic rights activist on fact-finding missions on human rights violations in Kashmir and Gujarat genocide or a creative writer, who can write with equal felicity in Punjabi, Hindi and English.

Satnam committed suicide in April 2016 after suffering from deep depression. He was 64 years old.

Read on:

- *Why Satnam committed suicide?* Daljit Ami, an independent documentary filmmaker who was pursuing PhD in Cinema Studies from Jawaharlal Nehru University, has written a very telling article. This article has been translated into English from Punjabi by noted author Amandeep Sandhu and can be read at http://www.countercurrents.org/ami0605016.htm

Shivcharan Jaggi Kussa

- *Struggle for Honour* by Shivcharan Jaggi Kussa; Translated from Punjabi by the author himself; Published by ibs Books (UK).

Struggle for Honour is the English translation of one of Shivcharan Jaggi Kussa's boldest and most famous novels, *Purja Purja Katt Marey*; the author himself has translated the work.

The novel deals with the black period of militancy in Punjab and the unfortunate involvement of the youth of Punjab in it. It was a time when the average man in villages was subject to untold atrocities committed by the Punjab Police, which was given unbridled power to crush the militancy. Juts about anybody could be accused of being a militant; the captured Sikh boys were then mercilessly tortured at police stations and were even forced to watch their families run into endless trouble shelling out large sums of money to ensure their release. This atmosphere drove many a young man into the arms of the militants – at least there they had the satisfaction of living and dying with honour.

The book is a realistic portrait of life in Punjab from 1984 to 1995. The midnight and early morning raids by the police, the gleam in their eyes at the thought of a promotion even at the cost of an innocent young man, the moles planted inside the militant network, the youth forced to act as informers against their friends and relatives, and the hushed up murders to prevent the police's sordid deeds from being exposed to the public... At one time, the Punjab police was the most dreaded police force in the country. In the governance system that India inherited from the British, it is the Indian Administrative Service that has control over the other services, including the police. And it was only in Punjab that IPS had the upper hand. However, this high-handed and brutal way of tackling militancy instead of rooting it out in fact fanned it.

The book also reminds it readers of the many people who went missing during that infamous period, including human rights activists. The most striking case was that of Jaswant Singh Khalra, the noted activist who unearthed thousands of cases of innocent Sikhs who were picked up by police, killed and then burnt, especially in the districts of Amritsar, Majitha and Tarn Tarn. Khalra was abducted in 1995 from outside his house by undercover commandos of the Punjab police and then murdered. The CBI investigated and found evidence that incriminated nine police officials in the death of Khalra. In 2011, after a long battle in court, the Supreme Court of India dismissed the appeal filed by four of the accused (they were appealing against their life imprisonment) and scathingly criticized the police's atrocities.

Even though justice was served for the family of Khalra, the book reminds us that in countless other cases, there was no justice for the common man. Many a young Sikh man fled India for good in light of these proceedings. This book is a powerful read and portrays that horrific period in a very accurate manner.

Author

Shivcharan Jaggi Kussa, popularly known as Jaggi Kussa, was born in the village of Moga, in the district of the same name. He immigrated to Germany in 1986 where he served with German and Austrian Police. Since 2006 he has been living in the east end of London and has produced a plethora of Punjabi novels. He is one of the most prolific contemporary Punjabi writers and his novels, stories, satires, articles and poems are published in various prominent newspapers, magazines and websites all over the world. His books regularly appear in online magazines and, like Roop Dhillon, he has embraced this medium. Despite living abroad, he has continued writing in Punjabi, and his works are well received.

Jaggi Kussa writes realistic satirical novels about corruption in the Indian Police force and in Punjabi society in general. Social issues like the dowry system, male dominance, female foeticide and frauds in the immigration system also appear in his work. He has won many awards, including seven gold medals and 17 further literary awards, including the Nanak Singh Novelist Award.

Sohan Singh Seetal

- *Time Has Taken A Turn (Yug Badl Gia)* **by Sohan Singh Seetal; Published by Punjabi University, Patiala.**

This novel is set in the village of Varn, inhabited by Jat Sikhs with a sprinkling of Hindus and Muslims. It is a quintessential village story with characters typical of any village, but where Sohan Singh Seetal scores is in the way he fleshes out the characters. The story seems so real that it transports us to era in which it is set and we live through the joys, pains and sorrows of its characters. While the society is predominantly patriarchal, Seetal demonstrates how, even in that milieu, strong women could manage to hold their fort and maintain their dignity.

The protagonist, Lakha Singh, is a prosperous Jat landlord who exploits the illiterate farmers of his village and usurps other's land through craft tactics. The farmers are bound by tradition and Lakha uses this to his advantage so that the farmers are constantly paying in debt. His wife, Basant Kaur is just the opposite – a pious and caring lady who always helps people in distress. She lovingly feeds all the workers and is widely respected. Basant is devoted to her husband, and they have two children. She takes in Duda, a congenitally deformed boy, and gives him a job and, for the first time in his life, three proper meals. Under her love and guidance, Duda becomes an intelligent and obedient worker.

It so happens that Lakha is bewitched by the beauty of Swarni, Basant's cousin. He uses his power to get his way and he forces Swarni's family to marry her off to him. Basant, devastated, underscores the vulnerability of women in society. Everybody watches in utter disbelief as Basant is almost kicked out of the house for not agreeing to Lakha's command.

Basant, heartbroken, stoically keeps serving Lakha and running the household efficiently. She treats her rival with her characteristic love and care. Incorrigible Lakha does not stop there and soon falls for another girl, Rajo – a low-caste girl with high ambitions. He marries her off to Duda but it is soon evident that she is his mistress and the marriage to Duda is just a ruse to keep her in his house. Duda is faithful to the house, does not utter a word and silently accepts. Swarni, however, cannot accept this arrangement and dies a bitter death.

Rajo and Lakha's son is named Jarnail Singh. He resents his illegal status, but Basant's love and care makes him channel his energy into getting a job in the revenue department. Partition occurs, forcing the family to leave their assets and rush to India. Duda and Basant die, and Jarnail forces Lakha to legally wed his mother, finally giving her societal status. Lakha Singh realizes that 'time has taken a turn.'

A typical rural drama enacted in the heart of Punjab – the tale goes on like the flow of a river. The chariot of life moves on. It knows no stopping and in its movement one finds grandeur.

Author

Sohan Singh Seetal is a Punjabi author, poet and lyricist. His novel *Yug Badl Gia* won the Sahitya Akademi Award in 1974.

Seetal entered the field of literary creation after 1947. He has written many novels most of which are romantic and sentimental. Among these *Dive di Lo* (The Flame of the Earthen Lamp), *Mul da Mas* (Flesh at a Price) and *Badla* (Revenge) deal with the eternal problem of women, about which most Indian writers become sentimental. Seetal has, in due course, travelled from sentimentality, which often becomes macabre, to competent realism, although here too the projection of problems and their solutions are not without a sentimental tinge.

Overall, Seetal has described in his novels the countryside of Central Punjab and the life of its people as a kind of parallel to Nanak Singh who deals with urban life in the same tract of land. Both are reformist and sentimental to start with and then grow into realists in their later work; but, while Nanak Singh tends towards a kind of Gandhian Socialism, Seetal's concern with the peasant's life takes a populist form.

Sohinder Singh Wanjara Bedi

- *Of Grime And Gold* (*Adhi Mitti Adha Sona*) by Dr. Sohinder Singh Wanjara Bedi; Translated by Dr. Jaspal Singh; Published by Punjabi University, Patiala.

Of Grime and Gold is the autobiography of the author that covers the first 22 years of his life; from the time he was born in Sialkot till just before Partition of India when he shifted with his family to Patiala.

As the author had a deep interest in folklore, the first chapter of the book is devoted to the folklore behind Sialkot, the place where he was born, about Kaliyuga, the age in which he was born, about Friday, the day he was born and even about Maagh, the month in which he was born. The second chapter deals with his ancestry, which he claims to be from Rishi Angiras as well as Guru Nanak Dev who was also a Bedi. There is a detailed description of the story of Angiras Rishi and many other Hindu Gods. The third chapter is about the divine benediction that his family was endowed with. According to him, in older times when the saints were fully pleased with the devotion of a disciple they used to bless him with powers to provide relief, which were bequeathed to his descendants. In his case, the family was endowed with a blessing for providing relief from malaria.

The author continues in the same way and, in the next chapter, deals with details of his family, from where they came and how they settled at Sialkot. He makes a very interesting observation that though his family was very religious, 'our faith and devotion in God has beguiled our generations. Our devotion has always mocked at us. Whereas we have gained a lot from limitless divine bounty, we have also suffered to the extreme. Our gain is spiritual and the loss is material.' This is a recurring theme in the book – the author's constant fight with the Almighty. He asks why God did not listen to his prayers even though he has been so devoted to God, worshipped Him whole-heartedly and led a pious life? He is besieged by this question throughout his childhood. He wants God to bestow upon him divine power, to grant him personal darshan and to not harm his family.

His grandfather had died very young leaving a huge responsibility on his father. Similarly, he is angry that his father too died when the author had just turned 21 and that too on the day he was to get married. And all this when, every waking moment, he devoted himself to reciting the name of God, baptized himself, and never indulged in drinks, tobacco and passions of lust. The book ends in 1946/early 1947 when he is heartbroken by his father's death. Angry with God, he tries to bring some sense of normalcy by getting married, finding a job and being the eldest by shouldering the responsibility of the entire family of 10 members. But soon Partition occurs and, shattered, they have to leave all their belongings and most of his writings and go to Patiala to start afresh.

On his train to India, he decides to make a clean break from his past, gives up his quest to settle scores with God, and, like the mythical phoenix, decides to rise again and decides to devote his life to books which would be his new spiritual calling, his new God.

Author

S. S. Wanjara Bedi (1924–001) was born at Sialkot, now in Pakistan. He did his M.A. in Punjabi from the Punjabi University and Ph.D. from the University of Delhi. He worked in a bank early in his career and as senior lecturer of Dayal Singh College, Delhi. He edited *Fateh*, a weekly and *Pritam*, a monthly magazine from 1949–1952. Bedi has written 80 books, which include three collections of poems, five books on literary criticism and *Punjabi Lokdhara Vishwa Kosh*, a collection of Punjabi folklore in 10 volumes.

Bedi developed a deep interest in folklore just after Partition when he shifted to Delhi. He felt the need to preserve the folk heritage of the Punjab, which was being neglected by the Punjabis themselves. Accordingly, he started writing an encyclopedia on Punjabi folklore. Bedi successfully contacted the refugees from Potohar, Jhelum, Gujarat and Mandi Bahauddin. He himself was well-versed in the folk tradition and collected invaluable material in book form.

He was a recipient of 15 prestigious literary awards, including Sahitya Kala Parishad Award. He held the post of General Secretary in the Punjabi Sahitya Sabha and published Punjabi's first tri-monthly, *Punjabi Lok Wave*.

Bedi's autobiography, *Galley Chikar Duri Ghar*, the book chosen for the Sahitya Akademi Award, not only records the autobiographical details of the author's life but also explores new dimensions of a person's total view of life. There is a remarkable balance between reticence and self-projection in the book. For the maturity of thought, sincerity of expression and chasteness of style, the book is considered to be a great contribution to Punjabi literature.

Swaran Chandan

- *The Volcano* by Swaran Chandan; Translated by himself: Published by Diamond Books.

The Volcano was originally published in Punjabi and then translated by the author himself in English. This novel is deeply felt and highly political, exploring the effect of cruel injustices on the minds of his characters. The novel has a curious mixture of styles – the historical works of Sir Walter Scott and Leo Tolstoy. It also owes much to Salman Rushdie's *Midnight's Children*.

The Volcano tells the story of the subcontinent's most turbulent times and is a sweeping novel about the Partition of India and the painful birth of Pakistan. This is a novel that brings India to life and gives a vivid glimpse of a way of life in the dying days of the British Empire and a compelling account of what happened to a group of friends and a typical village in the subcontinent before Partition.

Though the subject matter is pretty bleak, the book is laced with gentle humour and humanity and will appeal to anyone who wants to comprehend what happened during the years prior to our achieving freedom and its heavy costs and to someone who is keen to assess the tragic consequences of those heady days. Reading it is a journey of discovery of the recent past.

The book is full of the passion and restless energy of a teeming sub-continent. It is an ambitious novel of epic proportions that makes an important contribution to the growing literature dealing with the subject of the partition of India.

Very rarely does one find a novel that is so pleasant and heartwarming to read. *The Volcano* is much more than just about Partition, it is about self-discovery and finding your place in the world.

The novel is set in Quila Vasudev, which had Sikhs, Hindus and Muslims living in peace. The village has a mosque, a Sikh shrine and a Hindu temple. The people of each religion have houses in specified areas mostly in the vicinity of their shrines, possibly for easy access in case of an emergency. This village was typical of many others in the country. We have three characters, each recounting tales relating to his community. We are treated to the reminiscences of each. Especially noteworthy is the story of *Komagata Maru*, the ship that was sent back by Canada with Punjabis. We have detailed accounts of events in Indian history – Jallianwala Bagh massacre, Gandhi's call for Satyagraha, Salt Satyagraha, Cripps Mission, Quit India movement, Shimla Conference and finally the arrival of Lord Mountbatten with a mandate to partition India and to create Pakistan. The tryst with destiny was harrowing, painful and deeply agonizing.

The state of Punjab was divided. A land that was once the land of five rivers was now transformed into a formidable livid volcano with red-hot lava churning, raging, fuming and circling it. The vast volcano of unprecedented mutual detestation and hostility stood in red alert with its gigantic mouth roaring and snorting to engulf anything that came its way.

This is a novel that leaves an indelible impression on the minds of the readers. It is at once a work of fiction and a classic in historical writing.

Author

Swaran Chandan was born in Amritsar and is a highly respected Punjabi writer who bagged several awards – the Mohan Singh Vaid Award for his novel Kachche Ghar; the Shiromani Sahityakar Award from the Bhasha Vibhag, Punjab; the Balraj Sahni Creative Award from Dhudike Trust; and the Shiromani Samikshakar Award from I.W.A. He migrated to England in 1964.

An extremely prolific writer, he has written on a variety of subjects and in literary forms as varied as poetry, criticism, novel, short story. Besides a travelogue and a political treatise, he has authored eight novels, six collections of short stories, two volumes of verse and six books on literary criticism.

His novels include *Lal Chowk* (The Red Chowk), *Kacche Ghar* (The Tenements), *Kakh, Kan Te Darya* (The Straws and the Ocean), *Shatranjh* (Chess), *Kanjakaan,* (The Young Maids), *Ujara Khuh* (The Abandoned Well) *and Khali Palan Di Sanjh* (A Sharing of Vacant Moments).

Yashpal

- *Divya* by Yashpal; Translated by Anand; Published by Sahitya Akademi.

Three themes run throughout Yashpal's writings – gender equality, revolution and romance. He explored the distant past in novels such as *Divya, Amita* and *Apsara ka Shaap.*

Divya is the story of one woman's struggle to lead her own life. The story is set against the background of the conflict for supremacy between Hindu and Buddhist ideologies in India in the 1st century BC. Ancient India bursts in all its glory and vigour in this novel. It is rated as one of the great historical novels in Indian literature. It caused widespread furor because of the portrayal of Divya as a woman who refuses to live by the rules of a male society.

Divya, the granddaughter of the Brahmin Chief Justice of the Madra republic, is the most talented dancer of the state. Prithusen, Divya's lover, is an ambitious youth, whose father, the merchant prince of Madra, was once a slave. Prithusen is declared as the champion of martial arts, but the Brahmin aristocracy refuses to accept him as their equal despite his talent and wealth.

Divya, pregnant with Prithusen's child, is refused shelter in a Buddhist monastery because, as a woman dependent on her family, she does not have the permission of her father or her husband. In desperation, she throws herself and her child into a river. The child is drowned but she is rescued and begins a new life as Anshumala, the chief courtesan and artist of Shursen.

Divya's repute as the dancer reaches her former teacher Mallika, the chief courtesan of Madrayaspal. Mallika, in her old age, is looking for a worthy successor and travels to Shursen to meet Anshumala. She is surprised and overjoyed when she recognizes Divya and takes her back to Madra.

The Brahmin chief, Rudradhir, refuses to allow a Brahmin girl to be the chief courtesan. He asks her to become his wife and the first lady of the state. Divya turns him down because she does not want to lose her independence. By losing herself she cannot remain alive, she says. Prithusen, her former lover now a Buddhist monk, offers her the shelter of his religion. Divya again rejects the offer saying, 'A woman's religion is not Nirvana, but creation.' Marish, a philosopher who has no worldly possessions and who is an old acquaintance and admirer of Divya, offers his companionship as a male to an independent female. Divya accepts.

Divya does not represent a famous historical figure or event. It is an example of the author's commitment to social realism and of his perspective on history that analyses the circumstances and issues in the context of the situation prevailing at the time. Yashpal, in *Divya*, rejects both the inequalities of the Hindu caste system and its inherent contradictions about the position and role of a woman. He has made a sincere effort and performed an in-depth study of the oral and folkloric sources, taking the best from each, which is why this work is preferred over others.

Yashpal

- *This is Not That Dawn* by Yashpal; Translated by Anand; Published by Penguin India.

In 1956, Yashpal started writing *Jhootha Sach*, a classic, worthy to rank among the great Indian novels. The first volume is set in Lahore and is titled *Vatan aur Desh; vatan* being the land where one is born or one's motherland, while *desh* is the nation. It is a forcible split and an unnatural dichotomy introduced by Partition. It is a story from 1946 till independence in August 1947, giving almost a day-to-day account from May 1947. The announcement of transfer of power followed by the division of the country leads to the unforeseen event of mass movement of people and the brutal killings.

The second volume titled *Desh ka Bhavishya*, in contrast, covers a whole decade from 1947 to 1957 and is set in Delhi, Jalandhar and Lucknow. The longer period here shows that while lives can be uprooted and devastated in virtually a moment, it takes forever to pick up pieces that are left and to rearrange them in some residual pattern of survival. The novel carries on till 1957 for one other strategic reason, which is that Yashpal wishes to show a corrupt Congress minister losing in the general elections held that year. The scope and realism of this novel has resulted in its favourable comparison with Leo Tolstoy's *War and Peace*.

The English translation of both volumes has been done in one book and is titled *This is Not That Dawn*. The title has been borrowed from the famous couplet of Faiz Ahmed Faiz, 'Yeh daagh daagh ujala, Yeh shab gazidaa seher; Woh intezar tha jiska, yeh woh seher to nahi' (These tarnished rays, this night-smudged light; This is not that Dawn for which, ravished with freedom, we had set out in sheer longing).

The book is divided into two parts – the first part *Homeland and Nation* and the second *Future of the Nation*. The novel, with its profusion of well-etched characters, impressive narration and colourfully presented locale compels the reader to recall their own experience and touches a chord in everyone.

The book is based on events surrounding the Partition of India and is considered to be one of the best books on Partition. The first part of the novel narrates the lives, hopes and fears of the characters in the aftermath of the ensuing storm that violently attacks Lahore and its environs. We witness a descent into degeneration and the resultant abominable suffering.

It is the story of a simple Hindu community that lived in Bhola Pande's Lane near the Shahalami Gate in Lahore. Happenings of daily life are presented with great charm. The book follows a brother and sister coming of age in Lahore before the foreign ruler cuts the nation ruthlessly into two parts – India and Pakistan. The brother, Jaidev Puri, who wishes to become a famous writer, flees Lahore for the Indian towns of Nainital and then Jalandhar. The sister, Tara, a college student, is kidnapped by Muslim men.

In the second part, the characters heroically fight the tumultuous circumstances and forge a new life for themselves in the new nation – above all Tara, who at the end of the novel is an undersecretary with Government of India. Notwithstanding his ideological and personal differences with Gandhi (who had condemned his bombing activity) and Nehru, Yashpal ends up having Tara and the man she finally marries both work for the government. The *desh* certainly has a *bhavishya,* and the message that he wants to give is that the future of the nation is not in the hands of the leaders and ministers; it is very much in the hands of the people.

Professor Harish Trivedi has written a very enlightening introduction to this book.

Author

Yashpal (1903–76), born in Ferozepore Cantt in Punjab, was initially educated at Gurukul Kangri. After further schooling in

Lahore, he joined National College, where he met Bhagat Singh and Sukhdev and then became a prominent member of Hindustan Republican Socialist Army (HRSA), which worked for liberating India through revolutionary armed struggle.

The last significant armed act of the HRSA was the attempt on 23 December 1929 to blow up a train carrying the Viceroy, Lord Irwin. Yashpal detonated that bomb. It was around this time that he met his future wife, Prakashvati Kapur. Yashpal continued to work with Azad until the latter died in February 1931. He was arrested by the British in Allahabad and sentenced to 14 years in jail, a sentence that was eventually commuted to six years under an amnesty with the condition that he never returns to Punjab.

It was after Yashpal's release from prison that he began to write. Barred from Punjab, he made Lucknow his home. Marxism became his preferred ideology; he saw the Communist Party of India as the successor to the HRSA. He started a Hindi journal *Viplava*, and his wife set up a publishing company called *Viplava Karyalaya* in 1941 and a printing press, Sathi Press in 1944.

Yashpal is considered to be the most gifted writer since Premchand. He wrote around 50 books including essays, novels and short stories, as well as a play, two travel books and an autobiography. His last novel *Meri Teri Uski Baat*, won the Sahitya Akademi Award. He was a recipient of the Padma Bhushan.

POETRY

Amarjit Chandan

- *Sonata for Four Hands* by Amarjit Chandan; Translated from the original Punjabi by the author with Julia Casterton, Shashi Joshi, Amin Mughal, Ajmer Rode, Stephen Watts and John Welch; Published by Arc Publications.

The great writer and long-time admirer of his work, John Berger has prefaced Amarjit Chandan's *Sonata for Four Hands*, which has 61 poems. Painter and filmmaker Gurvinder Singh has designed the book cover. Sonata is a musical piece played on one or more instruments, and when that piece is played with four hands (two persons) on the same instrument, it becomes a sonata for four hands.

As Stephen Watts, in his introduction mentions, the present volume is an anthology of poems from the 1980s to the present day and represents the whole span of Chandan's work. He writes, 'Although the poems are not presented chronologically, they have been put in a themed order that accords with the poet's sensibilities, moving us as they do through language, silence, mother tongue and memory to love and loss.'

A lot has been written about his poems and most reviewers have mentioned eloquent silences and solitude as the main characteristics of his poetry. Poet Arundhathi Subramaniam writes, 'There is a silence in Chandan's poetry — a deep sense of the unspoken, and more accurately, the unspeakable. This is, no doubt, intimately connected with his years of solitary confinement in an Amritsar prison.'

The second-most important theme in his poems is his intense love for Punjabi Language. In an interview to a *Sunday Tribune* interview, Chandan said, 'I think, feel, and dream in Punjabi.

My language is my real home, my last retreat. I feel most secure, and at one with my own self in my ma boli. Freud says it is not possible to return to the womb. My poems bear witness that the return is possible through the ma boli, mother language. But sadly, we are losing our language, and this loss has been a severe blow to me.'

And it is this that drives him to continue to write in Punjabi despite all his years abroad. It also indicates his sense of rootedness. In another interview, he stated that 'There are people who criticize me for using archaic Punjabi language, but I must tell them that the source of my works lays in lokbani (folklore), Gurbani and Sufibani, which are the real sources of Punjabi culture and language.'

The force of this Punjabi identity is so strong in his poetry that its pull is not lost even in translation.

Poet

Amarjit Chandan (1946–) was born in Nairobi, Kenya. Chandan moved to Nakodar, his ancestral village in Jalandhar, East Punjab, when he was eight. As a student at Panjab University, Chandigarh, he got involved in the Maoist Naxalite movement of the late 1960s where he ran their publication section and befriended fellow poets Pash and Lal Singh Dil. He was later captured and imprisoned in 1971, which included two years in solitary confinement.

Later, he worked for various Punjabi literary and political magazines, including the Bombay-based *Economic and Political Weekly* before migrating to England in 1980, where he now lives.

Chandan has published eight collections of poetry and five books of essays in Punjabi. He has edited and translated over 30 anthologies of poetry, fiction and creative non-fiction of Brecht, Neruda, Ritsos, Hikmet, Vallejo, Cardenal and Berger into Punjabi, among others.

His work is included in many anthologies in Punjabi, Hindi and English published in India and abroad. His poetry has been published in English, Farsi, Greek, Turkish, Hungarian, Romanian and Indian languages (Assamese, Bengali, Hindi, Telugu, Urdu and others). His own works include *Jarhan*, *Beejak*, *Chhanna* and *Guthali*. He is undoubtedly the global face of modern Punjabi poetry.

Chandan received several awards and honours which include the Lifetime Achievement Award from the Language Department, Government of the East Punjab; and the Lifetime Achievement Award from the Punjabis in Britain All-Party Parliamentary Group, London and Anād Poetry Award, India. His short poem was carved in a 40-foot long stone by Eric Peever, both in Punjabi and its English version and is installed in High Street Slough, England. It reads as follows:

>dur bahut dur kisey nachhtar uttey,
>piá hai pathar geeta.
>Eh ankháN muNd ke takkná paiNdá,
>jeoN chetey ávey sohná mukh sajjanaN dá
>Far far away on a distant planet,
>There lies a stone unseen untouched.
>It can be seen only with closed eyes,
>as you see your loved ones.

Baba Farid

- *Baba Farid: Selected Poems*; Translation and Introduction by Paul Smith; Published by New Humanity Books.

One of Farid's most important contributions to Punjabi literature was his development of the language for literary purposes. Whereas Sanskrit, Arabic, Turkish and Persian had historically been considered the languages of the learned and the elite, and used in monastic centers, Punjabi was generally considered a folk language. Although earlier poets had written in a primitive Punjabi, before Farid, there was little in Punjabi literature apart from traditional and anonymous ballads. By using Punjabi as the language of poetry, Farid laid the basis for a vernacular Punjabi literature that would be developed later.

Among the famous people who have visited his shrine over the centuries are the famous scholar-explorer Ibn Battuta, and the Founder of Sikhism, Guru Nanak Dev, who met the then head of the shrine, Sheikh Ibrahim, twice, and his meeting led to the incorporation of 112 couplets (saloks) and four hymns by Baba Farid, in the Sikh Holy Book, the *Guru Granth Sahib*, by the fifth Guru, Arjan Dev in 1604. These verses are known to the Sikhs as the Farid-Bani.

Baba Farid lived in Punjab in the 13th century and composed hymns in Punjabi, the likes of which are yet to be composed. The language is Multani Punjabi, of an extraordinary power and sensitivity. There was something in his poetry akin to prayer. He spoke of his people in the people's dialect and asked them to use Punjabi for religious purposes.

The poetry, translated very ably by Paul Smith, brings out the following essential themes.

The main theme of Baba Farid's bani is vairag, dispassion towards the world and its false attractions. Farid lived a householder's life marked with contentment and perseverance. One of the greatest virtues of his life was his love and sympathy for all mankind. In an absolutely impressive manner, Sheikh Farid realized this manifest world, the reality of God. He advises us to overcome worldly temptations and remain devoted to God, the creator of the whole universe. He cautions us against the false attractions of the world through his Bani, which is deeply sensitive to the feeling of Empathy, Inevitable death and the waste of human life due to man's indifference to God and goodness.

He states that contentment resides in the heart purified of all traces of ego and greed. According to him, the detached person is also the wisest. He is the greatest who can face both pleasure and pain with equanimity. The richest person is the one with the most content heart.

According to Farid, self-realization or liberation from self is the other name for God-realization. One who is subject to desires of the senses is the meanest of all because such a man fails to control his mind, and the endless desires emanating from his mind make him a tool in the hands of the devil who makes him dance to his tune. Farid not only preached detachment and austerity but also made these the guiding principles of his life.

In Sheikh Farid, the relationship between God and man is that of husband and wife. In the very first three of his couplets found in the *Guru Granth Sahib*, he visualizes the relationship between man and God first as that between man and death and then gives it the conjugal parallel. The day woman was born, he says, the hour of dedication to the husband was fixed. Death, the bridegroom, comes and shows himself at the appointed hour. Death, the bridegroom, must take away in marriage the soul, the bride. Let the soul understand this that the appointed hour cannot be evaded. Like most men of renunciation, Sheikh Farid regards detachment from this world as the right path for man.

Poet

Hazrat Baba Fariduddin Ganjshakar (1173–1266), commonly known as Baba Farid, was a 12th-century Sufi preacher and saint of the Chishti Order of South Asia.

He is generally recognized as the first major poet of the Punjabi language and is considered one of the pivotal saints of the Punjab region. Revered by Muslims and Hindus, he is also considered one of the 15 Sikh Bhagats within Sikhism, and his selected works form part of the *Guru Granth Sahib*, the Sikh sacred scripture. Baba Farid was born in Kothewal village, 10 km from Multan in the Punjab region of Pakistan.

Baba Farid received his early education at Multan, which had become a center for education; it was here that he met his master murshid, Qutbuddin Bakhtiyar Kaki, a noted Sufi saint, who was passing through Multan from Baghdad, on his way to Delhi. Once his education was over, he shifted to Delhi where he learned the doctrine of his Master, and when Qutbuddin Kaki died in 1235, Farid assumed the role of his spiritual successor, though he did not settle in Delhi but in Ajodhan (the present Pakpattan, Pakistan). On his way to Ajodhan and passing through Faridkot, he met the 20-year-old Nizamuddin Auliya, who went on to become his disciple, and later his successor. His shrine is in Dera Pindi, and his descendants include Sheikh Salim Chishti. The city of Faridkot bears his name. The festival Baba Sheikh Farid Agman Purb Mela is celebrated in September each year, commemorating his arrival in the city.

Further reading

- *Faridnama* by Zahid Abrol, (the first-ever Poetical Translation of Sheikh Farid's Punjabi Verses in Urdu and Hindi Scripts); Ajanta Book.
- *Sheikh Fariduddin Ganj-i-Shakar Ain-e-Akbari* by Abul Fazal, English translation, by H. Blochmann and Colonel H. S. Jarrett. The Asiatic Society of Bengal, Calcutta; Volume III, Saints of India. (Awliyá-i-Hind), page 363.

- *Pakpattan and Baba Farid Ganj-i-Shakar* by Muhammad Abdullah Caghtai. Kitab Khana Nauras.
- *Baba Sheikh Farid: Life and Teachings* by Gurbachan Singh Talib. Baba Farid Memorial Society.
- *Baba Farid (Makers of Indian Literature)* by Balwant Singh Anand, Sahitya Akademi.
- *Baba Farid-ud-Din Masud Ganj-i-Shakar* by Jafar Qasimi. Islamic Book Foundation.
- *Sheikh Baba Farid aur unka Kavya* by Jayabhagavan Goyal, Atmarama & Sons.
- *Savanih hayat Baba Farid Ganj-i Shakar* by Pir Ghulam Dastgir Nami. Madni Kutub Khanah.
- *Baba Farid Ganjshakar* by Shabbir Hasan Cishti Nizami. Asthana Book Depot.
- *Love is His Own Power: The slokas of Baba Farid*
- *Hazrat Baba Farid-ud-Din Masood Ganj Shakar* by Sheikh Parvaiz Amin Naqshbandy. Umar Publications.
- *Baba Farid di dukh–chetana* by Sarawan Singh Paradesi. 1996, Ravi Sahitya Prakashan,
- *Hymns of Sheikh Farid* by Brij Mohan Sagar. South Asia Books, Sheikh Farid, by Dr. Harbhajan Singh. Hindi Pocket Books.

Beeba Balwant

- *Tale of a Cursed Tree* by Beeba Balwant; Translated from Punjabi by Rana Nayar; Ravi Sahit Parkashan, Amritsar.

There is a snippet of interesting and touching information about Beeba Balwant in the translators note: Beeba has refused to shut the doors of his home ever since his one-time beloved walked out on him, never to return. He has left the doors open in the hope that someday she would walk right back, straight into his open arms. Though it has not happened over several years now, Beeba continues to wait, refusing to give up.

As Aruti Nayar observes in *The Tribune* (25.10.2003), "Beeba channeled his failure to find true love in real life into poetry. Both the brush and the pen are tools that help him in his attempt to understand and explore "My own self and the world around". His poetry is born out of his disgust with the customs and rules of society and the hypocrisy that underlies social interaction."

> Piar ton jo sakhne hunde viah,
> Aadmi di zaat de hai sir suah,
> Jism chundan aarh lei lal lawaan di lok,
> Din dihare ho rahe aithe gunah.

(Loveless marriages, so frequently performed, are a curse upon the human race; people devour flesh under the garb of religious rituals. It is nothing short of adultery in broad daylight.)

However, the poetry in this book is different from the other verses of this incorrigible romantic. This book is not that of an ever-waiting sentimental lover. He is well anchored and not someone wringing his hands in desperation or wallowing in self-pity. As Rana Nayar writes, 'Beeba fine-tunes his lonely hours into a symphony of colorful words. He chases a fleeting desire to the skies with the same indulgence with which he returns to the warm/cold embrace of the stolid earth. For, Beeba is a painter of words and images, as much as he is a poet of colours.'

According to Nayar, Beeba writes just the way he paints, in small ponderous, deliberate strokes. Adding deeper tones to his word-brushes, he lingers over a mood or a feeling, allowing its nuanced shades to come alive through each and every experience he dips his colours in. It is no wonder then that he has been painfully slow with his poetic efforts, having published just three collections in almost two decades: *Terian Galan Tere Naan* (1980), an intensely personal, semi-autobiographical poetic overture; *Phulan De Rang Kale*, made of somber, meditative somewhat elegiac outpourings; and *Teeje Pehar Di Dhup*, songs of mellow fruitfulness.

Beeba is a versatile personality. He has acted and directed around 15 plays, written short stories, poems and ghazals; organized literary festivals and won numerous accolades. This book has 20 poems very ably translated by Rana Nayar who has done commendable work in translating a lot of Punjabi works in English, amongst other things. He is a master of both languages and therefore brings out the true essence and beauty of Beeba's poetry in its English translation. The book is adorned by drawings by Prem Singh, while Imroz has designed the cover page.

Poet

Balwant Singh, popularly known as Beeba, is a painter and poet, and is involved with the theatre. He was born in Jagraon in 1945. He is an alumnus of the Government College of Art, Chandigarh. His landscapes and portraits have evoked praise from viewers and critics alike. His medium is oil on canvas and the pigeon is a recurrent motif, a woman symbolized by a dove represents the spirit of womanhood, its travails and finally its crucifixion at the altar of tradition. He is also the recipient of the national award for designing the best poster for the Family Welfare Department.

His photo prints of Sobha Singh's paintings adorn the walls of the Sobha Singh Memorial Art Gallery at Sri Hargobindpur.

Along with his artistic pursuits, Beeba has been involved with theatre. He had begun his career along with Harpal Tiwana and Om Puri and acted in many plays of the famous playwright Kapur Singh Ghuman. Recipient of the Best Actor Award from the Indian Art Revival Group and the Best Director Award from the Punjab Naat Sangh, Chandigarh, he also studied Osho and stayed in his ashram at Pune. He continues to be an employee of the Department of Health based in Gurdaspur.

Bulleh Shah

- *Bullhe Shah: Sufi Lyrics*; Edited and Translated by Christopher Shackle; Published by Murty Classical Library of India.

Numerous authors have written books on Bulleh Shah because of the fragmented publication of his works. As this book explains, the turbulent conditions prevalent in Punjab during the 18th century and the lack of direct descendants who might have safeguarded his poetic heritage meant that the transmission of Bulleh Shah's poetry was entirely reliant on oral tradition for more than a century after his death. There appear to be no surviving manuscripts from the period preceding the first printed texts, which came only in the last decade of 19th century when Lahore became a major center of publishing.

The earliest substantial edition dates back to 1889 by Anvar Ali Ruhtaki and has 116 kafis; in 1930 came Mohan Singh Ubero's Gurmukhi edition of 50 selected Kafian; next, a Persian-script Kulliyat of 1960 edited by Faqir Muhammad Faqir (161 kafis); *Mukammal Kafian* of 1991 edited by Muhammad Sharif Sabir (155 kafis); Jagtar's *Bullhe Shah: Jivan Ate Racna* of 2008 (161 kafis). All these editions, however, differ in the language used and with regard to the volume of his total work. There are many English translations too but none of them have the translation of his work in its entirety.

This latest edition, published by the Murty Classical Library of India (MCLI) of the Harvard University Press has, for the first time, presented a complete translation of his entire body of work. The book has 157 kafis, miscellaneous short dohre (verses) on a range of topics and four of his longer poems – *Athvara* (The Seven

Days), *Baran Mah* (The Twelve Months), *Gandhan* (The Forty Knots) and *Siharfi* (The Thirty Letters).

MCLI has done a wonderful job. Named after the Murty family of India who made a generous gift to Harvard University Press, it aims to make available the great literary works of India from the past two millennia. Many classic Indic texts have never reached a global audience, while others are becoming increasingly inaccessible even to Indian readers. The creation of a classical library of India is intended to reintroduce these works to a new generation of readers.

The series will provide modern English translations of classical works by world-class scholars, many for the first time, across a vast array of Indian languages including Bangla, Hindi, Kannada, Marathi, Pali, Punjabi, Persian, Sanskrit, Sindhi, Tamil, Telugu and Urdu. It is a facing-page translation series and the original Indic text, in the appropriate script, is accompanied by a modern English translation on the opposite page. Thus, in this book, all the kafis, poems and dohres are given in Gurumukhi on the left page and the corresponding translation is given on the right side. MCLI has performed extensive research, making these volumes the most authoritative available. Till date, it has released 18 such volumes.

The book is a delight to read.

Poet

Bullhe Shah (1680–1757), born Syed Abdullah Shah Qadri, was a Punjabi Sufi poet, humanist and philosopher. His first spiritual teacher was Shah Inayat, a Sufi murshid of Lahore. Bullhe Shah is universally admitted to have been the greatest of the Punjabi mystics. In fact, no Punjabi mystic poet enjoys a greater reputation, with his kafis (a form of Sufi poetry) gaining unique popularity.

Bullhe Shah lived after the Pashto Sufi poet Rahman Baba (1653–1711) and lived in the same period as Sindhi Sufi poet Shah Abdul Latif Bhittai (1689–1752). His lifespan also overlapped with the Punjabi poet Waris Shah (1722–1798) of *Heer Ranjha* fame and the Sindhi Sufi poet Abdul Wahab (1739–1829). Amongst Urdu poets, Bulleh Shah lived 400 miles away from Mir Taqi Mir (1723–1810) of Agra.

Bullhe Shah practiced the Sufi tradition of Punjabi poetry established by poets like Shah Hussain (1538–1599), Sultan Bahu (1629–1691) and Shah Sharaf (1640–1724). The verse form Bullhe Shah primarily employed is the Kafi, popular in Punjabi and Sindhi poetry.

Bullhe Shah's writings represent him as a humanist; someone providing solutions to the sociological problems of the world around him as he lives through them, describing the turbulence Punjab is passing through, while concurrently searching for God. The simplicity with which Bullhe Shah has been able to address the complex fundamental issues of life and humanity is a large part of his appeal across formal religious and national boundaries.

Read on

- K. S. Duggal wrote a book called *Sain Bulleh Shah: The Mystic Muse* in which he has translated Bulleh Shah's Punjabi kafis into Urdu and English.
- Many people have put his kafis to music, from humble street singers to renowned Sufi singers like Nusrat Fateh Ali Khan, Pathanay Khan, Abida Parveen, the Waddali Brothers and Sain Zahoor; the synthesized techno qawwali remixes of UK-based Asian artists to the Pakistani rock band Junoon and Rabbi Shergill.
- *Dama Dam Mast Qalandar*, a *qawwali* composed in honour of Shahbaz Qalandar, has been one of Bulleh Shah's most popular poems and has been frequently rendered by many Indian, Pakistani and Bangladeshi singers.
- Bulleh Shah's verses like *Tere Ishq Nachaya* have also been adapted and used in Bollywood film songs including *Chaiyya Chaiyya* and *Thayya Thayya* in the 1998 film *Dil Se* and *Ranjha Ranjha* in the 2010 film Raavan.
- The 2007 Pakistani movie *Khuda Kay Liye* includes Bulleh Shah's poetry in the song *Bandeya Ho*.

- The 2008 film *A Wednesday* included a song titled *Bulle Shah, O Yaar Mere*.
- In 2009, the first episode of the second season of Pakistan's Coke Studio featured *Aik Alif* performed by Sain Zahoor and Noori, while a year later, the first episode of the third season featured *Na Raindee Hai* and *Makke Gayaan Gal Mukdi Nahi* performed by Arieb Azhar.
- In 2012, Bulleh Shah's poetry was featured in Coke Studio again, with Hadiqa Kiani performing *Kamlee*.
- Rabbi Shergill has sung his version of *Bulla Ki Jana*.
- Bulleh Shah's verses have been an inspiration to painters as well, as in the two series of paintings (*Jogia Dhoop* and *Shah Shabad*) by an Indian painter Geeta Vadhera inspired by the poetry of Bulleh Shah and other Sufi poets and saints.

Dev

- *Where Words End* by Dev; Translated by Gurbhagat Singh; Published by Sahitya Akademi, New Delhi.

Shabdant, Dev's award-winning collection of poems is the most important signature of contemporary Punjabi Poetry. There are some factors that have added to the scope of his poetry. His love of travelling has helped him to hold exhibitions of his paintings in the United States, France, Germany, Spain and Switzerland, where he is based at present. Interest in photography has given him a keen eye for the details, and the very fact that he is conversant in a number of languages has given him an exposure to different European cultures and literatures, which he has used frequently in his poems.

The thematic structure of his poetry is based on the Indian Diaspora, and his groundbreaking poetic styles are distinctive and historically significant. Dev is a nomad, a homeless vagabond who remains de-centered and his poetry is a 'passion for journey.' There is no center for Dev, and choosing between one end and the other, i.e. the East or the West, would be biased, missing out on the multicultural vision. And for him, the achievement of the polarities is important.

In this journey, in order to reach the other, raising bridges is necessary; Dev's preferred space is the middle of the bridge; and the 'multicoloured duality' thus creates a new 'space' in his poetic journey. The translator has very appropriately described this by differentiating between 'synthesis' and 'syncretism.' Dev prefers syncretism because 'in synthesis, both lose their identities, whereas in syncretism, they will co-exist in difference, enjoying a double membership in discourse.'

Dev feels that these 'Counterfeit Bridges' will be constructed with the flowing rivulets of love, and where this flow is blocked by repression and the hegemonic power game, no such bridge can be possible to reach out to the Other. And in this process of bridge building, the poet's role is that of a bridge-incarnate, not just the process of construction.

Love in Dev's poetry is both sacred as well as erotic at the same time; where love is 'silencing and enriching'; where bodily fires rise to 'reverence' and where the male protagonist becomes a 'pilgrim' of his beloved's body (The Water Fall). Love for him is a 'miracle' of the two sleeping rivulets. Dev's love for his homeland Punjab pervades his poetry; the Punjab of lofty dreams, of the readiness of the youth to change itself for a new beginning. Dev's repeated references to Guru Nanak, Buddha, Gurbani, Japji, Gita, Quran and Sufism represent about his rootedness and his religio-cultural orientation.

Additionally, his acquaintance with world literature and proximity to different cultures can be easily traced in these poems. *Dr. Faust*, *Spain*, *Kafka*, *Plaza de Mayo* and *For Lorca* are some of the titles that he has given to his poems; similarly, there are references to Godot, Polynesia, Tahiti, Babylon, Kohkaf, Che Guevara and Ho Chi Minh in different poems. With such a wide range and variety of themes, *Where Words End* can be called Dev's 'International contribution.'

Gurbhagat Singh was the best choice for the translation of *Where Words End*, because like Dev, Singh was highly influenced by the French and other post-modern, post-colonial trends in literature. Similarly, like Dev, he had a deep association and understanding of Sikh scriptures and their place in the lives of Punjabi people. Singh's grasp on Dev's poetry becomes quite clear in the way he has analysed the book in his Introduction; the final translation stands out as a work of deep critical insight. If Singh calls *Where Words End* as Dev's 'International contribution,' credit goes to him as well because of his excellent translation.

Poet

Dev, an eminent Punjabi writer-painter was born in 1947 in Jagraon, Ludhiana, Punjab. An autodidact, he is conversant in a number of languages including English, Swahili, German and Spanish. He is also a painter of repute, having held exhibitions all over Europe. Dev entered the arena of Punjabi literature in the 1970s, with the publication of his first book of poetry *Vidhroh* in 1969. Dev has established for himself an exclusive place as both a poet and a painter. These two art forms complement each other in his creations; there is poetry in his paintings and painting in his poems. His use of imagery, symbolism and figurative expressions provide a pictorial quality to his poetry and this dual qualification provides a vastness to his creativity. He has more than six collections of poems including *Doosre kinare Di Talash*, *Matabi Mitti*, *Prashan te Parvaz*, *Hun ton Pehchan* and *Shabdant* (Where Words End) to his credit. He has been greatly influenced by Puran Singh, Devendra Satyarthi, Surrealism and French, Spanish and Latin American poetry.

Faiz Ahmed Faiz

- *The Rebel's Silhouette: Selected Poems of Faiz Ahmed Faiz;* Translated by Aga Shahid Ali; Published by University of Massachusetts; Bilingual: Urdu/English.

During his lifetime, Faiz published eight books and received accolades for his works. Faiz was a humanist, a lyrical poet, whose popularity reached neighbouring India and even the Soviet Union. Throughout his life, his revolutionary poetry addressed the tyranny of military dictatorships and their oppressions, and Faiz himself never compromised on his principles despite being threatened by the right-wing parties in Pakistan.

Faiz's writings are comparatively new verse form in Urdu poetry based on Western models. He was influenced by the works of Allama Iqbal and Mirza Ghalib, assimilating the modern Urdu with the classical.

This book has poems and ghazals, both taken from various Faiz volumes. As the translator says in the introduction, Faiz in his writings, despite his left leanings, has the ability to balance his politics with his aesthetics without compromising either.

Don't ask me for that love again is a poem that glows with a passion long lost. The poet asks his beloved not to ask him for the love that he earlier professed to her. He says that time and situations force him to look at other things which many be very important at that point of time in his life. All the while he believed that her love was his sole comfort and that he cherished her sadness. But the world has shown him that there are worries and comforts that extend far beyond her.

Fragrant Hands is a poem dedicated to an anonymous woman who sent the poet a bouquet of flowers. He acknowledges the flowers as a breath of fresh air in the closed prison cells. He is reminded of the time he was with his loved ones, when life was not so painful. He says that however the world may cage him up, those who cherish him and his ideals will love him. They will never betray him. He will always feel grateful for their love.

Before you came is a poem that discusses how the life of a person changes once he has found love. Life was so simple and straightforward with a semblance of peace before he fell in love. It burst into a multitude of colours of passion once he falls in love. He requests his love not to leave, but to stay… stay as long as life returns to its constancy and familiarity.

In Search of Vanished Blood is a strong political commentary on the violence in society. The poet says that we try to hide the truth from generations to come and this could backfire on us. When we clean the past, we destroy the future. The bloodshed that has been rendered unto the world needs to be talked about so that future violence can be stopped. But we seem to be cleaning up our history, letting our future create more causes for confusion and chaos.

The book is a mix of poems that cry out passion for love of the beloved and passion for love of the nation. The poet seems to be telling us that these two parts of life are equally important. The passion that is inherent in the love of a beloved, in her hair, her face and her very presence that turns the climate into gold is as strong as the passion you feel for a nation embroiled in conflict with itself. The pain, the agony and the ecstasy are the same.

Poet

Faiz Ahmed Faiz (1911–1984), born in Sialkot in undivided Punjab, was an intellectual, revolutionary poet and one of the most celebrated writers of the Urdu language, having been nominated two times for the Nobel Prize in literature. Faiz also wrote poetry in the Punjabi language. A notable member of the Progressive Writers' Movement (PWM), Faiz was an avowed Marxist, for which he received the Lenin Peace Prize by the Soviet Union in 1962.

He did his BA with honours in Arabic, followed by Masters in Arabic as well as in English Literature. It was during his college years that he met M.N. Roy and Muzaffar Ahmed who influenced him to become a member of the Communist Party. In 1947, Faiz opted for the newly established State of Pakistan. In 1938, he became editor-in-chief of the monthly Urdu magazine *Adab-e-Latif*. In 1941, Faiz published his first literary book *Naqsh-e-Faryadi*.

In 1941, Faiz married Alys a British national and a member of Communist Party of the United Kingdom, who was a student at the Government College University where Faiz taught poetry. In 1951, due to his communist leanings he was arrested and given a long sentence in the Rawalpindi conspiracy case followed by exile from Pakistan. He then lived in London and returned to Pakistan in 1964. He again had to leave Pakistan in 1979 and took asylum in Beirut, Lebanon, and returned in 1982 in poor health and breathed his last in 1984 at Lahore. He was conferred Pakistan's highest civil award, *Nishan-e-Imtiaz*, posthumously in 1990.

Gagan Gill

- *Gagan Gill Poems*; **Translated by Jane Duran and Lucy Rosenstein; Published by The Poetry Translation Centre.**

In 2005, the Poetry Translation Centre, SOAS, London University, translated Gagan Gill's work as part of a project translating six international poets. *Gagan Gill Poems* is translated by Jane Duran and Lucy Rosenstein.

This book has 11 poems that are focused on women. *A Desire in the Bangles* is a poem that originates from the significance of bangles worn by the Hindu women. Culturally, Hindu women adorn their wrists with bangles when they are unmarried and married but are not allowed to wear them when they are widowed. They are supposed to break them when widowed. The poem very poignantly brings out the differences in what the bangles mean to a girl when she is a wife and when she is a widow.

Kanjika: Some Lamentations 2 is a poem that talks about the disconnect of the woman's true self to the society that she exists in. The poet lists out instances where she feels this disconnect. Her life is almost toxic with all the rules and regulations and even the joy she expresses is not hers.

Ants is hard-hitting and poignant at the same time. The first line 'The Ants had lost their way home' and the last line 'Long ago, perhaps they were women' is a stark comment on how we treat women in society. They are just the labourious ants slogging away day in and out, with no identity of their own. Each ant labours for the community just as the women labour for their community. They are doomed in their roles.

The poems are a reflection of women in society. They ring true to every woman who lives in India. Though the cultural references are very specific to the community that Gill is a part of, the pain is universal. The status of women as ants or as someone whose inner desires have no value over the cultural overbearing is true of any community.

Poet

Gagan Gill is a critically acclaimed poet with four collections of poetry and a book of essays to her credit. She is a full-time writer and lives in New Delhi. A prolific translator, she has also published 10 volumes of translations of the work of various writers like Zbiegnew Herbert, Harbhajan Singh, Sitakant Mahapatra and Shrikant Verma. Gill holds a Masters degree in English literature from Delhi University. She worked as a literary editor for 11 years with *The Times of India group* and *the Sunday Observer*. She has been a visiting writer from India at the International Writing Program in Iowa (1990) and a Nieman Fellow for journalism at Harvard University in 1992–93. However, she gave up a career in journalism in order to devote herself to poetry. Her poetry is taught in several American, English and German universities and is widely anthologized in English.

Harbhajan Halwarvi

- *Across the Bridges:* **Harbhajan Halwarvi; Translated by Pawan Gulati; Published by Sahitya Akademi.**

Harbhajan Halwarvi is a contemporary poet who cannot stop emphasizing simplicity in poetry. His poetry does not follow the laws of writing. It follows the heart. An oft-repeated theme of nature and loneliness runs through his poems. He writes from the heart and this makes his poetry ring true.

Across the Bridges (Pulaan Ton Paar), the award-winning book of poems, is written in the neo-Progressive tradition. However, the poet is conscious not only of ideology but of the structure and aesthetics of a literary creation as well. The present work is noted for its lyrical quality. The book is adjudged an outstanding contribution to Indian poetry in Punjabi.

The book is translated by Pawan Gulati who is a prolific translator. He has translated many works from Punjabi to English. These include novels and poems.

The book has 46 poems and 23 ghazals. They deal with varied emotions of the poet. The poet is highly melancholic and lonely. His loneliness comes through in most of the poems. He rues the fact that people are slowly getting detached from nature and the real world. Human egos are fragile, and pride is persistent.

The book begins with the poem *Across the Bridges*, which is also the title of the book. The sheer magnificence of the rivers is impressed upon the reader with very strong imagery of blood vessels. The land is muscular, and the river sculpts civilizations as it moves ahead. Every river is the same, just as human blood. It is the human that creates differences. Water brings all people together and nurtures growth. Yet people have found differences. People have discovered differentiators. Bridges have to be built to overcome these differences. But they are constantly breaking down and constantly being rebuilt. *Mending Walls* by the famous American poet Robert Frost resonates a similar theme, bringing out the fact that human ego is the same across nations.

The three-part *Loneliness* will ring true for every individual. Each one of us, even in the midst of activity, is lonely. The series begins with a poem that enumerates the scurry of the morning, yet brings in the huge spaces of loneliness that the poet can feel. The chasms are huge and difficult to cover up. Part Two talks about the maddening speed of daily chores. There is so much to be done and undone. Life takes shape every moment. Everyone is working, playing, laughing and talking. Yet the alarming loneliness overpowers. Part Three is the end of the day, when man and nature retire. Even as the birds go back home and people trudge to their abodes, the loneliness creeps in again. We cannot, says the poet, separate our lives from our loneliness.

Small Walls is a little yet powerful poem. The poet pities those who make issues of small, irrelevant things and create differences between people. Human egos are so fragile that we lose track of the bigger picture in life.

Flowing Water calls for adventure. The human spirit is restless and confused. It seeks contentment even as it is drifting. The stagnant waters soothe it and help it settle, yet the restless energy within makes us want to flow ahead like the river.

Murder is a very contemporary poem. The incident described in the poem is an oft-repeated act nowadays. We have heard stories of a waitress being killed by a young man for refusing to refill his glass or a dancer being shot dead because she didn't allow the young man to touch her while she dances. The poet makes a statement when he says that the sky is unaware of the blood shed on the land. He strongly brings out the indifference that has taken root in our society where such instances do not shake us. We go on with life as if nothing has happened.

The last section of the book is of ghazals. Ghazals are poems that are usually tuned into songs. The collection of ghazals here varies in theme from friendship to love. Loneliness returns in the ghazals. The ease of animosity and the difficulty to create and retain friendships is yet another theme.

The collection of poems stands out for its simplicity, strength and power. Yet the poems are subtle, hard hitting and thought provoking. They question your core. They show you a mirror, the reflection in which you may not be prepared to see.

Poet

Born in 1943, in Halwara, Distt. Ludhiana, Punjab, Harbhajan Singh Halwarvi is a postgraduate in Mathematics and Punjabi Literature. In 1977 he joined *Punjabi Tribune* as Assistant Editor; then he became Acting Editor and eventually Editor, of the same paper and worked there upto 1997 and again from 2000 to 2002. He has been guest Editor, *Jagriti* (Punjabi Monthly), Senior Research Fellow, Deptt. of Punjabi Development, Punjabi University and Editor, *Ajj Di Awaz* and Vice President, Punjabi Bhasha Academy, Jalandhar.

His works include four poetry collections, three travelogues, and a number of articles and book reviews. He has received several honours and awards, some of which are: Bhai Vir Singh Award by Languages Department of Punjab Government, Shiromani Punjabi Patrakar Award by Punjab Government Kartar Singh Dhaliwal Award for literature by Punjabi Sahit Academy, Ludhiana, and Harmony Award by the Organization of Understanding and Fraternity, New Delhi.

Harbhajan Singh

- *Tree and The Sage* by Harbhajan Singh; Translated by J.S. Rahi and Rita Chaudhry; Ajanta Books International.

We can see Harbhajan Singh's poetic genius at work in his long poems. In 1982, he published *Maththa Deeve Wala* (The Forehead with the Lamp), which was a distinctive experiment. Several voices appear side by side within this interior monologue. The significance of these poems in terms of the creation of a new poetic value is distinct not only in the development of the Punjabi poetry but also in that of Indian poetry as well.

In 1992, Harbhajan Singh published his famous long poem *Rukh Te Rishi* (*The Tree And The Sage*) that was honoured with the Saraswati Samman.

The Tree And The Sage is a deeply contemplative poem with six cantos, an untitled invocation in the opening and a titled *Antika* (epilogue) that forms an open-ended conclusion. The narrative is cast in the first-person account of an arduous search of a seeker who feels like a tree and aspires for a life brimming with the magnanimity of a tree. Caught between the duality of attachment and detachment, he ventures out from his abode to find the *Guru* who may reveal to him the meaning of life. He trudges through the claustrophobic cities and towns. He finds colonies standing alienated across roads and dotted by shadeless walls; he is bruised by thorny forests and crosses streams, desolate arid lands and deserts.

However, the guru he finds is no guru of flesh and blood. It is an awakening of the inner self just as it is revealed in the 15th Pauri of Guru Nanak's Japji: *Pancha ka Guru Ek Dhyan*. The *Tree and the Sage* is an odyssey of the seeker to rediscover the meanings lost in the materialistic, physical and psychological contradictions of existence. It is a tale of a 'journey from the body to the soul.' There is no going back from this state. The river lost in canals, tributaries and crops cannot be rediscovered. The self, dissolving every moment like a chunk of salt, cannot be put whole again. Life for Harbhajan Singh is an ever-going journey beyond the self. Herein lies the answer why Kabir could not return to his parents, Puran to Luna's palaces and the Buddha to the eternally waiting Yashodhara.

This poem by Harbhajan Singh is absolutely unique in quality. It is one long poem spreading over 80 pages. Singh has always been different than his contemporaries. In a class of his own, he excels himself in this work. The poet is free from the confines of religion, languages and pothis. His ideal is a man who unlike pothis is not circumscribed.

The translation is of exceptional quality. The poem is in a very readable format despite its length and the credit for it goes to both JS Rahi and Rita Chaudhry. The book has a very erudite introduction – to Harbhajan Singh, his craft, as well as to this poem – and annotations, spread over 14 pages, which explain everything in detail and with context.

Poet

Harbhajan Singh (1920–2002), a distinguished figure in Punjabi literature, was born in Lumding (Assam). He published his first collection of poems *Lassan* (The Marks of Violence on the Body) in 1956 and this very first poetic work brought him recognition as one of the major Punjabi poets after the Progressive movement, which had been dominated by Mohan Singh for a long time. Most of his poems tackled burning issues like nuclear armament, Emergency, Bangladesh program, war and its liberation. He is known for his long, dramatic and lyrical poems.

His poetry with its distinct modernist idiom dominated the Punjabi literary scene after his Sahitya Akademi Award winning *Na Dhuppe Na Chhaven* (Neither in the Sun Nor in the Shade) made its mark in 1967. He rejected all manners of idealism that the Progressive movement professed and advocated. Even the idea of realism was transformed. An anti-heroic and existential persona with a self-reflexive language became the epicenter of his poetic expression. A new mode of poetic vitality thus emerged. This was, in a way, similar to something that had happened within the Anglo-American poetry with the appearance of T.S. Eliot's *Wasteland* and the *Love Song of* J. Alfred Prufrock. It was in continuity with the same poetic sensibility that his *Sarak De Safe Ute* (On the Page of the Street) made its mark in 1970.

Harbhajan Singh

- *A Light Within: Selected Poems of Harbhajan Singh;* Translated by S C Narula; Published by Sahitya Akademi; Punjabi translated into English.

The book has 49 poems and the poet himself has chosen the poems for translation.

My Photograph is an introspective poem: the poet talks about searching for himself in a photograph that has been returned by a lover. Time seems to have stopped for him. Time and again, the poet has been forced to seek meaning in his life. He claims that he chose no one, neither his mother nor his lover. He does not live in the present. He lives in the hope that tomorrow will be his. Yet when he reaches tomorrow, yesterday comes back to him and he is seen seeking himself all over again.

A Light Within, for which the book is named, is a powerful poem. In it, the poet questions his dark existence. The imagery is a powerful reference to the violence and senselessness that exists in today's world. The stark nakedness of an individual, who does not have the time to cover himself, when he is suddenly exposed to the truth, hits hard. The image of a virgin having dreams of an adulterous birth is a reminder of the fall in morality in society.

Waits the Mother discusses the eternal wait of mankind. The mother waits for her child to be born, then to go discover the world, and later when she moves on into the next world, she waits for her progeny to join her. The mother depicts eternal hope, hope that keeps mankind going, hope that energizes man from the living and beyond. The last stanza of the poem is a very powerful image of the mother waiting for those who have reached their destination as well as for those who have not. The journey never ends. It just moves from one point to the other and we keep waiting for it to end. That is the paradox of life.

Our Worms deals with Partition. The scars of Partition have influenced literature from both the countries – India and Pakistan. Partitions of all kinds are painful, whether it is of family property, of states or of nations. Lines that draw boundaries in the heart hurt. However, man gets through it and then believes that the life he is leading is the most peaceful one and that the can of ugly worms now looks like a lovely bouquet.

This collection of poems is replete with imagery. The imagery is taut and powerful. The imagery is of the everyday life, yet it stands out for its individuality.

Jaswant Deed

- *Kamandal* by Jaswant Deed; Translated by Madhumeet; Published by Sahitya Akademi.

Jaswant Deed is a contemporary poet who writes in free verse. His style is not dictated by any fixed ideology. He writes as a free thinker who idealizes the man–woman relationship. His poems articulate the complexity of modern life, especially in this relationship. His poetry is vivid in its imagery and reflects his acute observations on society.

The book, *Kamandal*, has been translated by Dr. Madhumeet who is able to help create rich visual imagery for a non-Punjabi reader.

The book has 73 poems that discuss the life of the poet. As Deed explains in his introduction to the book, the compilation deals with his love, his relationships, his ancestors, inherited values, middle class life, woman–man relationship, family and himself. The backdrop of the poems moves from village to city, city to state, from state to country, and he feels that he is blessed to write in a language used by Sant Kabir, Sheikh Farid, Baba Nanak and Waris Shah.

The book begins with the poem *Prop*. The poet laments the loss of a mooring, an anchor. He says that in his journey from city to city he finds no prop for him to support himself. In a world where people leave their native homes looking for money and an elusive sense of prosperity, he feels the pain of being cut away from the umbilical cord and thrown into the throes of a daily, pulsating and colourful life, which still at times looks colourless and anchorless.

Dinner is another poem that catches one's fascination with its sheer simplicity. It is the tale of two friends meeting over dinner.

The poet takes the role of the narrator and describes how his friend calls him over for dinner. Friends bond over food and drink. Even as this bonding creates happiness, it sends them into nostalgia as they reminisce about times spent in the village, discuss how they had to leave the village and come to the cities. The power of alcohol takes over, lulling both the friends to sleep. The poet walks away quietly the next morning, only to insist on dinner at his place the next time his friend initiates it. And the process begins all over again.

Poems like *S.M.S* and *Truth* express his passion about the everlasting man–woman relationship. For Deed, love is eternal, beyond life, after life and in the next life. The pain of losing a loved one comes through in these poems. The pain of waiting for a loved one cuts through these poems.

26 January deals with the pain of a war widow. She is felicitated on the national day for the sacrifices made by her loved one. The medals and the applause raise questions in her mind. Where did her husband breathe his last? Whom did he remember at that moment? Could she see the place where he died? Could she stop time and bring him back alive? No, she shouldn't, she thinks as she dusts the medals and the applause.

The Beauty is again a poem that, with economy, communicates the immense pain of a young girl. The girl is called by different names, in the process of which she doesn't know her own name. Who are these people who call her by these names? Why is her name not known? And why is she weeping? The answers to these questions subtly bring about the reality of young girls who are thrown into prostitution.

The World is a simple poem on the daily lives of people. Each person mentioned in the poem is a person who you or I may know. We all have a Mr. Bhatia and a Mr. Goverdhan in our lives. But beyond all of them and above all of them is the Eternal player God, who moves silently, unseen and unheard.

These and the many other pearls that this book is endowed with definitely make for reading that is earthy and ethereal at the same time. The collection is funny yet disturbing. The poems force the reader to think of some very fundamental truths of life that most of us have probably forgotten long ago.

Author

Jaswant Deed (1954–) born in Shahkot Jalandhar, Punjab, is a Punjabi novelist and poet. He won the Sahitya Akademi Award in 2007 for his book *Kamandal* (Poetry). He worked for more than 30 years in Doordarshan Kendra and therefater left as assistant station director and is presently settled in Canada. He has produced approximately 50 TV documentaries/films on life and works of eminent writers/painters and other well-known personalities, chief amongst them being a documentary to commemorate the completion of 100 years of Ghadar Movement and formation of Ghadar Party and on the history of Shri Guru Granth Sahib and its message of Universal Brotherhood, Peace And Communal Harmony. His published works include one short story collection *Ik lapp Yadan Di*, 5 poetry collections – *Bache Ton Dardi Kavita, Achanchet Awaz Ayegi Aje, Ghundi, Dharti Hor Pre* and *Kamandal*. He has edited a short story collection *Desh Vand Dian Kahanian* dealing with Partition, for Sahitya Akademi and has translated Yashpal's *Jangal Di Kahani*.

Sidhu Damdami writing in *The Tribune* (6.1.2008) about Deed's poetry, states, 'In the early 1990s after the restoration of peace in Punjab, literary activities started picking up even in the absence of any visible social or political movement. This literature, which may be low on social and political concerns, is certainly high on concerns that affect the modern individual-personal, intra-personal and inter-personal conflicts. By his diction and form of treatment, Deed paves the way for Punjabi poetry to make a much-desired departure.'

Jaswant Zafar

- *The Other Shore of Words: Selected Poems of Jaswant Zafar*; Translated by Jasdeep Singh, Gurshminder Jagpal and Niranjan Tasneem; Published by Chetna Parkashan.

The decade of 1980–1990 in the province of Punjab in India was fraught with conflict and numerous events one after the other put the Punjabis and Sikhs on the boil again, having barely recovered from the onslaught of Partition.

Jasdeep Singh, one of the translators of this book writes in an article, 'During this time, Jaswant Singh Zafar was studying electrical engineering at the Guru Nanak Engineering College in Ludhiana. His first book of poems, written in Punjabi, *Do Sahan Vichkaar* (Within Two Breaths) has the gloomy disenchantment of these years. His second book, *Asin Nanak De Ki Lagde Han* (What are we to Nanak), explores the relationship of followers to the teachings and ideology of the Sikh Gurus. Many poems of the second book juxtapose Sikh principles of volunteerism, compassion and ecological concerns with the way these values are observed by the community in contemporary times. Then, in his third book *Eh Banda Ki Hunda* (What is a Human), Zafar looks at the relationship between humans, their sense of self, their surroundings, science, the Punjabi diaspora and the state of society in the era of consumer capitalism.'

The Other Shore of Words is an English translation of selected poems from his three-poetry anthologies written between 1985 and 2010. The poet has written a very delightful note at the beginning called 'From one shore to the other' in which he explains, among other things, how these three very different but gifted translators came to translate these poems. In the context of his first book, he says, 'Terrorism uses religion as an excuse and the ruling apparatus, in the name of fighting or curtailing terrorism, oppresses human rights. A blood feud ensues. Masses suffer in these two extremes.' He makes another very pertinent observation, 'Politics kills the soul of religion and occupies its body.' He further adds, 'in reality, religion turns out to be an excuse for expression of real character and flaws in man. Those who do not believe in religion may have many other excuses like morality or ideology.' These thoughts of the poet help us understand the poems that follow.

In the book, the Punjabi and English versions mirror each other on opposite pages. This device is often found in many poetry anthologies, but what distinguishes this book from others is that this bilingualism is carried throughout the book. The book cover, bearing the name of the book and that of author, is also written in both Punjabi and English. The poet's preface, From 'One Shore To The Other' has its Punjabi version facing it, titled 'Ek Ton Duje Pathan Di Yatra.' The index of chapters and the section, 'About the Translators' are bilingual too. Among the hundreds of books that were researched for compiling this book, I found Zafar's to be the only book of its kind.

The poet has beautifully explained the need for doing so, as this way reader can read the original or the translation and at the same time appreciate the translation process. People who know both languages can especially enjoy both and use this to improve their own linguistic proficiency, while those who are not fluent in either Punjabi or English can improve their language skills, as the case may be. While researching the books, I always wished for something like this, so that I could enjoy the Punjabi version alongside. Of course, it is appreciated that while this may be possible in poetry books, it may not always be possible in prose, especially in magnum opus of the kinds written by Ankhi, Baldev Singh, etc.

Amongst the poems, one of the most scathing is *Maryada* in which the poet laments the tendency of some of the followers of the Sikh faith to stick to Maryada (tradition) in a fundamentalist way – behaving in an exclusivist way rather than being inclusive.

The poet, in the other poems, reveals his humanist nature and his concern for social issues and even for the state of the environment. There is also a poem on wisdom gained while he is making his own house with his 'Ink, Sweat and Blood' when he realizes how an owner feels when the tenant sticks nails in the house built by his sweat. We can thus not only see the poet's sensitivity but also the breadth of his worldview.

Author

Jaswant Singh Zafar (1965–) is a writer based in Ludhiana, Punjab, India. He has written three books of poetry and two books of prose. An engineer by profession, Zafar's is a multifaceted personality, as he is not only a famed cartoonist but also has held photography and painting exhibitions.

Read on

- Canada-based Punjabi singer, composer and music director Gagandeep Singh has sung many of Zafar's poems in his album, *Zindagi De Rubroo*

Lal Singh Dil

- *Poet of the Revolution: The Memoirs and Poems of Lal Singh Dil*; Translated by Nirupama Dutt; Published by Penguin India.

Lal Singh Dil is a legend in Punjab, famed as much for his rousing poetry as for the brew of his tea stall. Born into the Dalit community in the years before Partition, he bravely challenged deep-rooted social prejudices through his crisp and stirring verses. His struggle led him to join the Naxalite movement – an experience that culminated in three horrifying years of torture at the hands of the police. In his later years, much to the dismay of his comrades, he converted to Islam because he believed that its tenets could be reconciled with the egalitarian and inclusive principles of communism.

He published his autobiography, *Dastaan*, in 1998, containing a foreword by Amarjit Chandan and an afterword by Prem Parkash. Although he had converted to Islam, he continued to publish his works under his name pre-conversion. This English translation by Nirupama Dutt of his autobiography, *Dastaan*, also has 20 of his poems. A powerful indictment of caste violence and discrimination, *Poet of the Revolution* describes Dil's most turbulent years in his clear, fiery voice. It is a must read.

Since this book has autobiographical content as well as his poetry, it was difficult to decide where to place this book. Since he was a poet, it was decided to place it under the genre Poetry.

Some of the poems that are included in this book are:

Fiery Furnace of Childhood is an essay about his childhood. Growing up in rural Punjab, India, in the post-Partition days is in itself an adventure that contains a hundred stories. He talks about how he began his education in Urdu, but that was discontinued when Urdu medium schools shut down because of the Partition. He narrates the tale of poverty and the pain of his grandmother. Women during that time had many a tragic tale to narrate with disease and death having a stronghold in every family.

Learning a Lesson talks about his school where he faced the realities of the caste system. He shares memories of his teachers. One of his teachers was an uncle of his and had a major role in shaping his education. His uncle was also a victim of the caste system. Despite his qualifications, he was treated differently at school because of his caste. The uncle won the Gurudwara elections but was not allowed to be the President due to his caste. These incidents had a lifelong impact on the poet.

In Custody talks about his experience in jail, as he was a major supporter of the Naxalite movement. The sheer violence of the police force and the ruthlessness with which the Naxalites were treated is brought to light in this essay. The Naxalites, though revolutionary in their approach, were also worried about the families of their near and dear ones and always took care to ensure their ideas and beliefs did not hurt the families.

Flowers of Blood is a poem that describes the futility of bloodshed across the world. The isolation that violence causes, the inner turmoil that people undergo, the rage and anger that overpowers sanity and causes them to shed blood is visible, yet not tangible. The pain is felt by all but expressed by none. When war overtakes peace and people kill each other, what is left is a river of blood. From this blossom the flowers of blood. And sadly they are all identical in a world that is trying to reinforce differences. Yet the poet laments that we are lazy at trying to establish peace.

My Country talks about the neglected people of the country – the poor, the oppressed, the lower caste, the women, the labourers or anyone who is marginalized by mainstream society. But society refuses to acknowledge their presence and, in fact, tries to dominate and even eliminate them. The marginalized sections of society are also my people, says the poet, wholeheartedly accepting all humanity into his fold. He is pained by the way these people are treated by the rest who create boundaries and keep those boundaries nourished by blood.

Caste is a strong poem that reflects the poet's personal life. The poet, who belonged to the lower caste, fell in love with a girl from a higher caste. The girl finds references in many of his poems. In this one, he brutally tells her that their love is doomed in a society that does not allow the mingling of castes, even after death. In such a place, there is no hope for the living. The caste system has plagued the Indian society for centuries, and the poet knows the reality that love has no voice in the madness of hatred that already exists.

Poet

Lal Singh Dil (1943–2007) was one of the major revolutionary Punjabi poets emerging out of the Naxalite (Maoist–Leninist) Movement in the Indian Punjab towards the late sixties of the 20th century. Referring to the impact of the Naxalite Movement in Punjab, Paramjit S. Judge says, 'The consequences of the Naxalite movement have been almost ephemeral and have hardly made an impact on the social and political spheres... Its positive contribution is that it has revolutionized Punjabi poetry which can never be traditional and romantic again.' The prominent poets belonging to this school are: Pash, Lal Singh Dil, Harbhajan Halwarvi, Darshan Khatkar, Amarjit Chandan and Sant Ram Udasi.

Dil had started writing poetry even while at school. Some of his poems were published in well-known Punjabi magazines, *Lakeer*, *Preetlari* and *Nagmani* even before his first collection of poetry was published. He published three collections of poetry: *Sutlej Di Hawa* (Breeze from the Sutlej); *Bahut Sarey Suraj* (So Many Suns), and *Satthar* (A Sheaf). A collected volume of all his poems titled *Naglok* (The World of the Nāgas) was published in 1998 and 2007. He also wrote a long poem titled *Aj Billa Phir Aaya* (Billa Came Again Today), which was published posthumously in 2009.

Read on
- The documentary filmmaker Ajay Bhardwaj filmed Dil extensively for his documentary *Kitte Mil Ve Mahi* (2005) that explores the relationship between Dalits and Sufism in East Punjab.

Manjit Tiwana

- *Our Sleepless Times* by Manjit Tiwana; Translated by B. M. Razdan; Published by Sahitya Akademi; Punjabi translated into English.

The book has 24 poems, intensely emotional and vivid.

Window Shopping is a simple poem that harbours the dreams and fantasies of young girls who visit the market place. Are they shopping for stationery or grocery? No, they are window-shopping boys. They look at each one, analyse them and find reasons to reject them. The shopping happens in the mind, each one keeping to her heart her stories and fantasies. The inner secret life of many a teenage girl is reflected in this poem.

Do Not Come is a powerful poem of how perceptions change over time. One of the partners has left the other one. She tells her partner not to return back to her. Even if all the forces of nature remind him of her, she doesn't want him to come back. He has been long gone and she fears he will come back a changed man. She doesn't want to break the image she has of him in her mind. She remains in love with this former self and wants it to stay that way. The pain is so real and raw that one cannot but sigh in anguish.

Day is a two-line poem but with the impact of an epic. The two words 'mischievous mendicant' are strong enough to bring to mind all the games that life plays with us. *Death* is another explosive poem. In four lines, the poet expresses the simplicity and complexity of death.

Warning is just what it is named – a warning to all those who misuse the power bestowed on them. It could be a political leader, a teacher or a boss.

Wedding is a scathing comment on the commercialization of writing that is happening in the world. As the creator, the poet cherishes all her thoughts. She wants to bind all her poems into the book of her life. As she goes through them, she realizes that each one is a valuable memory, either of her childhood or of her youth. Each one has a different story to tell. Some reflect her heart while some were for fame. She realizes that even if she did not consolidate her work, someone else would, as it would generate money after she has passed away.

The poems are sharp, stark and simple. Yet they hold in their heart explosive feelings that, if the reader cares to hear, can be disturbing. The straightforward approach of the poet transforms daily fare into transcendental experiences. The use of unpretentious words creates agonizing ripples and compels the reader to wonder at the evident yet unreachable truths of the world. The book is, in essence, a reminder of the sheer power of poetry.

Poet

Manjit Tiwana (1947–) was born in Patiala, Punjab. She did her M.A. in Psychology and English from the Panjab University in 1969 and 1973, respectively, and Ph.D. in Psychology. She also did Diploma in Indian Theatre (Acting and Direction). She was Head of the Department of Psychology in Government College for Women, Chandigarh. Tiwana's first poem was published in *Nagmani* when she was only 16. Her significant works are: *Ilham, Ilzam, Tarian di joon, Uninda Wartman, Savitri* and *Jin Prem Kiyo*. She is the recipient of the Sahitya Akademi award (1990) for *Uninda Wartman* (Poetry) and the Shiromani Punjabi Kavi Puraskar by Punjab State Languages Department for the year 1999.

Mohan Singh

- *Dreams & Desires: Seventy Poems of Mohan Singh;* Translated by Tejwant Singh Gill; Published by Punjabi University, Patiala.

This book is a collection of 70 of his poems selected from all his books except *Jai Mir* (1968) and *Nankayan* (1971). According to the translator, Jai Mir was left out 'as it sang paeans to peace arising out of triumph of socialism over capitalism.' He writes that, 'it was written more from ideological simulation rather than authentic experience and hence the poetic expression there is bound by rhetoric only.' *Nankayan* is an epic written on Guru Nanak and since only its entire translation can do justice to this magnificent work, the translator decided to forego the temptation of including a part of it in this selection.

Ten poems are taken from *Saave Patr* (*Green Leaves*; 1936), his first collection. To the reader of Punjabi poetry, these poems are very nostalgic, having been brought up listening to or reading them. *Ambi de Boote Thalle* (Under the Mango Tree) was the most celebrated of these. There are some patriotic poems as well, of which *Sipahi da Dil* (Soldier's Feelings) and *Sikhi* haunt the reader long after they are over.

Other than that, there are 10 poems each from *Adhvate* (Half-Way, 1944), *Awajan* (Voices, 1962) and *Buhe* (Doors, 1977); eight poems each from *Kasumbhra* (Red Oleander, 1939) and *Vada Vela* (Early Morning, 1958); and seven each from *Kach Sach* (Tinsel and Truth, 1942) and *Jandre* (Locks, 1964).

The collection contains Mohan Singh's famous poem *Kurrhi Potohar Di* (The Girl from Potohar), which describes the poet's encounter with a tall, beautiful maiden trying to cross a river with her bundle. As he, completely besotted, offers her help, she hands him the bundle and takes his hand. However, on the other side, as she thanks him, she says, 'May you live long, my *brother.*'

Her disdain for the simpler folks of Lahore comes from an anthropological rivalry, of sorts, which is explained in an excellent article by Nirupama Dutt. Despite Lahore's pre-eminent position in the hearts of Punjabis, there were some who never thought much of Lahore – they were the Rawalpindis. Rawalpindi is in the area known as Potohar, which forms a plateau, while Lahore is in the mainland of Majha, just as Amritsar is. The Rawalpindis held themselves to be a superior people – more cultured, better spoken, taller and fairer. It is this rivalry that the poet portrays.

Not all poems are as light-hearted though. Some talk about the exploitation of poor at the hands of rich (*Taj Mahal*), while *Yaad* (Memory) recalls the image of the legendary Heer and her tragic end. In *Rosenberg*, through the Rosenberg couple (American citizens who were hanged for being Soviet spies), the poet laments about how cheap life has become. These are just some of the many social concerns that Singh addresses in these poems.

Tejwant Singh Gill has done an excellent translation of these poems, and they are very reader friendly. As it has been mentioned elsewhere in this book, it is very shocking that the works of greats like Mohan Singh (who is called the father of Punjabi Poetry) have not been translated; in fact, none of his 10 books have been translated. This beautiful book is the only translated book available of this great poet, although individual poems have been translated and are available. The translator and the publisher (Punjabi University, Patiala) deserve all credit for the same.

Poet

Mohan Singh (1905–1978) is known as the father of modern Punjabi poetry. The other poets who contributed significantly to the growth of modern Punjabi poetry in the initial years include Amrita Pritam, Harbhajan Singh and Shiv Kumar Batalvi. Mohan Singh has been hailed as the greatest Punjabi poet of the 20th century. He received the Sahitya Akademi award in 1959 for *Wadda Vela* (Early Morning). Every year, his birth anniversary is observed at Village Nanoki in Nabha District in the form of a cultural mélange (Mela).

Singh was born in Mardan (Pakistan). From 1933 to 1939, he taught Persian language and literature at Khalsa College, Amritsar. In 1940, he joined as a lecturer at the Sikh National College, Lahore, but after some time he left the job and started a firm, Hind Publishers, and decided to promote the literary standards of Punjabi publications. In 1939, he had already started his famous literary Punjabi monthly, *Panj Darya*. In 1947, Partition disturbed his plans, and he shifted his business to Amritsar. For survival, he faced many odds. However, he soon closed down the firm and sold out the magazine *Panj Darya* and went back to teaching, first as teacher in Khalsa College, Patiala; later, he was appointed Professor Emeritus at Punjabi Agricultural University, Ludhiana, where he served till his death.

Singh was a major force in Punjabi poetry after 1935, and in the next 25 years, he influenced generations of Punjabi poets. He created new norms in Punjabi poetry and created the language of new metaphors. He is, therefore, considered the most important Punjabi poet after Waris Shah. Though a romantic in his earlier poems, he became a moving force under the impact of the Progressive Movement, and his poetry came to reflect social consciousness as he sang of liberty, equality and fraternity.

Munir Niazi

- *The Colours of Silence: Punjabi Poems of Munir Niazi;* **Rendered into English Verse by Anwar Dil; Published by Intercultural Forum and Ferozsons (Pvt.) Ltd., Lahore.**

Taiz Hawa Aur Tanha Phool, Jungle Mein Dhanak, Dushmanoon Kai Darmiyan Sham and *Mah-e-Munir* are some of his Urdu publications. In Punjabi language, he has published *Safar Di Raat, Char Chup Cheezan* and *Rasta Dassan Walay Tarey* (Stars that Show the Path). This book, *The Colours of Silence,* has 100 of his Punjabi poems translated into English from these three Punjabi works. The book is richly adorned by 64 illustrations – paintings, ink drawings, etchings, photographs, abstractions and calligraphy by eminent artists including Anwar Dil, who is also the translator of this book and who has written a beautiful introduction to the art and craft of Munir Niazi.

Niazi is known for his brevity and precision, and the very effective imagery in his poetry conveys pictures in a few words. Innocence, mythology, nostalgia, dreams, eroticism and romance are some of his most common themes. What also comes out of these poems is the concern for the suffering of his fellow humans, the shock at the indifference of humans towards each other's suffering and dismay over their petty hatreds. Dil writes, 'As a poet, he has often felt that he is one of those explorers who must look for oases in deserts… who all the time reflecting deep on the meaning and purpose of their experience…quietly building a more worthwhile universe within themselves before sharing with others.' Munir's poetry is universalistic and humanistic in outlook.

Since Niazi is known for his brevity, the average length of the poems in this collection is five to six lines. One poem is in fact of just one line and in fact the title is bigger than the poem; the title is *Vaqt ton agge langhan di saza* (Punishment for Going Ahead of Time) and the poem reads, 'One is left alone.'

Another shows his humility – the poem titled *Harf hijaab de parde andar* (Word within the veil of mystery) reads,

> One word the veil of another
> This mystery I do not comprehend
> Writing all my life
> I barely knew words

Poet

Munir Ahmad, better known as Munir Niazi, (1928–2006), a Sitara-e-Imtiaz Award recipient, was an Urdu and Punjabi poet from Pakistan. Munir Ahmed used to call himself Punjabi as the definition of Punjabi is cultural and geographical and most of his poetry was also reflective of the culture of Punjab.

Niazi was born in Khanpur, a village near Hoshiarpur, Punjab. He was initially educated at Khanpur. After Partition, he migrated to Sahiwal and then Lahore. Munir Niazi launched a weekly, *Saat Rang* (Seven Colours) from Sahiwal in 1949. Some of his poetry was used in films and these film songs became extremely popular among the Pakistani public, which established him as the foremost movie songwriter of Pakistan. His songs have been sung by the likes of Mehndi Hassan and Noorjehan. He also wrote for newspapers, magazines and the radio. In 1960, he established a publication institute, *Al-Misal*. He was later associated with Pakistan Television, Lahore, and lived in Lahore till his death. Munir Niazi mostly followed the poet's vocation, apart from brief engagements in publishing and film in Lahore. Besides, he was a popular poet at *mushairas* (poetry recitals/symposia) held throughout the subcontinent. Many of his poems are very popular on both sides of the border like *Der kar deta hun mein*.

Read on:
- English translations of selected Munir Niazi's poetical works were edited by Suhail Safdar and published in 1996 as *The Poetical Works of Munir Niazi, Pakistan Writings.*

Pash

- *Pash: A Poet of Impossible Dreams: Selected Poems;* **Translations from Punjabi by TC Ghai; Published by Pash Memorial International Trust, Canada.**

Pash, or Avtar Singh Sandhu (1950–88), was a Punjabi revolutionary poet who was gunned down by the militants for his atheism, non-conformism and outspokenness. Nevertheless, he has become an inalienable part of the Punjabi literary consciousness. He began as a Naxalite but soon broke out of the straightjacket of this ideology. Yet, he became a powerful symbol of rebellion against all oppression. His pen name 'Pash,' in the Farsi language from which it originally comes as a noun, denotes fragrance. Used twice in the same breath, the word used as adjective stands for sprinkling and that for a poet underlines communicating awareness.

He was born in Talwandi Salem, Jalandhar, Punjab, and grew up in the midst of the Naxalite movement, a revolutionary movement waged in Punjab against the landlords, industrialists, traders and others who controlled the means of production. He left his matriculation studies to join a training center in vocational training. However, he left that too in order to join the Border Security Force. After his discharge, he returned to his village; however, it was clear that he was not cut out for a career in the conventional sense. With his sharp intellect to sustain him, he launched several journals one after the other. *Rohle Baan* (Raging Arrows) was his first journal. He published his first book of revolutionary poems, *Loh-Katha* (*Iron Tale*), in 1970. His militant and provocative tone raised the ire of the establishment and a murder charge was brought against him. He spent nearly two years in jail, before being finally acquitted.

On acquittal, he became involved in Punjab's Maoist front, editing a literary magazine, *Siarh* (*The Plow Line*). He became a popular political figure on the left during this period and was awarded a fellowship at the Punjabi Academy of Letters in 1985. He toured the United Kingdom and the United States the following year; while in the United States, he became involved with the Anti-47 Front, opposing extremist violence. At the beginning of 1988, Pash was in Punjab for the renewal of his visa from the United States. A day before leaving for Delhi, however, he was gunned down by militants along with his friend, Hans Raj in his village on 23 March 1988. His other works are *Uddian Bazan Magar* (*Following The Flying Hawks*) (1973), *Saadey Samiyaan Vich* (*In Our Times*) (1978) and *Khilre Hoye Varkey* (*Scattered Pages*) (1989).

Khilre Hoey Varkey was published posthumously in 1989 followed by his journals and letters. A selection of his poems in Punjabi, *Inkar*, was published in Lahore in 1997. His poems have been translated into many Indian languages, as well as in Nepali and English.

Pash wrote around 200 poems, and this book presents translations of just over 100 of them. The selection is fairly representative of the earlier as well as the later, more mature man. He did not have much of a formal education, but his work created a storm in the literary world when it came out.

His poems rebel against almost everything – the Indian liberal democratic state and rejecting all its symbols, the Constitution, the parliamentary system, the concept of patriotism and national unity. He breaks all tenets of Sikh orthodoxy except his love for Gurus; he defies all the rules of the Punjabi literary tradition by spurning its subject matter, language, idiom, imagery and aesthetics; he rejects the city, the media, the ruling political class, the bureaucracy; he finds inspiration, first, in the likes of Marx, Lenin and Mao but later perhaps even questions those prophets of revolution. Here, in essence, is a rejection of the whole process of history and its various 'falsehoods.' The poems call out the march of civilization as illusory, fundamentally flawed and always against the interests of the marginalized and the poor.

The bulk of the poems reflect his angst against this exploitative system, and yet Pash can be tender and full of joy, longing and sadness. He can be pessimistic but is so without accepting defeat or losing hope. His zeal for life is evident, as is the fact that despite everything, he never stops dreaming. Moreover, he has written some dazzling love poetry. In the last poem in this selection, *Ma you are wearing out?* (Ma turehni hi janihai), he tells his mother that he has now returned to her, never to leave again. It seems that the kind of paradise he had set out to build as a young man – on the ruins of the blatantly unjust and inhuman state – could not be found.

Read on

- *Reckoning with Dark Times: An Anthology of 75 poems of Pash* by Tejwant Singh Gill is another translation of his poems in English.

Santokh Singh Dheer

- *To The Punjab of Farid And Other Poems* by Santokh Singh Dheer; Translated by Bhupinder Singh and Others; Published by Bhupinder Singh.

Santokh Singh Dheer's poetry collections include *Guddian Patole, Jadon Aseen Aavange, Poh Phutala* (Day Break), *Dharti Mangdi Meenh Ve* (The Earth Asks for Rain) and *Patt Jharhe Purane* amongst others. It is from these collections and others that the poetry has been chosen for this translated edition. Bhupinder Singh has translated most of the poems for this collection while the remaining ones are done by others. Bhupinder Singh is also a publisher of this book and, as he says, it is his tribute to the activist writer. The manuscript for this book has been prepared since 1988–1989 and was lying unpublished.

A veteran political activist, Dheer is bold, outspoken, down-to-earth and yet essentially poetic. His is the poetry of struggle. He yearns for change, for a fair deal to the downtrodden, the suppressed, the backward and the have-nots. He is invariably hard-hitting, because of which he went to jail several times. In fact, some of the poetry was written when he was in jail during 1981.

His search for truth is that of a socially conscious writer. He highlights the harsh realities of life. He shuns idealism, romanticism and sentimentality. He seeks truth, honesty and accuracy. His attack on anti-social elements is fierce and virulent.

Thus, the poems in this collection explicitly attack the senseless killings in the name of religion. The very first poem *I was not an informer* was translated by the veteran communist leader Satya Pal Dang and had appeared in many newspapers of the day. It is about a three-year-old girl who is shot by the terrorists along with her family members and before being shot she asks, 'Why do you kill me?' The terrorist replies, 'You are an informer.'

There are poems written from 1956 onwards and are on topical issues including the Vietnam War, Nehru, the Naxalite movement, the senseless division of the world into nations, the futile enmity between Hindus and Muslims in the land of Farid, the killing of Longowol who was trying for peace and the barbaric killing of an Harijan woman. About the last, he very poignantly says in his poem, *This was not barbarity* that perhaps it was not a barbaric act because, if it was, then some Rama would have picked up his arrow and slayed the Ravana of today or a Mahabharata would have ensued. But for today's insensitive people such acts are daily happenings, which fail to move them to action.

> Perhaps this was not barbarity
> Only a commonplace affair
> Had it been barbarity
> Some Rama's fire-arrow
> Would have pierced and killed
> The demon king
> The city of Lanka would have burnt
> And tethered
> In the flowery flames of fire

Poet

Santokh Singh Dhir (also spelled as Dheer) (1920–2010) was a noted writer and poet. He was known for his stories *Koee Ik Sawaar*, *Sanjhi Kandh* and *Saver Hon Tak*. Dheer was born in Bassi Pathana, Punjab. His life was a hard struggle raising a large family. He first worked as a tailor and then as a journalist for *Preetlari*, a monthly magazine and the daily *Navan Zamana* of the Punjab communist party. But journalism was a temporary vocation. Later, he started as a full-time writer and wrote about 50 books including four novels, nine story anthologies, 11 books of poetry, two edited volumes of folk literature, a travelogue, a book of essays, a translation of *Kabir Vachanavali* into Punjabi, a short autobiographical novel, *Yadgar,* and an autobiography, *Brahaspati*. He received the Sahitya Akademi Award for his story collection, *Pakhi* in 1996. The Language Department of Punjab honoured him with the Shromani Sahitkar Award in 1991, and Punjabi Sahit Akademi Ludhiana awarded him the Kartar Singh Dhaliwal Sharv Sharest Award in 2002. Punjabi University, Guru Nanak Dev University and Punjabi Sahit Sabha, Delhi, awarded him life fellowships. He was a member of Punjab communist party's state council.

Three of his works *Sanjhi Diwar, Ik Sadharan Aadmi* and *Mungo* have been turned into tele-films. *Pakhi,* the award-winning collection of short stories, presents heart-rending accounts of human lives caught in turbulent times.

Read on

- According to Amarjit Chandan, three translations exist of his story *Koi IK Sawaar,* done by the eminent writers Khushwant Singh, Amrik Singh and Balwant Gargi. A TV serial was made on it too.

Shah Hussain

- *Verses of a Lowly Peer* by Madho Lal Hussain; Translated by Naveed Alam; Published by Penguin Books.

Shah Hussain, the Imam of Malamti (self-deprecation) sect, is said to have more than a hundred thousand followers with 20 Khalifa.

Shah Hussain was probably the most defiant intellectual of Punjab, even by contemporary standards. However, like Baba Farid and Guru Nanak, he did not condemn the Mullahs with harsh words like his successors Sultan Bahu, Bulleh Shah and Waris Shah did. His tone, following his predecessors, was more of delegitimizing the Mullah/Qazi rather than outright condemnation. It is possible that the Mullahs and Qazis, up until the 16th century, were not as oppressive and corrupt as they became in the later period.

Hussain's poetry consists entirely of short poems known as Kafis and he is considered to be a pioneer of the Kafi form of Punjabi poetry. A typical 'Hussain Kafi' contains a refrain and some rhymed lines. The number of rhymed lines is usually between four and 10. Only occasionally is a longer form adopted. This book contains 152 of such kafis. The translator mentions that Dr. Mohan Singh Diwana, the Punjabi scholar acknowledged as the undisputed saviour of Hussein's Kafis in written forms, discovered around 138 of them. Subsequently, many more kafis were discovered, but there will always be a dispute about the exact number as singers and qawwals sometimes attribute disputable kafis to masters. Also, due to the prevalence of oral tradition, it made it possible for the traditionalists to suppress and censor many of his 'objectionable' kafis. The reverential texts try to portray him as a saint and the sexuality is ignored, downplayed or dismissed outright.

Hussain signs off at the end of almost each Kafi with fakir *nimana* (the lowly fakir), and his *malamati* style of self-humiliation is visible in many kafis. Being a weaver-poet, his work is replete with references to loom, spindle, thread and colour-dyes. In his kafis, he also alludes to the bad socio-economic conditions of the poor and in that sense was similar to Dullah Bhatti who was his contemporary.

Shah Hussain's period was known for freedom of thought as Akbar's policy of tolerance towards all religions made it difficult for Mullahs to condemn the Sufis. So his poetry openly talks of the superiority of the path of love over that of the Shariat.

According to N. Hanif, in his *Biographical Encyclopedia of Sufis: South Asia*, Shah Hussein excels all other Punjabi Sufi poets including Bulleh Shah on his metamorphism (use of metaphors and similes) and sentimentalism. Thus, a seeker is a bride who has to be accepted by God her husband, and the dowry stands for merit earned by practice of love of God. Similarly, the two-fold practice of the renunciation of the worldly pursuits and devotion to God have been described as *tanana* and *bunana* (warping and wafting); the worldly objects of attraction have been portrayed as deadly snakes, while the life of worldliness is likened to *Chitti Chaddar* (white sheet) and asceticism to *Bhuri* (black woolen blanket) and so on.

Naveed Alam has done an excellent job of translating the kafis so as to highlight that earthy flavour that Hussain's poetry has. As he says, it is not a literal translation but an attempt to represent the essence of Hussain's poetry.

Poet

Shah Hussain (1538–1599) was a Punjabi Sufi poet and the son of a weaver, belonging to the Dhudhi clan of Rajputs. He was born in Lahore.

Shah Bahlol Dariai of Chiniot initiated him into the spiritual path, and he remained a devout Muslim till the age of 36 when, while taking a lesson on tafseer (interpretation), he heard, 'This world is a place to play.' Shah Hussain ran out laughing and completely abandoned the path of organized religion. After that he was always seen dancing in a red dress with wine surahi (bottle) and piala (earthen cup) in his hand.

Shah Hussain fell for a Brahman boy, Madho, who became his lifelong love. Their love was so strong that Shah Hussain's name was changed to Madho Lal Hussain forever. It illustrates an essential tenet of Sufism, the merger of the lover with the beloved. Whichever way we interpret the relationship between Hussain and Madho, one thing is clear – they were openly in love and society accepted it. The story of the two lovers is a fascinating one and is unparalleled in the annals of Punjabi Sufism.

It is very likely that Hussain's relationship with Madho had a deep impact on his thinking, his mystical poetry and, most of all, on his religious life. In his passionate love for Madho, he bravely defied the norms of his own society, expressing a stern indictment of the orthodox theologians for whom religion had been reduced to a set of soulless rituals, rigid rules and strict restrictions drained of love, joy, compassion and emotion. It also made him profoundly tolerant in his attitude towards other religions. He celebrated Basant, the Punjabi spring festival, as well as the Hindu festival of Holi.

Hussain breathed his last in 1599, and his tomb and shrine is located at the Baghbanpura precincts, adjacent to the Shalimar Gardens, Lahore, Pakistan. Madho survived him by 48 years and was put to rest in a tomb next to Hussain's. The shrine, containing the graves of the two inseparable lovers, continues to attract large numbers of faithful pilgrims to this very day. His Urs (annual death anniversary) is celebrated at his shrine every year during the Mela Chiraghan (Festival of Lights).

Read on

- Hussain's Kafis are also composed for song and have been set to Punjabi folk music. Many of his Kafis are part of the traditional Qawwali repertoire. His poems have been performed as songs by Kaavish, Nusrat Fateh Ali Khan, Abida Parveen, Ghulam Ali, Hamid Ali Bela, Amjad Parvez, Junoon (band) and Noor Jehan, among others.

Shah Mohammed

- *The First Punjab War: Shah Mohammed's Jangnamah* by Shah Mohammed; Translated by P.K. Nijhawan; Published by Singh Brothers, Amritsar.

The decline of the Sikh kingdom within a decade of the death of Maharaja Ranjit Singh presents a saga of tragic events that touch the innermost feelings of the Punjabis even today. It is no wonder then that an account of the First Punjab War of 1845 presented by Shah Mohammed in his famous *Jangnamah* has been looked upon as the best requiem written on the fall of the Sikh kingdom.

P.K. Nijhawan, the translator, has given the text in Gurmukhi and Persian and has translated the text both into English and Hindi. *Jangnamah* is an exceptionally significant book.

One, the poem gives an accurate description of the events of those times as well as the important developments, social as well as political, that began to occur in the wake of the first Anglo-Sikh War. The second thing that stands out is Shah Mohammed's complete and unconditional identification with the *Khalsa Darbar*. Even six years after the death of Maharaja Ranjit Singh, his loyalty to the regime had not diminished in any way.

How could this have happened? The explanation lies in the manner in which Ranjit Singh governed the state. He ran that state in such an even-handed manner that even though the majority of the population in the state was Muslim, none of them had the feeling that the state was being run by a Sikh ruler.

Strict law and order was maintained and no high-handedness of any kind was permitted or perpetrated. He evolved a model of governance in which the Muslims, who constituted the overwhelming majority, came to look upon him as their wellwisher and benefactor. Even today Ranjit Singh is one of the Punjabi heroes recalled from time to time in Pakistan with nostalgia and warmth. There was complete identification between him and the people he ruled. Shah Mohammed's poem is a testimony to what happened.

The third point, which Nijhawan makes in his introduction, is about the Punjabi togetherness of the society. According to him, this is the only piece of literature or folk literature that is so full of Punjabi togetherness and even Punjabi nationalism.

Going back to what he knows about the 19th century, and the kind of atmosphere which prevailed in small towns and the countryside during his childhood, he makes a bold comment to say that co-existence amongst the various communities was a fact of daily life. It all began to change under the impact of the British rule, which as a policy, created divisions amongst the various communities. The introduction of the separate electoral system in the beginning of the 20th century and all that followed are recorded in countless books of history.

All this makes him call the First Anglo-Sikh War as First Punjab War taking cue from Shah Mohammed's original title *Jang Hind – Punjab*. According to him, the nomenclature of Anglo Sikh is an obvious distortion, done deliberately to rob it of its real pan-Punjabi character. This may be true, but a simple explanation can be what the eminent author Amandeep Sandhu wrote recently, that at the time of composing the poem, the British ruled Hind, Delhi and Maharaja Ranjit Singh's legacy ruled Punjab, therefore the war that broke out was called between Hind and Punjab. In stanza 92 it says, 'Jang Hind Punjab da hon laga (War broke out between Hind and Punjab).' The poem still has deep resonances. In the past few decades, the line has been often used in the context of the separatist militancy movement in the 1980s/90s when the militants dug deep into stanza 92 to get the phrase 'Jang Hind Punjab' to represent their war with the Indian State.

In any case, it portrays the popularity of the text in Punjab. Nijhawan is to be complimented on having made this exceedingly important literary text available to a wide-reading public. It is almost a filmic, yet truthful and sensitive account that unfolds reel after reel in the form of a documentary, which can be remembered and sung with great effect before different audiences by the itinerant singers of Punjab, called *dhadies*.

Before describing the actual war, Shah Mohammed goes into the events of the six years after the death of Ranjit Singh. That really supplies the essential backdrop of what, in fact, is going to happen. The killing of all important dramatis persona and finally the killing of Jawahar Singh, the brother of Maharani Jindan by the lawless troops described pejoratively as *Burchhas* (those who become a law unto themselves) forced the Maharani to break the stranglehold of the undisciplined army by getting them destroyed in a war with the British.

It is a heroic poem, which stands out even in India where there is a long tradition of *Vir Rasa* although classical *Vir Rasa* usually borders on exaggeration. But Shah Mohammed is very particular that he describes the whole thing in an undertone, seldom using a hyperbole or an extra word. Hence, while he fully praises the gusto with which the soldiers fought, he no less lampoons the cowardice with which they beat a retreat. Indeed, he does not mystify or mythify for the sake of it. His account of battles is summed up in a few apt similes and metaphors, which continue to haunt one for a long time.

Another great virtue of this poem is that it has been composed in the *baint* metre, the king of Punjabi folk metres greatly popularized by Waris Shah. Shah Mohammed is also no less a master of the *baint* and, therefore this ballad is sung along with *Heer* with almost equal effect, though the thought pattern and the subject matter are entirely different.

Poet

Shah Mohammad (1780–1862) was a Punjabi poet who lived during the reign of Maharaja Ranjit Singh and is best known for *Jangnama* written around 1846, which depicts the First Anglo-Sikh War that took place after the death of Maharaja Ranjit Singh.

Historians have pointed out that close relatives of Shah Mohammad were employed in Maharaja Ranjit Singh's army with whose help he pieced together a complete picture of the battle between the Sikhs and the British.

Soon after Maharaja Ranjit Singh's death, the entire edifice of his kingdom collapsed due to internal intrigues and British machinations. Poets projected, in the most appropriate words, the infighting among the Sikhs and the treachery perpetrated by the Dogras led by Dhyan Singh Dogra, making the descriptions a 'primary source' for all historians. The historical facts given in the Jangnama are verifiable from the Roznamacha (a daily diary), written during the reign of the Maharaja Ranjit Singh.

Shiv Kumar Batalvi

- *Luna* by Shiv Kumar Batalvi; Translated by B. M. Bhalla; Published by Sahitya Akademi.

The ancient legend of Puran Bhagat is part of the folklore of Punjab and other states of North India. In medieval times, Qadaryar wrote two versions of the story in Punjabi: *Puran Bhagat* and *Kallian Puran Bhagat*. Shiv Kumar Batalvi's *Luna* is based on this legend. Batalvi observes in the introduction that it is strange that there was a substantial difference in the two versions written by the same author. He has based his story on *Puran Bhagat* and ends it at the severing of the hands and feet of Puran. Beyond this, he does not find the story convincing or relevant to the causes he espouses. His recreation of the story of Luna is modern and realistic and is a powerful assertion of the Dalit and feminine viewpoints. He asserts that he has made appropriate changes to make the story more probable and realistic.

Puran was son of King Salvaan and Queen Ichhran. On his birth, astrologers told Salvaan that Puran is cursed and, if his parents see him, he will die. So he is kept in isolation. In the meantime, the ageing Salvaan marries Luna, a beautiful young woman. When Puran's curse is over, he comes out from isolation, and Luna is charmed by his looks. She offers carnal love to him. But Puran does not accept it as he considers Luna to be his Mother. Luna conspires and makes Salvaan punish Puran. Salvaan orders that Puran be executed, but Ichraan pleads for mercy for her son. The king does not have Puran executed but orders that Puran's limbs be dismembered and thrown into a well, from where Nath Jogis rescue him and teach him mysticism. Hence he becomes Puran Bhagat.

Luna is Batalvi's masterpiece. His poems are very popular in Punjabi but it is surprising to see that besides this work no other work has been translated into English. Some feel that it is difficult to adequately translate his work but this translator brings Batalvi's lines to life. The most alluring parts of the book are the changes that the poet has made to the story and his progressive thoughts behind them.

For instance, he says that in ancient times, the elderly kings used to fall victim to doubts and suspicions for petty reasons and their court poets, who were dependent on their masters' bounty, would not report incidents accurately. In the history and stories, the king would be absolved of everything, but the queens and their progeny would be depicted as immoral. Batalvi insists that a modern poet should not follow tradition blindly when there is no finality about any issue. When we talk of a new direction in literary creation, it amounts to flouting the tradition to some extent, and the artist has to search for the new meaning and interpretation in the traditional literature.

Similarly, the rulers were of high birth and in order to prove that were really great, the beauties such as Luna were depicted as the embodiment of lust – temptresses and handmaidens of evil, designed to deceive and mislead the righteous followers of the spiritual path to salvation. These beauties were normally of lower caste. So the blame would be cast upon them. Their misfortune was solely that they were poor and insignificant and there were none to stand up for their pain and sufferings. Batalvi claims that in his version he has dealt sympathetically and has tried to assuage this pain from the deep recesses of his soul where his feminism and his manhood lay simultaneously dormant.

Poet

Mainu Vida Karo (Bid Me Farewell)

Assan Taan Joban Rutte Marna
tur Jana Assan Bhare Bharaye

Hijar Tere di kar Parkarma
Assan Taan Joban Rutte Marna
(I am going to die in the season of youth,
I am going to depart without emptying my contents,
After completing a cycle of separation from you,
I am going to die in the season of youth.)

Shiv Kumar Batalvi (1936–1973) was an epoch in himself. A born romantic, introvert and passionate performer, he was blessed with a mellifluous voice laced with poignant emotions that left an impeccable impression on the listeners. He is most known for his romantic poetry, noted for its heightened passion, pathos, separation and a lover's agony.

He became the youngest recipient of the Sahitya Akademi Award in 1967 for his epic verse play *Luna* (1965). *Luna* is now considered a masterpiece in modern Punjabi literature. It is also credited with the creation of a new genre of modern Punjabi kissa. It is widely believed that Batalvi was unlucky in love and bereavement for loss is reflected intensely in his poetry. His first anthology of poems was published in 1960 titled *Piran da Paraga* (The Scarf of Sorrows), which became an instant success.

Read on

- Deedar Singh Pardesi, Jagjit Singh, Chitra Singh and Surinder Kaur have sung many of his poems.
- Nusrat Fateh Ali Khan's rendition of one of his poem *Maye ni Maye* is known for its soulfulness and imagery.
- In a recent album, Rabbi (2004) by Rabbi Shergill features his poem, *Ishtihar*.
- Punjabi folk singer, Hans Raj Hans created a popular album, 'Gham,' on the poetry of Shiv Kumar.
- In 2005, an album was released titled, Ek Kudi Jida Naa Mohabbat – Shiv Kumar Batalvi with songs sung by Mahendra Kapoor, Jagjit Singh and Asa Singh Mastana.

- Several of his poems have been adapted for songs in movies like *Ajj Din Chhadeya Tere Rang Varga* was adapted in the 2009 Hindi movie *Love Aaj Kal*, which became an instant hit.
- Bhupinder and Mitali have sung *Luna*.
- In 2012 an album titled 'Panchee Ho javan,' based on the poem written by Shiv Kumar Batalvi, was sung by Jasleen Royal. The album also contains another song 'Maye Ni' based on the poem *Maye ni Maye*.
- In 2014, rap duo Sweet Shop Boys, consisting of Indo-American Himanshu Suri and British-Pakistani Riz Ahmed, released a song entitled 'Batalvi,' which sampled Shiv Kumar Batalvi's own recitation of *Ek Kudi Jida Naam Mohabbat* from an interview done with Aikam TV in the early 1970s. The songs lyrics explore issues regarding cultural identity faced by many second-generation south Asians living in the West.
- In 2016, the same poem *Ek Kudi Jihda Naam Mohabbat* was adapted in a song featuring Alia Bhatt in the movie *Udta Punjab*.

Sultan Bahu

- *Death Before Dying: The Sufi Poems of Sultan Bahu;* Translated and Introduced by Jamal J Elias; Published by University of California Press.

Though Sultan Bahu wrote mostly in Persian, he got recognition in Punjabi due to his *Abyats*, which were written in Punjabi in *Abyat e Bahu* on the theme of Oneness of God. No contemporary Punjabi institution has made any efforts to preserve his writings (like they have for those of Baba Farid) and give them their due respect. Despite that, they delved deep into the hearts of the common people and continued to flourish. This is similar to how the writings of Pilu have not been preserved in the written form but they have been preserved in the minds of those who have memorized them and continue to recite them.

When folk singers present Bahu's *Abyat,* they begin with a long sustained note of hu as if paying gratuitous salutations to the goddess of musicology. People of every caste, creed, religion and community sing Bahu's sacred texts as if it were their own heritage, and Bahu became an integral part of the Punjabi culture in both the Punjabs.

At least 14 editions of Bahu's Punjabi *Abyat* have been printed, in both the Perso-Arabic and the Gurmukhi scripts. It has also been translated into Urdu and English.

The translator of the present edition has made a sincere effort and has performed an in-depth study of the various editions available, as well as of the oral and folkloric sources, taking the best from each, which is why this work is preferred over others. Jamal Elias has rendered the short poems of Bahu in a simple and readable form although, as he himself confesses, he has presented this translation keeping in mind the reader who may not be familiar with Punjabi terms (like bela, darya, papiha). Thus, he uses generic terms (like marsh, sea and bird, respectively) and the translation lacks that quintessential Punjabi flavour.

Bahu's poetry, like that of other Sufis, expresses dissatisfaction with formal and ritualistic forms of religion and talks of an individual spiritual relationship with God and of losing oneself within the divine. Detached from worldly affairs, devoted to the name of God, and guided by a Sufi master, the individual can undertake the mystical path with the ultimate goal of losing one's identity with God or to attain spiritual death before physical death. As Elias mentions, this quest for "death before dying" is based on a saying attributed to the Prophet Mohammad, "Die before you die!" Death before dying is thus a common refrain in Sufi poetry – signifying the importance of killing the selfish ego for the sake of attaining selflessness and thus qualifying for the beloved.

The imagery of Bahu's poetry is derived from the daily activities of the villagers like gardening and planting, and he presented them to the rural folk in a simple poetic form. Each of his verses ends with the word 'Hu.' People still read Bahu's Punjabi poetry and also listen to its musical renderings by qawwals. For the laymen as well as for the lovers of Punjabi literature, Bahu's fame is based on this one book.

Poet

Sultan Bahu (1630–1691) was a Sufi mystic, poet, and scholar active mostly in the present-day Punjab province of Pakistan.

Little is known of Bahu's life, other than a hagiography entitled *Manaqib-i Sultani*, written by a seventh-generation descendant. Sultan Bahu was born in Shorekot Village in Jhang District in Punjab, Pakistan. From his original name of Sultan Mohammad he came to be called Bahu (one who is with Him), for his constant remembrance of Hu (He alone).

More than 40 books on Sufism are attributed to him, mostly in Persian, and largely dealing with specialized aspects of Islam and Islamic mysticism. However, it is his Punjabi poetry that had popular appeal and earned him lasting fame. His verses are sung in many genres of Sufi music including qawwali and Kafi, and tradition has established a unique style of singing his couplets.

Sultan Bahu's education began with his mother, Mai Rasti, telling him to seek spiritual guidance from Shah Habib Qadri. Around 1668, Sultan Bahu moved to Delhi for further training under the guidance of Sheikh Abdul Rehman Qadri, a notable Sufi saint of the Qadri Order, and thereafter returned to Punjab where he spent the rest of his life. Sultan Bahu initiated an offshoot of his own order, which he named *Sarwari Qadiri*.

The shrine of Bahu is located in Garh Maharaja, Punjab, Pakistan. It is a popular Sufi shrine, and the annual Urs festival commemorating his death is celebrated there with great fervour.

Surjit Patar

- *Poems by Surjit Patar*; Translated by Gurshminder Jagpal; Published by Unistar Books Pvt. Ltd.

Main rahaan te nahi turda,
Main turda haan ta raah bande.
(I do not walk on the paths,
I walk and paths are created.)

Surjit Patar has made use of different poetic genres including ghazal, nazm, geet, using strict meters as well as blank verse and free verse. In *Poems by Surjit Patar*, the translator, Gurshminder Jagpal, has taken up 48 poems, randomly selected from Patar's various poetry books, and has picked all major forms of poems that Patar has written. One of the major forms that Patar has tried his hands on has been the ghazal. By writing ghazals, Patar has made a prominent place for himself among the leading poets of Punjabi, thus proving his creative potential. He took ghazal to new heights by taking it out of the ambit of romantic illusion and immersing it in the world of reality.

In Patar's poems, there is a conflict between desire and convention, nature and civilization, and it takes him back to the past where he rues the loss of Punjab's rich heritage. Some of the poems deal with the poet's concern with poetry as he feels that, at a time when human emotions and values are at a nadir, poetry, or rather poetic words hold the hope for their revival. Here, self-dialogue and self-critique become his poetic strategy to become the voice of humanity.

Patar is an idealistic and reflective poet whose poetry is absorbed in Nature, which for him is not a romantic refuge but a confidant of the modern alienated man. Trees find themselves alienated in an industrial society; nature becomes an index of longing and pain. Patar has been influenced by the Naxalite movement, which becomes visible in some of his nazms, where he speaks out against the corruption, political greed, tyranny, intrigue and exploitation of the weak, thus challenging the system.

Translating ghazal is an onerous task, as each couplet is an independent thought, yet it plays a significant part in the progression of thought of the whole poem. On the other hand, nazm has a unified thought written either in metrical or free verse or prose pattern, thus giving the translator a little more liberty. In some of the poems, Jagpal has tried to maintain the rhyme and meter pattern of the original whereas, in others, his translation has used the paraphrase mode. Yet, Jagpal is very conscious of the challenges of translating a highly disciplined poet like Patar whose poems display a keen sense of structure.

As the book is bi-lingual (it was the poet's suggestion), it allows the reader to look for deeper nuances of the original text in the translation. At the same time, it turns the reader into an evaluator to see how close the translation is to the original.

Poet

Dr Surjit Patar (1945–), renowned signature of Punjabi poetry, hails from village Pattar Kalan in Jalandhar District from where he got his surname. A teacher by profession, he retired as professor of Punjabi from Punjab Agricultural University, Ludhiana. Though Patar has been greatly inspired and influenced by great Punjabi poets Shiv Kumar Batalvi and Sohan Singh Misha, he has been able to maintain his individual poetic identity. He started writing poetry in the mid-1960s, with his poems published in different magazines and journals including *Preetlari*. He has about nine poetry collections including *Hawa Vich Likhe Harf* (Words written in the Air), *Birkh Arz Kare* (Thus Spake the Tree), *Hanere Vich Sulagdi Varnmala* (Words Smouldering in the Dark), *Lafzaan Di Dargah* (Shrine of Words), *Patjhar Di Pazeb* (Anklet of Autumn), *Sadi Dian Tarkalan*, *Surzameen* (Music Land), *Suraj Mandir Dian Poudiaan* and

Chann Suraj di Wehangi to his credit. His poems enjoy immense popularity with the general public and have won great acclaim from the critics. He is currently working on a book on the origin of language. However, he is not just a writer and poet par excellence; he is an excellent singer too.

Besides these creative works, Patar's literary achievements include his successful adaptation – into Punjabi – of the three tragedies of Fredrico Garcia Lorca, *Nag Mandala* of Girish Karnad, poems of Bertolt Brecht and Pablo Neruda, and plays of Jean Giraudoux and Moliere. He has written tele-scripts on Punjabi poets from Sheikh Farid to Shiv Kumar Batalvi.

Patar was honoured with the Sahitya Akademi Award for his book *Hanere Vich Sulagdi Varnmala* in *1993* and with the Padma Shri in 2012. He has also received numerous awards like Pash Puraskar, Bhartiya Bhasha Parishad Award, Saraswati Samman 2009 and Kusumagraj Literary Award 2014. Apart from Punjabi literature, he is a well-known figure in the country's literary arena.

Read on

- Surjit Patar has written the dialogues of the Punjabi movie *Shaheed Udham Singh: Alias Ram Mohammad Singh Azad*, a movie made on the life of Udham Singh.
- He also wrote dialogues for the Punjabi version of Deepa Mehta's movie *Heaven on Earth*.

Waris Shah

- *Waris Shah's Heer: A Rustic Epic of the Punjab*; Translation in Verse by S. N. Dar; Published by Anamaya Publishers, New Delhi.

In the (now) two Punjabs, *Heer* has perhaps touched more hearts than any other book. Since there is no copyright, it is not possible to know exactly how many copies have been sold, but the number must run into several hundred thousand in both Persian and Gurmukhi scripts.

Waris' diction is not restricted to any particular part of the Punjab, and that basic fact about *Heer* is the reason it is so universally popular. The Punjabi peasant knows no other book so well; no other story has a more familiar outline and environment. While the richness of thought and variety of similes and metaphors brings him emotional pleasure, his mind readily grasps the well-conceived situations and easy trend of arguments. There is no obscurity of language or ideas. He only has to hear it to understand it.

A few attempts have been made to render Waris Shah's *Heer* into English but none could engage the reader sufficiently. Sant Singh Sekhon's translation was published in 1978 and has been considered by many as one of the best. Richard Temple attempted another translation of the love-legend but it was not Waris Shah's *Heer* but the story as narrated by 'some jatts of Patiala State.' The translation in verse had appeared sometime early last century. Charles Frederick Usborne's narration of *The Adventures of Heer and Ranjha: Recounted in Punjabi by Waris Shah* follows the original text carefully and is used the world over as standard text on this poem. However, Usborne (died 1919) did not venture into verse; his translation is in prose. There are some other attempts too but they stop at a transliteration of Shah's magnum opus.

In S. N. Dar's English rendition of Waris Shah's epic, for the very first time, the complete text of Waris Shah's monumental poem has been translated into English, verse by verse. Dar died in 1971 at the age of 69. The masterly translation of *Heer* was his last offering to the literary world, but one for which he could not find a publisher. The manuscript lay in a corner of a dusty cupboard for over 35 years and was finally published in 2007.

Waris Shah's work is of a grand sweep and vision. His work stands out as a priceless literary legacy, even though the story that he recounted had been around since two centuries before he was born. A Hindu poet, Damodar, who claimed to be a witness to the star-crossed lives of Heer–Ranjha, had composed *Heer di Var* during Emperor Akbar's reign. Another dozen poets or so sang of the unrequited love thereafter, but it was Waris who made Heer into a Punjabi classic.

Apart from the literary merit of the long narrative in verse, the book throws interesting light on contemporary life in Punjab at the end of the Mughal rule – a time when the dividing line between the Hindus and Muslims was very thin. For example, the Muslim Kheras consult the Brahmins for fixing the date of Heer's marriage. It also gives anthropological details of that era, its fauna and flora, and its language and customs. For instance, the poet mentions in detail the types of sweetmeats that were prepared for Heer's wedding and who wore what during the rituals. Perhaps the most quoted and sung passages from Waris Shah's epic are those that relate to Heer's departure from her father's house in the bridal attire. Her heart-wrenching cry at being forced into marriage and her sense of loss of her home and her lover are poignantly captured by Waris Shah.

In an article about *Heer*, Kulwant Singh Virk wrote, 'the magic expressiveness and power that the Punjabi language enjoys in the pages of *Heer* has not been given to it in any other book. For those who suffer from a poverty of vocabulary in Punjabi, the cure is a study of *Heer* by Waris.'

Poet
Waris Shah (1722–1798) was a Punjabi Sufi poet of Chishti order renowned for his contribution to Punjabi literature. Waris Shah was born in Jandiala Sher Khan, Punjab, in present-day Pakistan into a reputed Sayyid family. Waris's parents are said to have died when he was young. Waris acknowledged himself as a disciple of an ustad from Kasur, namely Hafiz Ghulam Murtaza, from whom he received his education. After completing education, Waris moved to Malka Hans, a village 12 kilometers north of Pakpattan. Here he resided in a small room, adjacent to a historic mosque now called Masjid Waris Shah, until his death.

His mausoleum is a place of pilgrimage today, especially for those in love. Waris Shah is primarily known as the author of *Heer Ranjha* whose verse is a treasure trove of Punjabi phrases, idioms and sayings. His minute and realistic depiction of each detail of Punjabi life and the political situation in the 18th century remains unique, and the entire poem is an album of colourful and enchanting pictures of life in the Punjab, of varied views but always deeply absorbing.

Read on
- A 1964 Pakistani film titled *Waris Shah* featured Inayat Hussain Bhatti in the title role.
- *Waris Shah: Ishq da waaris*, a movie directed by Manoj Punj featuring Gurdas Mann as Waris Shah, won four awards at the National film awards 2006 including the award for best feature film in Punjabi.

Read on (Themes)
Bollywood has made numerous Hindi movies on almost all the immortal love stories of Punjab. Some Punjabi films made on these love stories of Punjab are as under:

- *Sassi Punnu*, directed by S P Bakshi won the National film award for best feature film in Punjabi, 1964.
- *Heer Sial* made in 1938 by K D Mehra had Noorjahan as the actress.
- *Mirza Sahiban* was made in 1993.

PLAYS

Atamjit

- *New Wave Punjabi Drama: Six Punjabi Plays in English;* Edited by Atamjit; Published by Punjabi Academy, New Delhi.

The history of Punjabi drama is one of colourful development since its very inception. Though it has always been a mix of English and Sanskrit drama, the influence of English drama has been more profound; Punjabi drama has largely followed the structure and formula of English plays.

There is a very common perception that Punjabi drama has not been able to take long strides like poetry, short story, and the novel, and that it lags behind the drama of other Indian languages. In the introduction to this book, Dr. Atamjit traces the history of Punjabi drama, its various influences, the various stages of its development, and major playwrights, giving a deep insight into the genre and preparing the reader to look at Punjabi drama from a new standpoint.

The six plays included in the book are written by writers who belong to the post-independence era (1942–1965). They thus belong to the new wave Punjabi drama and have some underlying unique qualities.

A Terrorist's Darling (Terrorist Dee Premika) is written by playwright and stage director, Pali Bhupinder Singh who has a number of plays to his credit, like *Iss Chowk Ton Shehar Disda Hai, Usnoon Kahin, Mitti Da Bawa, Tuhanu Kehda Rang Pasand Hai, Pyasa Kaan* and *Wrong Number.* In *A Terrorist's Darling,* Pali Bhupinder very skillfully highlights hypocrisy in a man–woman relationship. The supple, soft, lovelorn, poetic and idealist heroine is pitched against the hardcore radical revolutionist, known as a terrorist, with murder on his mind. The play also exposes the corruption that ails the Punjabi society.

Saavi's author, Jagdish Chander is known for his portrayal of authentic urban culture and characters. He celebrates basic human innocence and challenges the negative mindset of people. He has written eight plays, the most prominent being *Chowk Dholiaan* and *Sugar Free*.

Based on a folktale of the Himalayan region, *Saavi* deals with the dilemma of a woman who is a victim of the 'bride-exchange' tradition of the land; the play underlines the predicament of woman in a patriarchal society. *Saavi* was made into a film that had its World Premiere at IFFSA, Toronto, in 2015.

In *Dharam Guru*, Swarajbir uses material and dramatic action from history and mythology. Through a mythological story and mythical characters, it talks about the role of religion in politics. The play also attacks the class division and class discrimination prevailing in society through the ages. Throughout history, religion has tried to overpower society. The Brahmin, being the most superior class, had an upper hand in making the people bow to his diktats unquestioningly. Other prominent plays written by Swarajbir include *Krishna* and *Medni*.

The Meandering Canal is penned by Atamjit, a well-known signature in the New Wave Punjabi Drama. A playwright, director, theatre-scholar and the editor of the present collection, he is known as 'intellectual' playwright. As Rana Nayar says, Atamjit 'tends to approach the individual/collective psyche of the Punjabi community.'

A recipient of the two of the biggest literature and theater awards – the Sahitya Akademi Award and Sangeet Natak Akademi Award – Atamjit has written more than three dozen short and full-length plays, the prominent ones being *Kabristan, Chabiyaan, Hawa Mahal, Chiriyan, Rishtian Da ki Rakhiye Na, Farash Vich Uggia Rukh, Puran, Main Taan Ik Sarangi Haan, Kamloops Dian Machhian,* and the play in this collection, *Panch Naad Da Paani*, to name a few.

The Meandering Canal, based on two historical short stories set in 13th century Punjab and written by Manmohan Bawa, depicts the struggle of the time when Mangols were regularly attacking Punjab, which was defended by the Turks while the local Rajput rulers were reduced to mere spectators. The Mongols abduct a daughter of the Rajput nobleman and the other had to be given in marriage to the Turkish Governor. The girl creates history by accepting the proposal of the Turkish Governor. The play touches upon various issues like feminism, subalterns, Sufism and the struggle between good and evil.

The Melting Icicles of Life (Qtra Qtra Zindgi) is written by Devinder Daman, a director turned playwright who rose to prominence with his play *Chhipan to Pehlan* based on Bhagat Singh, the great martyr of Punjab. He writes most of his plays with the exact theatrical presentation and actors in mind but rarely does he use his plays as political statements. *The Melting Icicles of Life* is a somewhat autobiographical play with only two characters – a husband and his wife. When it was staged, Devinder Daman and his wife, Jaswant Daman played the roles. This play is a commentary on the lives of elderly couples who are left to look after themselves by the children who settle abroad, thus emphasizing the changing patterns in human life.

Waters of the Chenab (Jhana Da Paani) is written by Ajmer Aulakh, one of the prominent Punjabi playwrights who has established himself as the emissary of the agricultural lower-middle class of rural Punjab. Winner of many awards including the Sahitya Akademi Award and Sangeet Natak Akademi Award, Ajmer Aulakh has written a number of other plays including *Begane Bohr Di Chhaan, Satt Began, Bhajjian Bahaan, Kehar Singh di Maut, Ik Si Dariya, Salwan* and a collection of plays *Ishk Bajh Namaz Da Hajj Nahin.* The present play deals with the sale of girls from poor families, particularly from state of Bihar and also highlights the struggle of the rural poor folk.

All the translators deserve appreciation for their tireless efforts to recreate these plays in English, thus providing a wider space and a wider readership to these outstanding plays. Supriya Bhandari (*A Terrorist's Darling*), Dr. Manmohan (*Saavi*), Rajesh

Sharma (*Dharam Guru*), Snehlata Jaswal (*The Meandering Canal*), Ramnita Saini Sharda (*The Melting Icicles of Life*) and Paramjit Singh Ramana and Swaraj Raj (*Waters of Chenab*) have all done a brilliant job by keeping the essence and flavour of the original text intact. A number of plays have made use of poetry through chorus like *Saavi, Dharam Guru, The Meandering Canal* or through characters or flashbacks like *Water of the Chenab*. It is not very easy to translate poetry in the given context of the storyline but the translators have risen to the occasion wonderfully.

Kartar Singh Duggal

- *Water Sweet and Other Radio Plays* **by K S Duggal; Published by UBS Publishers Distributors Pvt. Ltd.**

K. S. Duggal was a celebrated name in the world of radio drama in the 1940s. His plays, written originally in Punjabi, have been transcreated into several languages including English and have been broadcast by AIR network.

He is credited with developing a form of the radio play in Punjabi. To meet the needs of the radio play, he uses his characters as symbols. His play *Puranian Botlan* (The Old Bottles) is a meaningful critique of the unscrupulous behaviour of the urban middle class. His other notable plays include *Auh Gaye Sajjan Auh Gaye* (There goes our good Friend), *Ik Siffer Siffer* (One Zero Makes Zero) and *Mitha Pani*, all of which have been produced, very successfully, several times over the radio. In these plays, Duggal seems to have been impressed by the technique of T.S. Eliot and Christopher Frye in the use of rhythmic prose.

Mitha Pani (Water Sweet) reveals that Duggal's plays are real portraits of everyday life in the sub-continent. Every time it is broadcast, listeners in India and Pakistan come looking for Sakina, a lead character in the play.

In his acknowledgements, Duggal writes, 'The play Mitha Pani, written originally in Punjabi, was translated into Hindi by an unknown admirer. It was then rendered into English by a JNU teacher whom I have not been able to locate despite my best efforts. It was then transcreated by me into its Radio version for this volume to figure along with a selection of other Radio Plays written and broadcasted in Punjabi, Hindi, Urdu and other regional languages including English.'

This book has seven of his plays including *Mitha Pani*.

Mitha Pani is the longest of these plays and runs into more than 100 pages. It is a story of Partition and begins with a family displaced from Pakistan and allotted a land at Hissar, now in Haryana. The family has lost all its belongings, and the daughter Savitri was abducted. They are totally devastated. Additionally, the land allotted to them is sandy and dry and has no canal or water source for irrigation. As the family tries to settle in the allotted house (of a Muslim family), a girl, Sakina, comes for shelter as she too was abducted and has managed to flee. Reeling under the loss of their daughter, the family gives her shelter. The family then tries to build a life with all the meager resources at their disposal, and after some years, the Bhakra Nangal Dam brings water and electricity to their village. Also, the women relief committee locates and brings their daughter back to them. In the meantime, Sakina has won their heart by her devotion to family and they have decided to make her their daughter-in-law. But the cruel hands of destiny that brings back their daughter takes back Sakina. The family, obeying the diktat of the law, sees Sakina off in full bridal attire – red dress, jewellery, her coloured seat and fan. It is a very touching play.

The Upper Storey is a soliloquy in which the male narrator reveals the story of his life, the betrayal by his wife as she falls for an army officer who comes to live across their house but is eventually left alone when her lover goes away. Even then, he is willing to welcome her back into his life. Set in an urban space, it is in contrast with *Mitha Pani* and its rural setting.

The third play, *Roopmati* again showcases Duggal's versatility. It is based on the historical account of the legendary Rajput beauty Roopmati who falls in love with Baj Bahadur, the ruler of Mandau, and finally marries him against her family's wishes. This leads to the destruction of her Rajput clan in the ensuing battle. However, the same beauty attracts the attention of Adam Khan, the Mughal commander. Baz Bahadur flees away from the battle scene, leaving Roopmati to her fate. Despite the pressure to marry Adam Khan, Roopmati prefers dying for love.

To Each a Window is a play in which Duggal uses dialogues between two sisters Mira and Radha, who are on a visit to Mussoorie, to reveal their respective Krishnas, as they look out from their hotel window for him.

In *Once There was a Sparrow,* Duggal again tackles the issue of marital infidelity, but in a different manner. On a day when it is raining very heavily, a stranger seeks shelter in a house where the woman is alone with her child and is waiting for her husband, who then calls her to inform her that because of the rain he is staying at a friend's place. The woman is sure that he is spending the night with another woman, as she can hear a woman in the background ordering coffee.

Soon the woman, seeking revenge, asks the stranger to stay back and starts preparing coffee for him, when she finds him calling his house and making the same excuse that her husband had made to her. This gets her thinking and she drives that man out. Duggal leaves it for the readers to decide about the infidelity of the husband.

In *Between Two Men*, a similar predicament befalls Farooq, the second husband of Salma when he learns that the first husband, Lateef, has prohibited Zeenat (the daughter from first marriage) from visiting Salma. He starts castigating Lateef, saying that children should not be kept away from their mother. However, his self-righteousness soon disappears when Salma offers to stay with Lateef for Zeenat's sake and asks him to send Farid (their son from the second marriage) to meet her there.

In *The Blind,* Duggal depicts the ambivalence that Sajni feels towards her husband when he becomes blind while on army duty just four weeks after their marriage. She wants him to see and admire her beauty, her make-up, her dresses, the flowers tucked in her hair. She is not content with merely his undying love and adoration for her. She wishes him to see her long flowing hair, her vivacious lips, their tenderness when she is sad and their languor when she is asleep, the intoxication in her eyes and the dimple on her cheeks. Circumstances finally make her realize the real depth of love, which is above these ephemeral longings.

Manjit Pal Kaur

- *Sundran: A Poetic Drama* by Manjit Pal Kaur; Translated by Tejwant Singh Gill; Published by Ravi Sahit Parkashan, Amritsar.

Manjit Pal Kaur (1948–) has based this poetic drama on the life of Sundran, taking forward the legendary story of Puran Bhagat. Puran was son of King Salvaan and Queen Ichhran of Sialkot in the first century. On his birth, astrologers told Salvaan that Puran is cursed; if his parents see him, he will die. So, he is kept in isolation for 12 years. Meanwhile, Salvaan marries Luna, a beautiful young woman. When Puran's curse is over and he comes out from isolation, Luna is charmed by his looks and she offers carnal love to him. But Puran does not accept it as he considers Luna to be his mother. Luna conspires and makes Salvaan punish Puran. Puran is punished and is to be executed, but Ichhran pleads mercy and he is thrown into a well from where Nath Jogis rescue him and teach him mysticism. Hence, he becomes Puran Bhagat. As the Nath Jogi's disciple, Puran, during one of his sojourns, goes to Sundran's palace for agape. Sundran is smitten by Puran and wants to marry him, but Puran is not ready. On her request, Nath Jogi grants her togetherness with Puran for seven days. During these seven days, she tries her best to persuade him to live with her but Puran finally forsakes her after seven days and goes back to the jogi.

It is on this segment of the legend that Manjit Pal bases her poetic drama. Sundran is visualized as a beautiful and wealthy princess. She had lost her father, mother and brother in a coup, but those traumatic events did not affect Sundran and she continued to be a kind and caring woman. The translator, eminent writer Tejwant Singh Gill, in his introduction to the play, writes,

'The impulse for thus endowing Sundran's personality seems to have come to Manjit Pal from feminism's sober claim to the effect that centuries of oppression and suppression have generated in the female greater potential for such endowment.'

After Puran leaves, her first impulse is to commit suicide but finally she decides to live and deliver the child conceived through Puran. In that era, the decision to be a single mother is quite revolutionary and bold.

Qadaryar, Professor Puran Singh and Shiv Batalvi, each with their own interpretation, have written the story of Puran Bhagat. In the story by Qadaryar, the encounter between Puran and Sundran is almost a normal meeting where she wants to marry Puran but the latter is not ready. Professor Puran Singh, on the other hand, focused more on the mother–son relationship between Puran and Ichhran, and the infatuation of Sundran for Puran is secondary. In Shiv Batalvi's *Luna*, Sundran does not feature at all. Batalvi is more focused on correcting the centuries-old stigma on women as seductresses and the lower caste as responsible for society's ills. Manjit Pal's story is focused on Sundran and is enriched by gender-specific concerns.

The book has been published bilingually with the Punjabi text given alongside the translation, which is an innovation for Punjabi playwriting. As already mentioned, among the many translations that I went through to select the following 100, very few bilingual publications were found. A bilingual publication is, indeed, a treat to read.

Read on

- The original story of Puran Bhagat was written by Qadaryar (1802–1892) who was born near Gujranwala, West Punjab. A poet of the court of the Maharaja Ranjit Singh, Qadaryar is best known for his heroic narrative poem, *Qissa Puran Bhagat*. The poem is written in siharfi (an acrostic format) with the first word of each octave beginning with a letter in the order of the Punjabi (Shahmukhi) alphabet. Randeep Singh has translated it into English.

- *Feminising the Patriarchal Legends: A Study of Manjit Pal Kaur's Sahiban and Sundran* by Pankaj Singh; Published by Indian Institute of Advanced Study 1992.
- The *Oxford Companion to Indian Theatre* is the first reference work embracing both rural and urban modes of Indian theatre spanning its entire history of over 2000 years. It consists of 750 entries encompassing forms and personalities across India geographically and historically, in 22 languages and has 63 contributors, edited by Ananda Lal, who is professor of English at Jadavpur University, Kolkata. He also directs and translates and is theatre critic of *The Telegraph*, Kolkata. The book describes Manjit Pal Kaur as 'The only woman dramatist of note in contemporary Punjabi theatre; also a feminist poet.'
- Sahit Kala Prakashan, Ludhiana, published Pal's first play, *Sahiban*. Pal has also written one more play, *Sarap*. All these are poetic plays in Punjabi.

Mazhar Tirmazi

- *A Lifetime on Tiptoes* by Mazhar Tirmazi; Script in three languages; Published as an e-book; Originally written in Punjabi by Mazhar Tirmazi; English translation by Gurbaksh and Ruth Garcha; Welsh Translation by Menna Elfyn; Introduction by Dominic Rai; In association with Man Mela Theatre Company.

A Lifetime on Tiptoes is based on stories his mother told him about life in British-India prior to Partition in 1947. It has been performed/read in English, Welsh, and Punjabi in India, Pakistan and the United Kingdom. The story of how it came to be developed as the play has an interesting history.

Umran Langian Paban Bhaar (a lifetime on tiptoes) is a Punjabi poem written by Tirmazi in 1973 and published in the literary journal *Rut Lekha*. Tirmazi's family was one of the millions uprooted by the Partition when they were forced to migrate from Jalandhar district to what had suddenly become Pakistani Punjab. The experience of being removed from the homeland and the inevitable feelings of loss, ambiguous loyalties and deep longings for what cannot be recovered are the predominant themes of Tirmazi's poetry, which is regarded as some of the best in contemporary Punjabi literature.

The poem was best known as a song. It was set to music and first performed by Pakistani singer Asad Amanat Ali Khan in 1975. It has gone on to become one of the best loved songs to come out of Pakistan and is still enchanting new audiences today, almost a decade after Asad Amanat's death in 2007.

In the introduction, Dominic Rai writes that he first heard Tirmazi reciting this poem in 2005. He immediately translated the title, *Umran Langian Paban Bhaar*, into English as *A lifetime on tiptoes*. Then, along with the writer, he developed the poem into a Punjabi play. Subsequently, the play was translated into English and then into Welsh. This e-book has all the three versions. He further adds that it is incredible that the poem that become a song in the 1970s has become a play in Britain 40 years later and continues its journey to engage with Punjabi, English and Welsh audiences. The scripts have been published as an e-book to reach new and younger audiences.

In the afterword, Tirmazi writes that though he had been listening to the stories from his mother, he got a better understanding of the pain of migration and separation from his motherland when he went to England from Pakistan. He writes, 'I discovered myself to be living under the shadow of my mother's suffering and I can heal myself through telling the "qissa" of our partition.'

In the play, he says he has tried to recreate the actual scene of Partition by combining realism and surrealism. In a way, this play is one of the very few written in recent times on the subject of Partition. All the others were mostly written up to the 1990s.

In light of the rising hatred between faiths in recent times, his play acts not only as a nostalgic reminder of the peace and unity of the past but also as an active instrument of struggle for peace and harmony in today's world. The main sufferers of Partition were Punjabis and Bengalis, and it is hoped that his attempt, and that of the present compilation, will help achieve the longing for some sort of harmony in the Punjabis at least.

Author

British-Punjabi poet Mazhar Tirmazi, born in Pakistan in 1950, is a distinct voice in modern Punjabi literature as he explores the theme of separation from the homeland with persistence and in all its manifestations, till it evolves into a constant longing for the lost or the unattainable.

Tirmazi is the author of four collections of poetry and his work is a part of the curriculum in Punjabi language courses at Chandigarh University. His published work includes *Jag da*

Sufna (dream of awakening), *Thandi Bhubal* (cold ashes), *Kaya Kagad* and *Dooja Hath Sawali*. His poetry also features in the Kings College anthology *Mother Tongues* and in a collection of underground poems titled *Waiting Room*.

Tirmazi has worked as a journalist in London for Urdu–English bilingual daily newspapers *Awaaz International* and *Akbar Wattan*. He has organized conferences to promote the Punjabi language in Britain and Australia. He is a recipient of the British parliamentary award, Punjabis in Britain that recognizes poetic acumen, linguistic ability and promotion of Punjabi culture.

Read on

- Recently, the song, by now a classic of the Pakistani songbook, was updated for Coke Studio's eighth season and sung by Ali Sethi, with Nabeel Shaukat Ali coming in midway with a folk song originally sung by Faisalabad's Allah Ditta Lonaywala.
- Before that, in 2011, musician Kuljit Bhamra released a new version of Tirmazi's song with a younger singer, Shahid Khan.
- The play was performed at, among other places, Palace of Westminster, London, in the Gladstone Room, the very chamber where the Partition of India was debated 60 years earlier.

Sant Singh Sekhon

- *Seven Plays On Sikh History* by Sant Singh Sekhon; Compiled and Translated by Tejwant Singh Gill; Published by Sahitya Akademi, India.

Sant Singh Sekhon [1908–1997] wrote many plays. His one-act plays are *Chhe Ghar* (Six Homes), *Tapia Kyon Khapia* (Why the Ascetic Got Confused), *Natsunehe* (Dramatic Messages), *Sundrepad* (Beautiful Feet), while *Wiaholi* (Bride) and *Baba bohar* (Old Oak) are his verse plays.

Kalakar (Artist), *Nal-Damayanti* (Nala and Damayanti), *Narki* (Denizens of Hell) [originally written as – *Eve at Bay* – in English] are his full-length plays and *Moian Sar Na Kai, Bera Bandh Na Sakio, Waris, Banda Bahadur, Vada Ghalughara* and *Mittarpiara* are his historical plays on the theme of Sikh history.

Out of these Punjabi plays, *Mittar Piara* won the Sahitya Akademi Award in 1972. Sahitya Academy has published this English translation of seven of his plays, which are based on episodes in Sikh history.

The wide canvas of *Baba Bohar* takes us on a journey from the times of Guru Gobind Singh to the Independence of India. The bohar tree that has withstood the ravages of time and has been witness to history tells its myriad stories to young boys. The writer uses poetic license and history is a backdrop to his creativity. The play resonates with the reader because it is drawn from the familiar.

Vadaa Ghallughara, or the Great Holocaust (called the 'Big Holocaust' in the book), was a siege of the Sikhs by the forces of Ahmad Shah Abdali in 1763 between the villages of Raipur and Gujarwal in Punjab, which resulted in thousands of deaths, many women and children among them. Singh weaves in popular narrative in the play and, remarkably enough, ends it on a positive note.

In *Waris*, we meet Waris Shah (whose Heer has made him immortal for those who know Punjabi), his love Bhagbhari and the Fauzdar with a glad eye.

The decay of the Lahore court after the death of Maharaja Ranjit Singh is the focus of *Bera Bandh Na Sakio* (They Could Not Anchor the Fleet). The same theme continues in *Moian Sar Na Kai* (The Dead Were Not Aware), in which Singh also makes a powerful plea for unity among Punjabi people.

Singh fulfilled his desire to write a play 'on whatever contacts there might have been between Lenin and Indian patriots.' *Mittar Piara* (The Beloved Friend) came out of this endeavour. Bhai Santokh Singh and Bhai Rattan Singh are 'infused with the self-sacrificing spirit of Gurbani. They have come to grasp the theory and practise of Marxism,' says Tejwant Singh. These Gaddar (revolt) leaders participate in the deliberations of the second Comintern and then interact with their beloved friend.

Tejwant Singh Gill, the master translator, has done an excellent job in translating these plays. As one reads the plays, one can feel the original Punjabi even through the English text. In the introduction, the translator has given a critical commentary on Singh's work as well as a handy glossary.

SHORT STORIES

Ajeet Cour

- *The Other Woman* by Ajeet Cour; Translated from Punjabi by various authors; Published by Academy of Fine Arts and Literature.

The Other Woman has 14 short stories. The stories have been translated from Punjabi by Khushwant Singh, Satjit Wadva, Jasjit Mansingh, Devender Assa Kaur, Sudhir and by the writer herself.

The stories cover a wide range of subjects such as the apathy and corruption of government servants (*Ali Baba's Death* and *Happy New Year*), the brutality and insensitivity of Punjab police (*Bloodhounds*), the militancy issue in Punjab (*Dead-End*), the Sikh genocide of 1984 (*November 1984*) and the preference for a male child and the slow subjugation of the female child (*Initiation*). However, it is the issue of the status of women that predominates most of the stories. Cour illustrates the pathetic attitude of Indian society in general, and that of Punjabi society in particular, towards its women.

Thus, *Mami* is a sad story of a wife who is rejected on the first night of marriage because she has a dark complexion. Her parents refuse to take her back and she lives alone in a rented house nearby and depends on a meager allowance for food from her 'husband' who goes on to marry another woman. After his untimely death, the second wife refuses to pay that agreed amount, even though she gets the husband's entire property. Finally, the first wife is forced to work as a servant in her erstwhile house to survive.

Similarly, the title story *The Other Woman*, which is autobiographical in nature, deals with men who get entangled with women outside of their marriage but who don't give the respect and care due to those women and may even renege on their promise to marry them. The women, though madly in love with the men, are always hanging by a thread and can be maltreated and even discarded anytime. Cour, like Amrita Pritam, has been remarkably open about her relations with men and this story is a part of what is fully given in her candid autobiography, *Khana Badosh*.

November 1984 is a somber story of the senseless, vindictive and state-supported violence unleashed by the ruling party after the death of Indira Gandhi. The author and her daughter (noted painter Arpana Cour), along with some other like-minded citizens, were involved in relief work at the camps where the distraught Sikh families had been housed. The first-hand account of the victims given by the author is gut wrenching and reminiscent of the violence of the Partition and the massacre of Jews by the Nazis. It is one of the very few stories written on this subject by Punjabi authors in the books mentioned in this compilation.

Death Where Is Thy Sting and *Returning Home* are two delightful stories in the anthology. In the former, Rashid discovers he has cancer and just six months to live. Since his wife is dead and his only son lives in the United States, he toils and lives alone in Delhi. He re-examines his life, decides against making his life more miserable by subjecting himself to meaningless doses of radiation, chemotherapy and other such treatment and relocates to his village home where he spends his last days in joy and gay abandon, doing what he likes.

Similarly, in *Returning Home*, petty issues of daily life do not bother the grandfather; instead, he spends his time in meditation, talking to the sun and the sparrows and enjoying every moment despite the indifferent care by his son and daughter-in-law and the constant nagging by his wife. As the protagonist, his granddaughter who finds her grandfather mystical and says in the story, 'Probably my grandfather never grew up in the usual sense. He belied Time and Space and everything that we call and consider normal. He kept his dialogue going with the sun and God and sparrows.'

The translation of the stories is excellent, and the cover page is a beautiful painting by Arpana Caur.

Author

Ajeet Cour (1934–) was born in Lahore and, after Partition, her family came to Delhi where she did M.A. (Economics). She has written 20 books of short stories and novellas, which have been extensively translated into almost all Indian languages and into some foreign languages like Polish, Russian, French, Bulgarian and Spanish. She has also translated several classics into Punjabi but she has made a mark as a short-story writer. Her well-known works in the genre are *Gulbano, Mehak di Maut, But shikan, Faltu Aurat* and *Maut Ali Babe di.* She has also written two volumes of her autobiography, one of which, *Khana Badosh* won The Sahitya Akademi Award of 1985. The other volume is *Koorha Kabaarha*. The hallmark of Cour's creativity is her relentless search for the truth and her dedication to get at it.

Her short stories portray the situation of women in society, suffering from underprivileged positions in relation to their husbands and lovers. She is a crusader for women's issues and has displayed courageous convictions.

She has bagged many awards like Shiromani Sahitkar Award, International IATA Award, Sahitya Akademi Award, Bharatiya Bhasha Parishad Award, Punjabi Sahita Sabha Award and the Padma Shri. She has the honour of being selected as 'one of the thousand peace crusaders of the world for the collective Nobel Peace Prize.'

Cour is the founder chairperson of the Academy of Fine Arts and Literature and the Foundation of SAARC Writers and Literature. She is also involved with a lot of charity work.

Amrik Singh Kanda

- *Overreach* by Amrik Singh Kanda; Translated by Dr. Rajinder Singh; Published by Unistar Books Pvt. Ltd.

Overreach contains more than 40 of Amrik Singh Kanda's stories. In his stories, it is very refreshing to read about the day-to-day problems that we face. His stories are not about great and abstract issues like existentialism, religion, or politics but about what you and I face each day.

Thus, there are issues like a husband's dilemma when his wife starts working late hours and when people start coming by to drop her home (*Pigeons*). In another story, a man is principled and refuses to make money by unfair means but is not liked by his wife and children, as they want to lead a luxurious life like others (*Dreams and Non-dreams*). In *Dodder*, the wife and son indulge in corrupt practices but the daughter refuses to do so and sides with her principled father.

In *Strands of Attachment*, when the lady gets a heart attack, the husband and son, who are both terribly busy with their business/job, advise her to rest and recuperate somewhere near the hospital as it was difficult for them to come so far for regular checkups. There, she meets an old man who is also aimlessly whiling away his time after being forsaken by his family. Both find solace in mutual loneliness.

Then there are stories about the misuse of official positions by bureaucrats, their debaucherous lives and how even people working for them live base lives (*Why should we bother...*). In *The Dwarfs*, a retired bureaucrat thinks himself the repository of all knowledge and cynically treats a humble do-gooder as a fraud but finally realizes that he was a dwarf before that simple man.

In *Helplessness,* we see a young new teacher at a medical college who comes from a poor family and has a blind mother and a sister to marry off. The principal advises her that to keep the job and be successful she will have to teach 'harmonium' to the five trustees at their home. The teacher realizes that, while she has to teach anatomy to the children at college, she is supposed to show her body to the grown-ups in the evenings. Only then would she have all the comforts of life.

In *The Dragon*, a young student, after working hard and doing numerous errands for his supervisor, finally realizes that his doctorate would not go through unless he gives his supervisor some big 'gift.' In *Agony of Dead Yearnings*, the problem of domestic help is dealt with. Those who employ them treat them with insensitivity – things like suddenly changing their work hours to suit their own needs without sparing a thought for the help's family or personal matters. *The Man-Eaters* is the strongest indictment of the ruling class and portrays the servility of the subjects. It is a remarkable story where the author excels himself in describing the sorry state of affairs around us.

Though the stories are simple and tackle these 'mundane' issues yet the author treats them very intelligently and subtly. He exposes the ills of the society but without any rancor or value judgement. The reader is left aghast when confronted with these ills and, hopefully, some people treading these ill-advised paths will be brought back on track.

Author

Dr. Amrik Singh Kanda is a writer based in India, a satirist, a business and immigration consultant, a journalist, lyricist and publisher. He has published many books and articles on subjects ranging from humanity to civilization. He is also a columnist and writes a column, *Kande da Kanda*.

His work includes *Leehon Parey, Aj De Chankiya, Kujh Heere Kujh Panne* and *Chite Khamban Da Bharam* (Punjabi short stories), *Kanda Arz Kare* and *Kande da Kanda* (social and political satire), *Na Dharti Ki Na Aasman Ki* (Hindi short stories) and *The Thorny*

Path (English short stories). His new books include *The Race* and *Overreach*, both of which are translations of his short stories.

He is one of the younger Punjabi authors and has a distinct down-to-earth approach. His stories are concerned with social evils and with a decline in the values, especially in bureaucracy, teachers, schools, colleges and universities. As the translator writes, 'Kanda does not leave any situation untouched, no evil unnoticed and no good deed un-praised.'

Baldev Singh Dhaliwal

- *Burning Soil* by Baldev Singh Dhaliwal; Translated by Inder Singh Khamosh; Published by M.P. Parkashan.

Burning Soil is an English version of 16 Punjabi short stories written by Dhaliwal, which have been translated by Inder Singh Khamosh. 14 of these are from his book *Opri Hawa* and two stories were published in magazines. Individually, every story of this collection has gained recognition on one platform or the other. The story *Aut* (Issueless) was selected by Dr. Gurbux Singh Frank while editing a collection titled *Sajrian Pairan* published by the Sahitya Academy Delhi in 1998 containing Punjabi stories by the young writers blossoming in the last decade of the 20th century. The story *Opri Hawa* (Mysterious Ailment) earned a place in a collection of stories edited by Dr. Raghbir Singh Sirjana named *Veehwin Sadi Di Punjabi Kahani* published by Sahitya Academy Delhi in 2000. Doordarshan Kender, Jalandhar prepared a telefilm named *Wapsi* in 1997 based on Dhaliwal's story, *Adam and Eve*. All the stories of this collection have been translated into Hindi, English and other Indian languages.

    The dominant feature of these stories is the topical presentation of the socio-economic conditions of Punjabi people. The narrative deals with the situations arising from the complex mode of life, particularly in the spheres of culture, politics, religion, the folkloric basis of social-cultural ethos and human psychology. Under the influence of modernity, urbanization has caused massive cultural transformation, but the contradictions of urban and rural dwelling results in severe anguish. Dhaliwal has tried his level best to portray the real nature of human beings.

    Since Dhaliwal belongs to a family of middleclass peasants, his understanding of the middle and marginal peasant life is remarkable. Many of his characters shuttle between the town and the country; in fact, they belong nowhere. Dhaliwal also uses a vibrant Malwai laced with rustic idioms and proverbs. The translator has tried his best to retain the essence of that Malwai dialect, which is rooted in witticism, sarcasm, irony and puns.

Dhaliwal's stories deal with contemporary situations. The complex caste equation in villages is a reality; technology has reduced the bargaining power of the rural workers; the landowning gentry too have their own economic problems… All of these issues come out loud and clear in *Between the Two Grindstones*.

Mysterious Ailment is a different kind of story. From the village, the narrator's brother, Naranj descends upon his brother in his cramped house in the city and stays for over a week without explaining why he has come. Perhaps he was affected by a mysterious ailment that has attacked him in the past. Finally, the ailment turns out to be a tough situation at his village house, where his parents and wife cannot live together and are demanding separation. But he cannot afford two households.

In *Terrorist*, the protagonist, his wife and children who live with lot of constraints in Chandigarh come to the village house of his parents to ask for some monetary help, as the wife wants to buy a house of her own. For this, his father offers no help as he has a daughter to give off in marriage. The usual tension and skirmishes follow.

Though most of the stories are village based some, like *Last Half of the Name* and *Adam and Eve,* deal with urban issues where the educated wife wants to work but the man cannot bring himself to accept that. *Honeymoon* is about a village boy who is bent upon erasing his past of poverty and works hard as a lawyer. However, in the process, he makes his life mechanical and fails to provide care and affection to family.

Although all the stories are very realistic and based on every day life, stories like *Snake Charmer, Prohibited Line* and *Issueless* are a bit too realistic and can be painful to read. In *Snake Charmer,* the egotistical father does not take lightly being snubbed or sidelined.

But he doesn't rave or rant like a normal person; instead, schemes and plots to bring his enemy down even if that enemy is his own son and at stake is that son's marriage. In *Prohibited Line,* the husband is used to having his way at home. All acquiesce before him, except his second wife who is misled to revolt and hence crosses that prohibited line and ends up paying with her life. *Issueless* is about uncle Bhima who sacrifices for family, remains a bachelor, even goes to jail, but his nephew wants to go against him and sell their land to their arch enemy. Worse, the hero of the story – the second nephew – on whom Bhima relies, tells a lie, runs away and leaves them to sort the mess.

Author
Baldev Singh Dhaliwal is the author of *Uche Tibe Di Ret* (Poetry), *Opri Hawa* (Short Stories), *Motian Di Chog* and *Thames Nal Vagdian* (both travelogues) and 10 books of criticism. He was awarded the Bhai Vir Singh Galap Award by GNDU, Amritsar, for *Opri Hawa*. He did his BA Hons, M.A., M phil. and Ph.D in Punjabi from Panjab University, Chandigarh, and was a reader at Punjabi University, Patiala.

Balwant Singh

- *Balwant Singh: Selected Short Stories;* **Selected and Edited by Gopi Chand Narang; Translated by Jai Ratan; Published by Sahitya Akademi.**

This anthology is a superb selection of 20 of his short stories. They have been selected and edited by Professor Gopi Chand Narang, eminent scholar and critic, and have been wonderfully translated by Jai Ratan. Not much of Singh's literature is available and no information about him is available online. Therefore, this book is a wonderful initiative by Sahitya Akademi to bring Singh out of this oblivion. The icing on the cake is an erudite introduction by Professor Narang 'on the art of Balwant Singh.' Although slightly long at 50 pages and a bit repetitive, the introduction provides significant details of the writings of Singh, his style, depiction of characters, his romanticism, the cultural significance of his stories, Punjabism in them, his place in Urdu literature, and how his fellow contemporaries viewed him as an author, amongst other things.

The anthology contains few of the stories which earned him a special identity and which he loved himself like *Jagga, The Granthi* and *Baba Mehnga Singh,* although his acclaimed story *Saaza* has not been included.

Many of his stories are steeped in romantic tradition. The hero in his romantic stories would invariably be a man six-foot high, with unusually broad shoulders, veins standing out on his hands and forehead, with a swarthy complexion, powerful jaws, a thick solid neck, ears pierced with large rings, a long *kurta* with a striped *tehmat* and carrying a *lathi* or some other weapon. According to Narang, such valiant characters that stride through Singh's fiction satisfy some hidden, unconscious urge of their creator.

This is coupled with his choice of locales and personas – the village, countryside, mud houses, tracks, *havelis, rahats,* wet dykes, hard-working farmers, women making dung-cakes and lighting *chulhas,* ruminating cows and buffaloes. Then, in these villages, the placid nights resound with the recitation of Waris Shah's *Heer,* while in the melas the musicians sing Shah Mohammed's epic poem, *Jangnama.*

However, Singh's repertoire is not limited to such stories. The stories in this collection deal with a variety of subjects like hypocrisy, Partition trauma and infidelity. There are stories that deal with the movement from countryside to the city and the attendant frustration caused by urban corruption. Stories like *The First Stone, Webley 38* and *The Patriot* depict the baseness, meanness and barbarity of man and highlight pathos, devastation and exploitation. Then there are stories in which the pivot is the sexual urge or the lack of it. Stories in this category are *Paperweight, Termite, The Hard Way Around* and *Soorma Singh.*

The two stories that stand out are *The Wayward Boy* and *Lala Nihal Chand,* both based in urban settings. The former is a story of a boy of 12 who regularly excuses himself from his class and, when the father follows to see where he goes, he finds his son enjoying nature and meeting people. The father realizes that his son is abundantly endowed with a zest for life and its warmth while the father had severed his connections with vital streams of life and had become trapped in a dreary hectic routine. The latter is about Nihal Chand, an endearing and guileless shopkeeper in Amritsar, who wins over the readers with his vitality and cheerfulness and is indifferent to the pleasures and pain of the world.

This book thus manages to present the versatility of Singh as an author and proves that, although he may not be as recognized as Manto, Bedi and Chander, his short stories merit equal importance, if not more.

Author
Balwant Singh (1921–1986), was born in village Bahlol, district Gujranwala (now in Pakistan) where he received his early

education. Later, when his father Lal Singh was appointed as lecturer at the Military College, Dehradun, Singh also moved and did his matriculation from there, followed by graduation from Allahabad University. After completing his graduation in 1942, he spent some time in Lahore where he came in contact with Rajinder Singh Bedi, Manto and Krishan Chander and started writing. His story, *Sazaa* published in the monthly *Saaqi* (Delhi) made him a known figure in literary circles. Even before Partition, Singh had established himself as a notable writer of fiction in Urdu.

After Partition, he found a job at the Publications Division of Ministry of Information and Broadcasting and managed the publication of three Urdu journals, *Aajkal, Bisaat-e-Aalam* and *Nau Nihaal*. After his father's death, he moved to Allahabad where his father had set up a hotel. He began handling the hotel but spent most of the time reading and writing. Although he deserved the highest awards, Singh never got any recognition except UP Government's Award, Bhasha Vibhag Patiala's Prize and the Shrimoni Sahityakar Award from the Punjab Government.

Singh is the author of more than 40 volumes of fiction, which include 22 novels and about 300 short stories. He wrote more novels than short stories but his genius found his best expression in his short stories. He wrote in both Urdu and Hindi.

Singh depicted rural life in the Punjab with penetrating insight, and his perception of the Sikh psyche is unrivalled. He had the courage to delve deep into the intricacies of the human mind, and he illuminated hidden terrains of the human experience and explored new meanings, which not only made his stories unique but also made the characters memorable.

Bushra Ejaz

- *Snake and Shadow* by Bushra Ejaz; Translated by Kumar Sushil and Raenee; Published by Unistar Books Pvt. Ltd.

Ejaz was married at the young age of 12 and her experience in an alien atmosphere led her imagination to burst out into stories and poems. Her books, *Baran Anaya Di Aurat* (The Lady Worth Twelve Anna), *Aaj Di Shaharzad* (The Story Teller) and *Kataran Ton Bani Aurat* (The Shattered Self) are available in the Gurmukhi script. *Snake and Shadow* contains the translation from Punjabi into English of 15 selected stories from these three story collections.

The book begins with an endearing story, *Umbrella Man* – the tale of a lonely army captain posted in Murray who happens to meet a sad, young woman teaching in a school there. Though they become friends, she stonewalls all queries about herself. When, one day, the captain finally professes his desire to marry her, she simply disappears. Many years later, he meets her again and realizes that she had become a widow of an army man at a very young age and had dedicated her entire life to the mission of education in the army and society.

The trend is set, and the stories that follow depict the sufferings and anguish of women in different settings. In *Witness*, the affable schoolteacher, Master Sadique joins the army in a surge of patriotism, leaving his wife Zubaida alone. Soon, he is martyred, the whole village celebrates his martyrdom, and Zubaida is left with only a pension. She follows the footsteps of her husband and continues to serve society but is often misunderstood. The village labels her as a loose character without understanding her good deeds. She refuses to say anything in her defense and is condemned.

The story, *Earthworm* is about an urban woman who has to suffer the tortuous treatment meted out by her husband, Sajjad. She is an artist who specializes in abstract painting. In his race for doubling his business, the husband neglects his wife and uses her only for sexual gratification. Mentally, she feels that earthworms have invaded her body and starts painting earthworms in her incomplete painting of a woman.

Little Ammi is the story of Amina – the youngest of all brothers and sisters and always pampered. She is like a living toy with blinking eyes, laughter and tears. Suddenly, her mother dies and the mantle falls on little Ammi – she takes up the responsibility and cares for the entire family. It is a poignant tale of how circumstances transform a young girl into a responsible adult.

Snake and Shadow is the story of Rabo who suffers from fits of epilepsy. Her parents take her to a Pir who is noted for exorcising ghosts and evil spirits. The Pir claims to have cured Rabo but her stomach starts swelling. She believes that a snake had entered her and was growing in size. Rabo ultimately stabs her belly and claims that she is releasing the snake.

The story, *Guilt* is about a highly respected Sayyad Ghulam Ali. As he returns home from an early morning visit to the Mosque, he hears a meek crying voice of a new born from near a trash can. He wants to hurry away as his only son, Vilayat, was expecting his child any minute. When he looks at the little bundle wrapped in a dirty rag, he is astonished to see the birthmark on the boy's wrist – a newly opened pomegranate flower – similar to the mark on his wrist and that of Vilayat. Meanwhile, the boy dies of cold and hunger. At that precise moment, his servant comes running to announce the arrival of his own grandson. He is offered congratulations but he is in a fix. Should he accept greetings at the birth of a grandson or mourn the death of a grandson?

Author

Bushra Ejaz is a renowned fiction writer of Pakistan. She has produced a significant body of work – short stories, travelogues, poems, autobiography and columns. She writes in Urdu and in Gurmukhi. Her work is attuned to women's issues and is universal in its theme. The problems faced by women in general, issues between men and women, desire for love, unrequited love, older men marrying young women and the problems arising out of that. Though they are placed in the contextual framework of her country and religion, most of us can identify with the characters and their sorrows and happiness.

Through her stories, she examines the inwardness, silences and ambivalences that form a major share of the survival manoeuvers of women who are caught up in the oppressive discourse of patriarchy. These manoeuvers are unconsciously internalized through the sedimentation of continuous repressive rituals and existences. Ejaz's women characters defy all cultural barriers and strike a kinship with both Pakistani and Indian women. Her feministic stance is bound to surface although hers is a latent, passive and non-activist brand of feminism.

Read on

- *Just Before the Dream* has poems of Bushra Ejaz that were translated from Urdu into Punjabi by Mohammad Idris and have further been translated into English by Ishmeet Kaur; Published by Twenty First Century Publications, Patiala.

Gurnam Gill

- *Only Dreams: Short Stories* by Gurnam Gill; Edited and Translated by Gurdial Singh Aarif; Published by Unistar Books Pvt. Ltd.

The spread of the Indian, especially the Punjabi, diaspora is often described as the revenge of the colonized. Those who migrated to the United Kingdom took their language and culture with them and cross-pollinated there to leave a lasting impact on the culture scape of what was once truly Great Britain. However, things were never easy for the early migrants to the United Kingdom. Besides linguistic and cultural alienation, they had to contend with the insidious and brazen forms of racism. This volume dwells on these aspects but also showcases how the diaspora came to terms with the not-so-friendly socio-cultural environment, eventually taking firm roots there.

Gill's stories are written lucidly, like the stories of Guy de Maupassant and O'Henry, and leave a lasting emotional impact on the reader. 17 of his stories are included in this anthology. However, his choice of subjects is not restricted to diasporic concerns and the nostalgia about homeland and Punjab; he also writes of urban and modern issues.

Thus, in *Right or Wrong*, the protagonist is attracted to a shoe polish woman at the station in Mumbai. He tries to go to her and to find ways of befriending her but finally realizes that she is also working as a prostitute trying to make her ends meet. The author displays the underbelly of Mumbai where immense poverty flourishes.

In *Across the Breakwater*, Bhushan, after the death of his wife, marries his wife's younger sister, Renu at the insistence of his relatives, as a child needs to be brought up. He is aware that Renu was in love with another man but she bows to family pressure and marries. Bhushan soon realizes that although she does all her duties, including looking after him and his daughter, she is not happy and is only going through the motions. He, in his mind, wants to set the young girl free, but his selfish self-interest wins, and he is unable to do so.

I Know is about a Punjabi girl who wants to become an actress in Mumbai and defies her mother to go there. She carves out a career for herself but, torn by the separation from her mother, she is often saddened and finally loses her mother without even being able to meet her before she breathes her last. The author very poignantly portrays this struggle between ambition and family duty and honour.

Shazia is about the Partition and the misery that follows, while *The Tale of Sad Moments* tackles the issue of militancy and police excesses. In *How Long*, Bindu, who has separated from Joginder, tries to pick up the threads of her life and starts meeting Deb. However, her daughter, Alka does not like this and Bindu is caught between her heart's desire and her daughter's happiness.

The Need is a distinctive story in which Mr. Virk is still young at heart and with a healthy sex drive but his wife, in keeping with the advice of relatives, tries to not sleep in the same room because 'what will children and grandchildren think?' In *Nude & Naked*, Subhash arrives in Mumbai to choose a wife and sees two different women, spending time with both. It is a very urban story showcasing today's more open society. In *Plunder,* Gill tackles the dispute between mother and daughter. In *May Green*, Maninder Grewal goes to Goa where she meets a fellow Punjabi, but he soon repulses her as he tries to force himself on her. Thus, the author constantly pushes the envelope and takes up realistic issues, often making very pertinent observations.

Even in the stories relating to diaspora, the author tries new issues and subjects. The title story, *Only Dreams* is about Kirpal (called Paul by his English neighbours) who is infatuated with Jeena. He backs off when he realizes that Jeena's husband, Charlie is similarly infatuated with his wife, Santosh. In *Two Yards Space*,

Gill tackles the issue of the old man who cannot decide whether he wants to finally die in London or in his native place, especially after his wife dies, while in *The Strangers*, the old couple arrives in India to breathe their last in their native village, but their relatives refuse to let them live in peace and they have to go back to England.

In *My Native Land,* Balraj goes to Canada and sees that people are so busy earning dollars that they do not have time to meet him. He is also surprised to find a great transformation in his simpleton aunt who, in the Punjab village, never spoke a word but is now driving a car, working, drinking and is almost the boss at home. Similarly, *Defeat* and *Their Own Respective Worlds* deal with life aboard while trying to cling to traditional values.

Author
Gurnam Gill (1943–), born at village Dhoori near Jalandhar, migrated to England in the mid-1970s where he started writing both poetry and short stories with equal felicity and flourish. He has also written novels and a book on health. His works include *Sooraj Da Vichora* (Sun's Separation; Short stories), *Sagar Vichle Registan* (The Desert inside an Ocean; Poetry) and *Te Hava Ruk Gayi* (Novel).

Read on
- *Life Under One Roof* (Fictional Innovation) is a series of short stories. The author explains, 'It does not fit in the genre of a novel; but can be enjoyed as a novel. It may seem autobiographical but is absolutely imaginative.' Unistar Books Pvt. Ltd has published it.

Harbans Singh

- *Mahindi and Other Short Stories*; **Translated by Harbans Singh; Published by Navyug Publishers.**

Navyug Publishers first published this anthology of Punjabi short stories in its English translation in 1984. It contains 16 short stories and they are not only the most representative of their authors but also have come to be accepted by wide consensus as the classics of Punjabi short fiction as it has evolved over the years. Professor Harbans Singh, a connoisseur of literary excellence, has shown immense sensitivity in choosing these stories, which is so characteristic of all his work, whether academic or literary.

The authors included in this anthology are all stalwarts – Kulwant Singh Virk, Sant Singh Sekhon, Surinder Singh Narula, Nanak Singh, Mohan Singh, Amrita Pritam, Kartar Singh Duggal, Santokh Singh Dhir, Gurmukh Singh Musafir, Gurbaksh Singh, Ajeet Cour, Balwant Gargi, Mohinder Singh Joshi, and Navtej Singh. Thus, we have the all-time-favourite *Pemi's Children* by Sant Singh Sekhon, *The Milkman & His Neeli* by K.S. Duggal and *The Blades of Grass* by Kulwant Singh Virk, which are invariably included in any anthology of Punjabi stories.

Kulwant Singh Virk's other story in this anthology, *The Bull Beneath the Earth,* is a very poignant story of an army man who, as promised to his colleague Karam Singh, visits the latter's family, unaware that his friend had attained martyrdom. He is initially upset by the restrained welcome that he gets at the friend's house but, when he comes to know about Karam's death, he is extremely touched by the family's attempt to hide their grief so as to not spoil his holiday.

Santokh Singh Dhir's *The Common Wall* is a heart-warming story of a feud between cousins over the construction of a wall.

The Sarpanch fuels the feud but the brothers finally rediscover their love for each other in times of need.

The title story, *Mahindi* is by Mohinder Singh Joshi and tackles the issue of dowry, while that of Amrita Pritam's *Kanjak* talks of child widowhood of one-generation versus the changing times and loosening of morals in the next generation. *Bua* by Nanak Singh is a funny take on rural hospitality, which the urban people are unable to now digest. Gurbaksh Singh's *Kehru the Rascal* is again an endearing story of a village toughie and how he turns out to be a man of a golden heart.

The Derby Sweepstake by K. S. Duggal is a delightful and funny story of Shaikh Sharif who is perpetually waiting for his promotion in office. When finally it happens, it changes his life a lot but he his jolted when the promotion is suddenly reversed. A sweepstake ticket finally gives him the courage to stand this ignominy.

Balwant Gargi's *The Old Woman's Tincan* is a poignant story of a woman travelling on a train and a bunch of girls trying a prank to see the contents of her tincan, while *Fragrant Charm* by Mohan Singh is again a touching story of a Kashmiri girl who in her innocence and love for the sweet fragrance of a perfume bottle does not think of the consequences and takes risks.

The stories thus tackle a variety of subjects and are a delight to read. The quality of the translation is wonderful as Professor Harbans Singh has perfect mastery over both English and Punjabi.

Hina Nandrajog & Madhuri Chawla

- *Santalinama: Partition Stories*; Edited by Anna Sieklucka and Sutinder Singh Noor; Translated by Hina Nandrajog & Madhuri Chawla; Published by Punjabi Academy.

As the Punjabi word *Santali* (the number 47) in the title suggests, the book is about 1947, the year of the Partition of India. The Punjabis were the most affected by this cataclysmic event and have thus written a lot about Partition.

However, most anthologies end up choosing representative authors and representative stories whereas, as the editor, Professor Anna Sieklucka from Warsaw University, Poland, points out, that there are many more stories written in Punjabi on Partition. After extensive research in several libraries all over the world, she collected over 500 partition stories written in Punjabi. 31 of these priceless stories have been presented in this volume. Punjabi Academy, the editors and the translators, deserve full credit for bringing this exclusive anthology on Partition and, in turn, bringing some new Punjabi authors to the notice of the English-reading public. Even in the case of well-translated authors, their newer stories have been selected. There is only one more exclusive anthology of Partition stories in English and that is by Mohinder Singh Sarna, while in Punjabi there are just two anthologies – Jaswant Deed's *Desh Wand Diyan Kahaniyan* and Ram Swarup Ankhi's *Kala Santali*. It is hoped that the Punjabi Academy will publish the rest of the stories from Professor Sieklucka's collection soon.

Hina Nandrajog and Madhuri Chawla have translated the stories into English. The other editor, Professor Sutinder Singh

Noor has a doctorate and has more than 37 years of teaching experience. He retired as a professor from the Department of Punjabi, University of Delhi, Delhi.

Amongst others included here are stories by three Pakistani writers – Afzal Ahsan Randhawa, Afzal Tauseef and Iliyas Ghuman. The entire Punjabi community (on both sides of the present border) shared the wounds of Partition – their land was divided, they were uprooted and were forced to live separately. Further, as Professor Noor points out, they have included not only the generation of authors who suffered the trauma of Partition directly but also contemporary writers who wrote about Partition much later. Their stories also depict the trauma of Partition with great poignancy.

Gurbaksh Singh Preetlari, in *You Will Always Be My World*, talks of a young Muslim boy who was left behind in India and was brought up by a Sikh family. When he turns 18, they tell him the true story of his birth and give him the freedom to decide to stay or leave. It is a story of courage, conviction and character. *Chasm* by Mohan Bhandari is also along similar lines and the boy brought up is always aware of his real parentage and the mindless carnage that caused him to be left behind. *Incomplete Men* by Sujan Singh depicts similar tragedies that befell people fleeing from Dhaka.

The full fury, inhumanness and brutality exhibited by both the sides is depicted in stories like *Jathedar* by Santokh Singh Dhir, *Carnage* by Gurdev Rupana, *Il-Koko: The Mysterious Kite* by Iliyas Ghuman, *Midwife* by Navtej Singh, *Sport of Demons* by Sant Singh Sekhon, *Triad of Trees* by Mohinder Singh Joshi and *Ladhewala Waraich* by M.S. Sarna. Though these stories are vivid and honest, it is hard to imagine the extent to which humans can be beasts at times.

The Para Trooper by Ram Sarup Ankhi, *A Bard Named Fattu* by Gurbachan Singh Bhullar and *Lost Again* by Gurdial Singh all deal with the pull of the motherland even when the nation has been divided. All three protagonists cannot bear to be away from their native village, even though two of them are now soldiers in Pakistan's army and are finally apprehended by forces.

Similarly, the stories *Not a City, But a Shell* by Ajeet Cour, *The Dust of thy Feet* by Lochan Singh Bakshi, *Grapes have Ripened* by Devendra Satyarthi, *Disfigured Jutti* by Gurmukh Singh Musafir, *Lost Fragrance* by Afzal Ahsan Randhawa, *The Mortar* by Sukhwant Kaur Mann, *My Beloved Trees, My Children* by Afzal Tauseef, *Come, Sister Fatima* by Baldev Singh and *Neighbours* by Dalip Kaur Tiwana are all about nostalgia for the land left behind and about hope – rebuilding lives and moving on to mend fences between the two countries and the two communities. These stories inspire confidence in humanity once again.

Waryam Singh Sandhu, in *Shadows*, talks about both the trauma of Partition as well as about the militancy issue in Punjab. *The Exile* by Naurang Singh does not directly deal with Partition but is more about the freedom movement and India attaining Independence. Similarly, Amrita Pritam, in *The Five Sisters*, talks more about women's issues and how life unfairly treats women at all levels and strata in our society. It is women who bore the worst kind of brutality during Partition.

This is a very important anthology as, except for some stories like *The Resilience of Weed* by Kulwant Singh Virk and *Ladhewala Waraich* by Mohinder S. Sarna, all the other stories are available for the first time in English.

Jarnail Singh

- *Towers: Stories Beyond Borders* by Jarnail Singh; Edited by Gurpal Sandhu and Jasminder Dhillon; Translated by various authors; Published by Unistar Books Pvt. Ltd.

The book has a collection of six stories based on his experience of living in multicultural Canada. Mr. Gurpal Sandhu, one of the editors of the book, has written a very in-depth introduction to the book titled *Katha Across the Edge*, where he deals with subjects like Katha, the form of south Asian narrative tradition, the influence of Western literature, the growth of Punjabi short story and finally the Punjabi diasporic short story writing. As far as Punjabi diasporic literature is concerned, it can be seen that while the first generation of diasporic authors portrayed the romantic scenes and astounding images of the Western world, the second depicted the nostalgia for the homeland – an outcome of the anguish caused by the racial discrimination suffered by them. Now, the third generation (or contemporary writers) of the Punjabi diaspora are trying to go beyond the strict boundaries of the nation state, racial discrimination, bitterness of alien-land and the longing for homeland.

Jarnail Singh is one of the best examples of such writers as his stories contain descriptions of global events and universal values in accordance with the Punjabi sensibility – a sensibility that has a general character of resistance towards every type of oppressive behaviour. Sandhu believes that a distinctive feature of the Punjabi narrative tradition is resistance towards the repressive regime and inhuman traits, and this is very intricately woven into Singh's stories even when they talk of people of different communities, nations, ethnicities and events like 9/11 or environmental threats to public places in Canada.

Towers depicts the tragic scenes in the aftermath of 9/11, highlighting terrorism and its impact on ordinary Americans. William Thompson and his family justify the oppression by the U.S. forces in the Middle East and Afghanistan but soon their daughter, Stacy, becomes a victim of the attack on the World Trade Centre. The concrete Towers collapsed, as did the Towers of hope of ordinary people. Then, their son Dennis, who is in the U.S. army, loses his life in the military action against Iraq.

Identity is a story that narrates the tale of a couple that has an insatiable lust for money, which led them to ignore their parents and children. *Identity* depicts the society that hankers after a comfortable lifestyle and exploits close relationships, and presents, graphically, the degeneration of human relationships.

Similarly, in *Water*, Sukhjit Kaur is worried about the materialistic lifestyles of her son and daughter-in-law as well as what she perceives to be their insensitivity, selfishness and self-centered natures. Through the depiction of these characters, the author tries to stand for a progressive and humanistic value system.

Celebrity Bodies has portrayed another aspect of inhuman character through the ideas of power and supremacy. The model, Manisha is crazy about possessing the title Top Model. Manisha is well aware that modeling is an art and wants to stand by this commitment. However, powerful business houses have captured this art and instead of displaying well-designed clothes, they have turned it into an erotic playhouse of undressed and attractive feminine bodies.

In *Snow and The River,* the narrator loves Shawn, a boy from an aboriginal community with a pure soul but no money. Then she meets a rich classmate, Saunders and is captivated by his rich lifestyle. He soon leaves her and she, realizing her folly, goes back to her old love. Besides these human failings and values, the author takes up issues of the preservation of natural resources, which the rich are constantly trying to usurp in the name of development.

In Circles and Circles of Pain, the author juxtaposes two wars – the Indo-Pak war of 1971 where the narrator loses his dear friend and the Canadian army's intervention in Bosnia where another of his friends, Steve loses his life. The author flags two very important issues through the characters. First, in both cases, he depicts the life of the widows who have to undergo tremendous hardships. He writes, 'Navtej was killed in a war which lasted only two weeks. But his widow Jeetan died innumerable times in her lifelong battle for survival.' Similarly, 'Although Steve's life came to an end abruptly, the war raged on… Nancy's life…had been converted into a battle ground, a very rocky battle ground.'

The second issue is whether moral courage is greater than physical courage in a war. Steve's son, who gets very disturbed on his father's death, asks that if one is not convinced about the issue for which the war is being fought, do the soldiers have the right to dissent and not fight in it? Do they have the moral courage to stand by their conviction or should they just obey orders?

The stories have been very ably translated by Tejinder Kaur, Swaraj Raj, Kiron Heer, Gurpal Sandhu and Jasminder Dhillon.

Author

Jarnail Singh was born into a modest peasant family in the village Meghowal near Hoshiarpur, Punjab, India. After completing high school, he joined the Indian Air Force in 1962 and, while in service, he earned his Masters' degrees in English and Punjabi. Upon obtaining release from the Indian Air Force and before migrating to Canada in 1988, he worked at a bank as an accountant.

While in India, he produced three collections of stories: *Mainu Kee*, *Manukh Te Manukh* and *Samen De Haani*, all related to the realistic depiction of the miseries and hardships of the peasantry as well as of military personnel.

In Canada, he worked for two decades as a supervisor at a security company. The immigrant experience of life in Canada brought creative richness to the range of the subject matter of his later stories.

He has written three collections of short stories in Canada, *Do Taapu*, *Towers* and *Kaale Varke*. The first two deals with the struggles of Punjabis living in Canada, the clash and assimilation of East-West cultures, the growing generation gap, breaking up of relationships and problems of teenagers. These short stories deserve to be identified as a distinguished work of Punjabi diaspora in terms of the assortment of themes and novelty of ideas.

Jarnail Singh's *Kaale Varke* (Black Pages) bagged the Dhahan Prize 2016 for Punjabi Literature. The Punjab Government in India has also honoured him with the Shiromani Sahitkar Award.

Jasjit Mansingh

- *Time Out: Stories from Punjab*; Edited by Jasjit Mansingh; Published by Srishti Publishers 2002.

This volume incorporates 18 stories by 14 writers who represent some of the most widely known names in modern Punjabi literature. So besides the well-known names like Amrita Pritam, Ajeet Cour, Kulwant Singh Virk, K.S. Duggal and Prem Prakash, we have the pleasure of reading stories by authors like Buta Singh, Manmohan Bawa, Ramindra Ajit Singh, Jaswant Singh Virdi, Krishen Singh Dhody, Baldev Singh, Raj Gill and even Tauquir Chugtai, who writes in Punjabi from Pakistan. The cover is a delightful painting, *Earthen Pot* by Arpana Caur, based on the Sohni Mahiwal story, and the book contains pen and ink sketches by Manmohan Bawa.

The editor has grouped the stories, each group representing a distinguishing part of the life of the people of Punjab who have undergone several vicissitudes of life placed as they were in different regions of the country. The reader is afforded a bird's eye view of the persona of the Punjabis, especially as they overcame times of travail and agony.

The stories have been carefully arranged to provide the readers with 'a sense of the layers of time and events' that have shaped 'the modern Punjabi.' She has included the bloodcurdling Partition stories. These stories are accounts of individual human compassion beyond religious divisions.

Ajeet Cour's *November 1984* is not a short story but an eyewitness account of the violent attacks on Sikhs following the assassination of then Prime Minister Indira Gandhi. Cour mentions three specific stories that particularly struck her during her work in the refugee camps. While officials were complicit in the brutal assaults targeting Sikhs, common people reached out to the victims to console them in their tragic losses. Kulwant singh Virk's *The Weight of the World* and Prem Prakash's *He Is Not That Jasbir* are well-known stories repeated in most anthologies.

The stories that stand out in this collection are *Bhabhi Morni* by Amrita Pritam, a saga of selfless love and devotion by a bhabhi and her devar, and *Sardarni* by Buta Singh, which is powerful story of a matriarch who dominates the joint family.

Baldev Singh's *Her Last Cries* similarly deals with the issue of identity but at a much earlier time. The character, Bhagwan Kaur is the well-loved matriarch at the heart of a large Jat family. At her death, her old friend quietly reveals to another relative that Bhagwan Kaur's real name was Miriam. Her whole family had been killed in front of her but she was saved by a neighbour who then brought her up in his family. This secret is kept deeply buried even from her own children and grandchildren. This aspect of women's silence, especially during the Partition, has been well documented in the oral histories recorded by other writers.

One of the most moving stories in the book is Jaswant Singh Virdi's *A Miracle*. Once again, it is set during Partition and recounts an incident from the point of view of a male narrator who sees a young Muslim girl of the neighbourhood being led naked through the streets by a mob. People watch, but nobody comes forward to help her. The young man finally takes off his turban and covers her. As a knife comes whistling through the air towards him, the young girl steps forward and is killed. Not only is this a heart-warming story of communal tolerance and respect that redeems one's faith in individuals but also the use of the turban as a symbol of honour and dignity is insightful and complex.

This is an astonishing collection of deeply moving and heart-warming stories. The translators have done a wonderful job. Jasjit has translated most of the stories while Tara Meenakshi Sekhri and Satjit Wadva have translated others. Jasjit credits her mother, Mrs. Devinder Kaur Assa, for her valuable help in translating these stories and also Bhapa Pritam Singh of Navyug Press, the leading publisher of Punjabi Literature for his help in selecting the stories.

Jaswinder Singh

- *The Elusive Fragrance* by Jaswinder Singh; Translated by Hina Nandrajog; Published by Punjabi University, Patiala.

The Elusive Fragrance is a collection of 10 short stories written by the Sahitya Akademi winner Jaswinder Singh and translated by Hina Nandrajog.

In the short stories included in this book, the author has beautifully and eloquently captured the domestic life of both rural and urban society in Punjab. He has depicted the close relationship that was prevalent earlier but is slowly crumbling in the modern age. What we glean is that close-knit families are disintegrating, and members once displaying love and affection are now spewing hatred and anger. Senseless fights have become common and what we behold in placid families is the rapid growth of greed and jealousy.

The inhumaneness and the selfish nature of men in high posts are depicted in *Deadstock*. Bhupinder Singh was brought up and educated by his maternal uncle, but now that he has a good job in town, he is surrounded by people (including his wife and friends) who discourage him from doing anything for his relatives. He meekly submits to them, suppressing his conscience.

The same imperviousness is depicted in *The Outsider*, in which the relatives are happy to take the most from Karam Singh but conveniently turn their back on him once he stops obliging them. However, he regains his confidence and once again hope springs in his heart.

The Smouldering Truth is about a happy, idealist man who is a dedicated comrade of the party. But everybody, including his wife, advises him to be 'practical' and 'diplomatic.' Reading the story, it is easy to sympathize with the wife who suffers because of his idealism. But, at the same time, it is difficult to work out how much one can bend to be accommodative.

Singh's stories have strong woman characters like in *Elusive Fragrance, Wheel of Life, Bitter-Sweet Shores, The Smouldering Truth* and *Dancing Serpent,* although they are not always positive. Thus, in *Bitter-Sweet Shores,* the mother lives happily with a son and daughter-in-law but a death wish seizes her and she forces her obedient son to marry again for the sake of a child, in the end losing her son's love and respect. The whole house is in turmoil thereafter with everybody at each other's throats. In contrast, in *Dancing Serpent,* when the whole family is bitten by the Canada bug and is ready to do anything to get the 'Beeja' (visa), the wife refuses to be party to this, especially when a fake marriage has to be performed before the Granth Sahib.

Singh's stories, unlike those of many Punjabi writers, end with a ray of hope and do not have gloomy endings. In most stories, the characters rise above the injustice and stand up for their rights or for the truth. In *The Wheel of Life*, when her husband leaves her for another woman, Santo very bravely and gracefully brings up the children. Initially, she signs a petition against her husband demanding maintenance charges. However, she decides to withdraw her petition and decides to become independent. Her father-in-law, recognizing her bravery, supports her to the hilt against his son.

Author

Jaswinder Singh (1954–) is a Patiala-based literary critic and an eminent scholar. He got the Sahitya Akademi Award 2015 for his maiden novel, *Maat Lok*. The novel was published in 2011 and is set in the 1980s. It deals with moral and cultural questions cropping up due to contemporary socio-economic changes. Singh is better known for literary criticism in Punjabi literature and retired as a professor of Punjabi literature from Punjabi University, Patiala.

Khushwant Singh

- *Land of Five Rivers;* Stories Selected and Translated by Khushwant Singh; Published by Orient paperbacks.

In the introduction to the book, the celebrated author, Khushwant Singh says that he had translated a large number of stories from Hindi, Urdu and Punjabi into English and the same were published in various magazines, largely *The Illustrated Weekly of India* during the nine years that he was its editor. This special compilation, *Land of Five Rivers,* is of stories written by Punjabi authors in any language. And not all stories are about Punjab as some of the authors, like Khwaja Ahmed Abbas, though born in the state, did not live there or could not speak or understand Punjabi.

There are 19 stories by some of the best-known writers from Punjab and, like in every such compilation, it is the compiler's choice as further constrained by what is available. So, it has stories from well-known authors like Manto, Amrita Pritam, Rajinder Singh Bedi, Balwant Gargi, Yashpal, Krishen Chander and K. S. Duggal and from those from the relatively new (at that time) like Ajeet Cour and Usha Mahajan. Khushwant Singh has translated most of the stories while some are by other translators; in the case of Balwant Gargi, Satindra Singh and Gurmukh Singh Jeet, the authors are the translators themselves. Khushwant Singh has also included one of his own stories, *A Punjab Pastorale,* the only story in this book that was originally written in English.

Singh makes a very interesting observation in the introduction. He asks a pertinent question – is there anything distinctive about writers born in the Land of Five Rivers? He then answers it, 'I believe there is. Male writers try to project a macho image of men of their state – macho with a sense of naiveté simplicity. But even within this stereotype they have plenty of variations. However, no such Punjabiness is visible in the stories written by Punjabi women or men writing on feminine themes. They paint on a larger canvas and are, oddly enough, less inhibited in expressing their emotions.'

In a way, this anthology is a microcosm of what my book is. While all other anthologies contain stories written in Punjabi, this anthology celebrates all Punjabi authors who wrote in any language – Punjabi, Hindi, or Urdu. Thus, we have some authors featured here who are otherwise not featured in any other anthology; authors like Khwaja Ahmed Abbas, Upendra Nath Ashk, Yashpal, Krishen Chander and Usha Mahajan. This makes it an extremely significant anthology of stories by authors from Punjab.

Some of the stories in this are by stalwarts and are very well known – *Toba Tek Singh* by Manto (titled as *Exchange of Lunatics* in this anthology), *Lajwanti* by Rajinder Singh Bedi, *The Night of Full Moon* by Kartar Singh Duggal and *Soorma Singh* by Balwant Singh.

The anthology features Krishen Chander's very endearing story, *Tai Eesree*, a word sketch of Aunt Eesree, a kind and benevolent lady. Another very moving story is that by Amrita Pritam, *Stench of Kerosene*, which is the story of Manak who doesn't want his dear wife, Guleri, to make her annual trip to her parents this year. Guleri, safe in her husband's love, fails to see the resentment in her mother-in-law's heart for Guleri's failure to sire a child even seven years after marriage.

A Hundred Mile Race by Balwant Gargi is tale of Boota Singh who can run a 100 miles and is hopeful of going to an international sports meet. *The Night of the Full Moon* by Kartar Singh Duggal is a hair-raising story of the hidden desires of a mother. *Hunger* by Krishen Singh Dhodi is the story of a poor teenager whose sole ambition is to eat a loaf of bread and a pat of butter.

A number of stories are from the era of Partition and talk about the pains of Partition. Apart from the story by Manto, *The Death of Shaikh Burhanuddin* by K. A. Abbas is a touching story of a Sardar who protects his Sikh-hating Muslim neighbour during the Partition. The original story was titled *Sardarji*. Similarly, *Gods on Trial* by Gulzar Singh Sandhu is the story of the conversion of Muslims to Sikhism and being slaughtered despite that.

Khushwant Singh and Satindra Singh try their hand at lighthearted humour. *A Punjab Pastorale* by Khushwant Singh is about a missionary in Punjab and how he tries to 'improve' unclean locals. However, he is frustrated by his failure and the story ends with him finally finding solace in seeing a beautiful and youthful village lass. Similarly, *The Mahabharata Retold* by Satindra Singh is the story of little boys who force their parents to take them to watch the play Mahabharata and the queer happenings therein.

As the *Deccan Herald* in a review states, 'the stories in the books are timeless and most of them have been readers' favourites for many years. All of them depict the life in Punjab. The stories smell the earth of Punjab. The loud life, the big heart, human emotions and relationships are expertly captured. Khushwant has an uncanny eye for the biting edge in short fiction, for the farcical and the sublime.'

Krishan Chander

- *The Full Moon Night* by Krishan Chander; Translated by Jai Ratan; Published by Asia Publishers.

This anthology contains nine of Krishan Chander's best stories and Jai Ratan has ably translated them.

The title story, *The Full Moon Light* is one of his most loved stories in which he takes a break from his focus on the ordinary man and his struggles; the story is based in Kashmir. A trifling misunderstanding leads to a lifetime of separation for two young lovers, and when they meet 48 years later they, along with the readers, realize how human beings often form judgements and jump to conclusions without bothering to clarify. We all regret the loss of their innocent love and the wasted opportunity, although the lovers have been long reconciled to their fate.

Aunt Isari and Her Debt is again one of best known and translated stories and it finds a place in many anthologies. Isari is a very lovable and humane character and she reminds us of many such people in our own Punjabi households. She rose above her grief and was always there to help and love everybody and to give her famous four-anna coin.

Kalu Bhangi is a very powerful account of a typical ordinary man in whose life nothing changes despite the fact that he slogs for hours, days and years, gives himself selflessly to those whom he serves and never complains. The author, while cheekily emphasizing that no story can be written on such ordinary people, goes on to write one about his simple but powerful character. Such people are the unsung heroes but sadly nobody even takes notice of their struggles and everyday battles.

Same ordinary lives are depicted in *The Mahalaxmi Bridge, Dreamer,* and *Dani,* all of which celebrate these brave warriors.

Like Jarnail Singh in his story *Circles and Circles of Pain* mentions, while we remember the bravery of those who die in war, we fail to take into account the bravery of those left behind who have to fight a war every day. They are also the brave ones. Chander highlights and sensitizes us to the plight of such brave warriors who are all around us but we fail to see them or appreciate their struggles.

At the Hotel Firdaus is again a delightful story set in Gulmarg, Kashmir, with its myriad cast of Indian, English, Jewish and Italian populations. Though it talks of the futility of war, the subtext again celebrates the ordinary people and exposes our insensitivity towards them. Thus, as the poor water carrier, Abdullah dies and his son tries to come to terms with his dead body, the hotel manager, unaffected by the tragedy, reminds the son to deliver hot water to the Gora Sahab who is waiting for his bath.

Shehzada is a story of a woman who, because of her plain looks, does not find a suitable match. The person she likes ends up marrying a good-looking and rich lady who turns out to be characterless. Chander depicts society and its obsession with external qualities. The end of the story is dramatic and makes it a very different Chander story, hence showing his versatility.

Author

Krishan Chander was one of the most prolific and influential writers in the Progressive Writers' Movement, along with Saadat Hasan Manto, Ismat Chugtai and Rajinder Singh Bedi. He is most famous for his short stories and novels. Born in Wazirabad, Punjab, and raised in the valleys of Kashmir, he was strongly influenced by natural beauty. He penned over 20 novels, 30 collections of short stories and scores of radio plays in Urdu. His short stories are the stories of Kashmiri villages, as well as those of displaced expatriates and rootless urban men.

He continued a ruthless campaign against the abuse of power, poverty and the suffering of the wretched of the earth, casteism and terror. Chander put things in perspective in the larger framework of society, class and the perennial tensions and conflict between the privileged and the deprived, the pampered and the neglected, the elevated and the marginalized.

He was involved with leftist, socialist and Marxist groups and joined revolutionary Bhagat Singh in his struggle. He was imprisoned for two months because of his political activities. He wanted India to be free and admired the Russian Revolution.

A director in the film industry heard his story, *Annadatta* on the radio and asked him if he would write for a film, *Dharti Ke Lal*. Chander agreed and shifted to Pune and then Bombay. He wrote film scripts for movies such as *Mamta, Do Phool* and *Sarai Ke Baahar*.

Kulwant Singh Virk

- *Selected Writings of Kulwant Singh Virk* **Edited by Gulzar Singh Sandhu; Stories Translated by Sandeep Singh Virk; Published by Publication Bureau, Punjabi University, Patiala.**

While selecting which book of Kulwant Singh Virk to include in this selection, this notable effort by Punjabi University, Patiala, came to light. Not only does it have 28 of his best Punjabi short stories, which have been very ably translated by his son Sandeep Singh Virk, but it also has a good compilation of middles, which he wrote for various papers as well as articles, written for journals in English. Since none of these middles and articles would be available in any other book, the present book offered itself as the best alternative compared to other anthologies, which only have the translated short stories.

The book has been edited by Gulzar Singh Sandhu who was close to the author as well as to other members of Virk's family. The family had preserved the writings of their patriarch and they also worked hand-in-hand with Sandhu to select the stories. The book has an able associate editor in Masha Simrat Kaur and due to all this talent and collective effort, the book is a highly readable one and clearly shows the versatility of Virk as an author.

His short stories in the volume justify Virk's title of one of the best storywriters of Punjabi, especially his stories depicting the Punjab peasantry. Sandhu mentions in the editor's note that Kartar Singh Duggal had labeled Virk as 'son of the soil with a golden pen.' The very first story in this compilation, *Do You Know Me* is a beautiful story of a migrant who has suffered the personal trauma of Partition. With just few sympathetic words from the narrator, the migrant gets the (mistaken) impression that the narrator knew him from before. Just this fact of finally meeting somebody from his past galvanizes the migrant, and he is back on track to 'live' again with zest.

The other stories in this volume like *Tigresses, A Pond of Milk, Blades of Grass* depict Virk's vast repertoire.

Similarly, the articles in this volume that he wrote for journals show his mastery over various subjects. His articles on Grand Trunk Road, Cremation of Maharaja Ranjit Singh, Upper Bari Doab Canal, and The Sirhind Canal are works of meticulous study and research of history. For lovers of literature, there are his very informative and erudite articles on language and literature especially Indian and Punjabi Literature and his observations on some of the famous Punjabi authors. There is a very humorous piece on the travails of being a Punjabi writer.

The last section contains middles that are not based on research or deep study but are 'Vignettes from Everyday Life' – about incidents happening around him and keenly observed by him. From *Anatomy of a Literary Meet* to his meeting with a Russian woman who knew Hindi, they are all very interesting and show the society of that time. The book ends with two very significant articles – *People Who Have Influenced Me* and *What Life Has Taught Me*.

Author

Kulwant Singh Virk (1921–1987) was an eminent short story writer who wrote mostly in Punjabi but also extensively in English. His short stories were translated into several languages including Russian and Japanese. His portrayal of the rural society of central Punjab is gripping in its intellectual, rational and psychological approach.

Born in the village Phularwan (now part of Pakistan), he received his Master's degree in English from Khalsa College, Amritsar. He joined the army in 1942, serving as a Liaison Officer during the partition. Later, he edited the journal *Jagriti* (in Punjabi) and *Advance* (in English).

He also worked as the Director of the Communication Centre at the Agriculture University of Ludhiana. Known for his psychological but realistic portrayal of characters, he selects some common incident of life and then renders it into a story. His *Chah Vela* (Breakfast Time), *Dharti te Akash* (Earth and the Sky), *Tudi di Pand* (A Bundle of Straws), *Ekas ke Ham Barrack* (Children of the Lord), *Dudh da Chapped* (A Pool of Milk), *Golhw* (The Figs) and *Nave Lok* (New People) reveal different facets of peasantry and their changing milieu because of changes or lack of changes in education and economic development. His stories are epiphanies of life.

Honoured as an eminent writer by the Department of Languages in 1959, his collection of short stories, *Nave Lok*, earned him the Sahitya Akademi Award in 1969. He was also recognized by the Literary Forum of Canada in 1984 and acclaimed for his contribution to literature by the Punjab Arts Council in 1981 and by the Punjab Sahitya Academy in 1986.

Manjit Inder Singh

- *Contemporary Punjabi Short Stories: An Anthology*; Edited by Manjit Inder Singh; Published by Sahitya Akademi.

This volume is the result of a three-day workshop of Punjabi–English translation of short stories organized by the Sahitya Akademi in Shimla in 2008. It was a unique workshop where a small group of academics, teachers, critics and translation experts gathered. Translators learnt a lot about the dialectical subtleties of Punjabi stories by writers from Majha, Doaba and Malwa. Manjit Inder Singh was the director of this workshop and is the editor of this book. The stories have been very ably translated by Dr. Tejinder Kaur, Dr. Rajesh Kumar Sharma, Dr. Hina Nandrajog, Dr. Madhuri Chawla, Dr. Swaraj Raj, Hartej Kaur, Madhumeet and Kuljit Singh.

As the title suggests, the majority of the stories are of contemporary Punjabi authors, although there are older texts like that of Kulwant Singh Virk (*The Wild Grass*), K.S. Duggal (*Miracle*) and Sant Singh Sekhon (*Pemi's Children*). Also, this anthology has some authors like Harbhajan Singh, Jaswinder Singh, Talwinder Singh, Sanwal Dhami, Ajmer Sidhu, Jasweer Singh Rana, Kirpal Kazak and Balwinder Singh Grewal whose stories are not readily available in English. There are 18 stories in this collection.

The anthology also features the famous stories *Towers* by Jarnail Singh, *Snow* by Sukhjeet (it is titled as *Blizzard* in one another anthology) and *A Purchased Woman* by Veena Verma.

The story, *Agni Kalash* by Gurbachan Bhullar is about Surinder, a librarian at a college. He is attracted to Saraswati, a teacher at a nearby school. She, however, is a Brahmin and marries a Brahmin boy who incidentally turns out to be Surinder's friend. So, they keep on meeting and finally, one day, in the absence of her husband they both spend the night together. The author makes it look very natural and the easy acceptance of infidelity by both characters makes it disturbing. The story has shades of D. H. Lawrence and Jean Paul Sartre.

Serpent and the City by Sukhwant Kaur Mann is a Partition story where a Sikh, after Partition, is mistaken for a Muslim and killed. It also tackles superstitions relating to snake bites. But the most important point that Mann makes in the story is that the nomenclature that was given to people uprooted during partition ('refugee') was wrong. They had not come from any other country; in fact, they had been uprooted from one part of their own country and sent to another. So, they should be called 'displaced people' and not refugees. It is sincerely hoped that the writers would take note of this very important distinction and help rectify this serious mistake that has crept into the parlance, literature and hence history. This is similar to the distortion in describing the killings of Sikhs after Indira Gandhi's assassination as 'Anti-Sikh Riots,' or 'Sikh Riots,' or 'Hindu–Sikh Riots.' It is felt by many that it was pure massacre or genocide where helpless Sikhs were targeted and killed, and their properties identified and looted. They point out that the dictionary meaning of genocide is 'the deliberate killing of a large group of people, especially those of a particular nation or ethnic group.' Whereas the meaning of riot as per various dictionaries is 'a noisy, violent public disorder caused by a group or crowd of persons, as by a crowd protesting against another group, a government policy, etc., in the streets.' The correct usage of words cannot be overemphasized especially for writers, because whatever they write becomes a part of recorded history. We are therefore very thankful to Sukhwant Kaur for being alive to this sensitivity.

Jinder's story, *Murder* is about father–son relationship; the father has been a very vocal man, does what he likes, and speaks his mind. He is respected in the society for his courage but he could never get along with his wife and so his son hates him. At Bapu's deathbed, the son is surprised and perplexed to see his mother serving Bapu with devotion. He wishes that she would actually kill Bapu so that her sorrows would also end.

Ajmer Sidhu's *Iqbal Hussain Isn't Dead* is also a Partition story and a abducted Muslim woman who marries a Sikh, yet she never comes to terms with the husband or in-laws and is only happy when her son befriends a Muslim Faqir. *The Bridge* by Sanwal Dhami is also related to Partition and is a long story about a maverick and debauch who revels in all kinds of jobs, both legitimate and illegitimate, to make his living.

It is Talwinder Singh who excels with his story *The Woman Within*. Chann and Raavi are a young loving couple; fate snatches away Chann leaving Raavi a young widow at 23, with a small daughter, Chenab. The parents are shattered at the loss of their only child but rise to care for their daughter-in-law and granddaughter. The family, with the support of Raavi's parents, soon settles down to an idyllic life caring and living for each other. Chann's friend Sohan pitches in and tries to fulfill all the duties of a son of the family. But slowly the woman within Raavi rises and is attracted to Sohan. It is a very beautiful story and we wish we had such Punjabi families, replete with care for one another.

Mohan Bhandari

- *Selected Short Stories of Mohan Bhandari*; **Translated by Paramjit Singh Ramana; Published by Punjabi University, Patiala.**

During his 60 years of writing, Mohan Bhandari wrote 70 stories. This book is a collection of 21 short stories translated by Paramjit Singh Ramana.

Bhandari's stories are characterized by their economy of style and efficient, effortless denouements. As Rana Nayar says, 'He is a self-professed miniaturist and his consistent, unsparing efforts at verbal minimalism; tireless almost poetic concern for the language and his unqualified humanism, put him among the front runners of short fiction, not only in Punjabi but other Indian languages as well.' Most of the stories in this collection are just 2000–3000 words long but, despite their brevity, they do not fail to highlight very important issues while giving voice to the marginalized and exploited sections in contemporary Punjabi society. This collection has two long stories too, *The Nose-Ring* and *Tarn Taran*.

The story, *Gangajal* targets caste prejudices in society. An orthodox Brahmin's hypocrisy and bigotry are exposed through a very simple but humorous plot.

Make Me Tagore O Mother…is the tale of a highly talented, low caste, poor young boy who is compelled by his family circumstances to drop out of school. His life is difficult and a few hours of his life reveal the tragedy. He loves life, poetry and music. Vital social issues are tackled, and the story is told in a highly readable and enjoyable manner.

In *Tarn Taran*, amongst other issues, the issue of militancy in Punjab is tackled. It also briefly touches on the killings of Sikhs at Kanpur in 1984. *Footprints of a Man* has an interesting twist in the tale at the end, while in *Somnath Temple*, a very understanding father tackles the news of the love affair of his daughter skillfully and humanely.

Nose-ring has a very wide canvas, with the characters based in places like Bombay, Rishikesh, Saharanpur and Malerkotla. It is a story of degenerate Nawabs, prostitutes, film producers and their henchmen. Thus, a very wide range of issues is tackled, and they reveal the author's felicity in writing on all of them with the same sensitivity. *Grudge* is another remarkable story in which some very stark truths of our families and societies are revealed.

Middle-class shallowness and selfishness are portrayed clearly in the story, *The Birth of a Thief*. The narrator vividly captures the scene of humiliation of an innocent, starving and helpless man. He makes fun of the snobbery of the people who take pride in their Indian culture but lack sympathy for the distressed. Even in his lightly told humorous tales, Bhandari manages to convey his genuine pain at the transformation taking place around him that causes deep anguish and pain to the ordinary people.

Tilchauli is a character portrait of a petty street hawker who succeeds in becoming one of the richest businessmen in the area. One theme of the story is that money does not bring peace or joy to anyone. The story is effectively woven around the ritual feeding of the ants as a religious act for bringing better luck. There is a comic twist and a moral dimension to the story.

One impressive quality of Bhandari's stories is his distinctive use of language. He uses simple short sentences with folk similes, refrains and fragments of popular songs and rustic comparisons that make for joyous reading. There is a heartfelt affection for the Punjabi landscape and cultural heritage in Bhandari's work.

The translator, Professor Paramjeet Singh Ramana, has done a remarkable job in translating Mohan Bhandari's stories in simple, readable English with remarkable lucidity of expression while remaining close to the original text as far as meaning and significance are concerned.

Author

Mohan Bhandari is a Punjabi writer who was born in 1937 in the Banbhaura village of Sangrur district, Punjab. He became a government employee and passed M.A in Punjabi and Bachelor of Law, both privately. He was a self-made man and had an intimate knowledge of his society. Problems of life in a fast-growing city like Chandigarh, where he lived for 52 years, provide the major thematic concerns, characters, backgrounds and locations to his stories. However, villages also provide the background to some of his best stories. There is a lingering nostalgia in his stories for the sense of fraternity, kinship and the close-knit social structures of rural India. In his writing, he has caught the entire flavour of an age. Some of his best stories explore a small section of an individual's life, like a vital aspect or a single event, but they all become symbolic of the larger social structures.

Deeply influenced by Russian writers like Tolstoy, Gorky, Dostoevsky, and Chekhov and Urdu writers like Manto, Bhandari is credited with 15 books of stories, of which *Til-Chouli, Kaathi di Latt, Gora Basha* and *Moon di Akh* are extremely popular. He received the Sahitya Akademi Award in 1997 for his collection of short stories, *Moon Di Akh*. He has also edited and published introductions, biographical sketches and articles on many well-known writers like *Gaatha Gargi Di* on Balwant Gargi, *Manto De Rang* on Saadat Hasan Manto, *Shiv Kumar: Birha Da Sultan* on Shiv Batalvi and *Eh Ajab Bande,* a collection of pen portraits of 22 well-known Punjabi Litterateurs.

Read on

- Another collection of Mohan Bhandari's Punjabi short stories has been translated by Rana Nayar as *The Eye of a Doe and Other Stories*; Published by Sahitya Akademi.

Mohinder Singh Sarna

- *Savage Harvest: Stories of Partition* by Mohinder Singh Sarna; Translated by Navtej Sarna, Rupa, India 2013.

The present choice of stories is only a small representation of his impressively varied and large oeuvre. These are his most powerful, most significant and well-known short stories on Partition. Only two of the stories relate to the Sikh genocide of 1984. Despite the brutality in each story, there is always a humanitarian perspective present. Fittingly, the book is dedicated to 'the defenders of humanity,' the small numbers of seemingly insignificant men and women who refused to be a part of this madness and did their bit to restore some sort of semblance of humanity by giving some sort of burial to the dead. It needs to be remembered that dead bodies were found rotting away in fields and dumped all over the place.

Thus, we see characters like Dina in *Savage Harvest* who is a blacksmith. The killers, including his son, use axes made by him. He is revolted by his work and tries to run away in a desperate attempt to save people known to him. Or Hussain in *A Defender of Humanity*, who, being a truck driver, manages to drive Hindus and Sikhs across the border while risking his life. There is Abnash, who, despite her husband and children being stuck in Pakistan, refuses to occupy any looted property in Delhi and saves two Muslim girls from the mob and takes them to the refugee camp.

She and I is a favourite story in which the protagonist working at the post office gets a lady assistant who has suffered untold miseries in Pakistan and has finally been rescued after two years. After getting to know her hellish experiences and sufferings, the protagonist, in a supreme act of bravery, compassion and humanity, decides to marry her. Although there are many heroes and heroines in other stories who exhibit similar acts of compassion, who escort other people to safety, who hide virtual strangers in their homes, who refuse to kill or loot, I believe it takes a very brave character to personally decide to accept such a woman when many families had refused to accept back their daughters and daughters-in-law after they were rescued from across the border.

The underlying social message in Sarna's stories is that hate and violence cannot have a place in society and those who propogate hate and violence have no religion. Basic human values must be the guiding spirit in any society.

Author

Mohinder Singh Sarna (1923–2001) was born in Rawalpindi. He joined the Indian Audits and Accounts Service after his B.A. (Hons.) and retired as Accountant General in 1981. He started writing at the age of 20, and his first collection of short stories *Pather de Admi* (Men of Stone) was published in 1949. He wrote more than 225 short stories, which have appeared in 11 books of short stories. He also penned four novels and four epics in verse dealing with the lives of Sikh Gurus and heroes, besides a literary autobiography.

Several of his books have been made textbooks. The innumerable awards and honours he received in his lifetime include Giani Gurmukh Singh Mussafir Kavita Puraskar, Bhai Santokh Singh Kavita Puraskar, Nanak Singh Fiction Award, Delhi Sahitya Kala Parishad Award, Shiromani Punjabi Sahitkar Award, Waris Shah Samman, 'Zenne Jadid' Award and Bawa Balwant Trust award. His book, *Navain Yug de Waris* won the Sahitya Akademi Award in 1990. This is a collection of short stories that cover a whole historical epoch right from the days of Partition in 1947 up to 1990.

However, it is his Partition stories that stand out. The Partition of India witnessed the largest mass migration in human history – around 14 million Hindus, Sikhs and Muslims were displaced and around 6 lakh people were killed (though the estimates vary from 2 Lakhs to 20 Lakhs) in the retributive genocide between the religions.

Sarna was himself affected by the riots and the displacement caused by Partition. He was witness to the untold brutality and barbarism of that era, the riots, rape, pillage and killings. He lost his newly wedded sister and was stuck in Rawalpindi for a while. He was finally able to escape to India but had to leave behind everything, including his father and brother who could come to India only much later. While looking for them, he observed that the killing and brutality, the misery of refugees and the senseless vengeful violence was identical on both sides of the border. As the translator mentions in his introduction, it was something of a miracle that Sarna managed to keep his hope in humanity intact in his treatment of Partition in his writings. Some of the pain and horror was written away in his writings, while the rest resulted in his nervous breakdown 15 years later.

NarinderJit Kaur

- *Voices in the Back Courtyard: Punjabi Short Stories*; Translated by NarinderJit Kaur; Published by Rupa & Co.

This book is an intriguing compilation of 15 stories by eminent Punjabi women writers, writing about their experiences in Punjabi society. The stories are as varied as their authors are – the blurb reads, 'Right from Amrita Pritam of the 50s to Veena Verma of the 21st century, this book traces a sinuous path of struggle, emotional turmoil, unfinished dreams and social rejection, which becomes a source of strength for these writers.'

Despite the varied subjects the stories cover, most of them are extremely dark or have bleak endings. Perhaps this darkness is the true barometer of the state of women in Punjab. A lot has been written about the skewed sex ratio in Punjab and of the preference for a boy child, despite the importance and freedom that is given to women in Sikhism. These stories lend some weight to that sad aspect of life in Punjab. Of course, in the background of these tales, one sees unmistakable depictions of the vigour and celebration of life that characterizes social life in Punjab.

The stories cover universal issues like old age and its problems (*Bhubbal di Aag* by Bachint Kaur), the mother–son relationship (*Putra Eion Nahi Bhul Jayida* by Balwinder Kaur Brar), bulldozing a colony and the uprooting of innocent and helpless people (*Jeeonjoge* by Sukhwant Kaur Mann) and even incest in *Ikkurhee Chup Si* by N. Kaur.

In fact, only the stories of the three of the greatest Punjabi authors don't have such gloomy and sad endings. The story by Amrita Pritam (*Shah Di Kanjari*) takes us back to pre-Partition Lahore and its famous Heera Mandi and the colourful courtesans. Dalip Kaur Tiwana's *Rub te Ruttan* is about the seasons and how we have stopped enjoying them. In the story, the seasons rush to God and request Him to take them back as nobody at Earth seems to need them. The translator has very ably captured the various sights and sounds of the monsoon season depicted so vividly by the author in the story. It is a delightful read. Similarly, Ajeet Cour's famous satirical story *Intezar* is about greed and the manipulation of a child's dead body for monetary gains. Even the parents of the dead child join in this money making exercise and continue to hold on to the body even as it starts stinking and rotting.

However, the story that stands out is Veena Verma's *Muull Di Teeveen* or *The Purchased Women*. The story is based in rural Punjab and depicts a quintessentially Punjabi lifestyle. It is the story of a Sikh truck driver who is tall and sturdy, enjoys his drinks and women, and is feared by his nosy villagers. But, at heart, he is still a true Punjabi who cowers on seeing his father, cannot disobey him, or even raise his voice when his father is around. He is very sensitive and is moved by the love and devotion of a Bengali woman who he had purchased on his trip to eastern India. Though he had bought her for his enjoyment, he finally ends up marrying her.

Nirupama Dutt

- *Stories of the Soil*; **Edited and Translated by Nirupama Dutt; Published by Penguin 2010.**

This anthology is exceedingly comprehensive as it celebrates a century of the Punjabi short story. It has 41 stories by 39 authors. One cannot get a better representative anthology of Punjabi authors. And then, it tries to include authors from all periods. It has eight categories and these cover Partition stories, stories by women authors, Dalit literature, Diaspora authors, and even has a separate section on authors from across the border. Other anthologies that have been included by me have either stories by one author or are on specific subjects like Partition stories or are stories only by diasporic authors.

The book thus opens up a whole new window to this genre. Dutt has put together an interesting amalgam of stories that take us on a guided tour of both the Punjabi story and the socio-economic evolution of the community. She has done a stellar service to Punjabi literature and to non-Punjabi readers by bringing 41 Punjabi stories into focus. Dutt's selection includes the parable-like stories of Nanak Singh and Sant Singh Sekhon as well as the vociferous voices of Amrita Pritam and Balwant Gargi. Post-Partition Pakistani writers, affording a peep into composite Punjabi culture take up another section. We have glimpses of the fight for freedom, the independence, the Partition, the riots. Gloriously presented is Punjab, the land of five rivers, its forefathers, legends and stories.

Each story is delightfully penned and brilliantly translated. Dutt's love of Punjabi and her clear grasp of the social and literary milieu make for easy reading.

There are some stories which are ever famous and often a must in any anthology, for example, *Pemi's Little Ones*, *Bhua* (titled here as Spilt Milk), *The Shah's Harlot, Raaslila, Grass, A Matter of Faith, Jasbir, Then and Now* and *God and Seasons*.

K. S. Duggal's *Majha Is Still Alive* has shades of Chekov. The story is set in New Delhi, the capital of a newly independent country, which, as it moves towards modernization, sheds many of its values. But Majha, the tongawala, will not budge from what is sacred to him even though he and his horse face hunger.

Race by Balwant Gargi is a tragi-comic tale of a village lad who is a good runner and who goes for help to the Patiala Ruler.

Mirror by Gurdev Singh Rupana is the sequel to his earlier famous Partition story *Hawa* and, as Dutt mentions in the introduction, 'it is a sort of confession of the facts concealed in the previous narrative.' *Junction* by Gulzar Mohammad Goria is on the Sikh Genocide of November 1984, and he is one of the rare storywriter writing on this subject out of the more than 100 Punjabi-writing authors whose work is featured in my book. *The House with a Pipal Tree* by S. Tarsem is a surprising story about men permitting their wives to be polygamous for child bearing.

However, it is the stories by the Dalit voices and by the Pakistani authors that are refreshingly unique, as we do not find many of them in other anthologies. The Dalit stories talk of low-caste men going to town and taking an upper caste name – the caste dynamics that are ever present. Prem Gorkhi's story is about gender discrimination while Mohan Lal Philauria talks of discrimination faced by upper-caste people in England.

Azra Wakar's simple and beautiful story, *Ganga Ram* bemoans the loss of the composite culture of Punjab. *Ideal Town* by Iliyas Ghumman and *Paying Guest* by Mohammad Mansha Yaad are realistic portrayals of Pakistani society. A wonderful narrative by Zubair Ahmed in *Doors and Windows on a Rainy Day* takes us into the bylanes of Lahore where the author grew up, giving us a literal peep in each house.

But it is the story of Ahmed Salim, *Proclaimed Offender* that stands out. Originally titled *Ishtiaria*, it is an ode to the culture of Punjab represented by the Sufi poet Waris Shah. The author writes, 'There are posters in town of the proclaimed offender and he is none other than Waris Shah and his sin is that he was born in united Punjab. Punjab has been partitioned but the name of Waris Shah has not yet been partitioned. As long as he is not partitioned he will be sent to gallows again and again.'

Veena Verma's *Shadows* is a very delightful yet poignant story about two women looking forward to meeting their husband.

Overall, given its wide variety and an easy-to-read translation, this collection is a substantial read and a good way to get acquainted with the lesser-known aspects of Punjabi fiction.

Prem Prakash

- *The Shoulder Bag and Other stories* by Prem Parkash; Translated by Rita Choudhary; Published by Guru Nanak Dev University (GNDU), Amritsar.

GNDU, like Punjabi University, Patiala, has been doing its bit in promoting English translations of major Punjabi literary texts. This collection has 12 of Prem Prakash's quintessential Punjabi stories structured around themes of love and relationships, gender and caste, and individual and collective spaces. Prakash tells the stories simply, honestly, and naturally, through prose that is lucid, flowing and flexible. The translator, Rita Choudhary, who is a teacher of English Literature, has done a wonderful job in translating the finest pieces of Prakash's oeuvre, remaining true to the spirit of the original work. An added advantage of the book is the interview between the translator and the author; it is very biographical and one gets to learn about Prakash's early life, his influences and his works, all of which is very insightful.

The author employs various different narrative styles in his short stories. Some of them are epistolary like *Ghar* in which Rita Bhullar, the female protagonist, narrates her entire life in a letter to her friend Sushma. Similarly, in *Arjun, Let the Chariot Roll*, Gurdev Chand returns to his village in Punjab to look after his chacha (uncle) who is breathing his last. Through a letter to his English wife Catherine, he recounts the story of his village and his family.

The title story, *Shoulder Bag*, goes even further. Shoulder Bag 1 is a story of a writer who writes about his unsuccessful affair with a married woman who eventually goes away with his friend, as he is ambivalent towards her. Shoulder Bag 2 is in the form of a letter in which that woman, after reading Shoulder Bag 1, reacts to the allegations and insinuations made against her and tries to set the record straight. It is a refreshing style and makes the story extremely interesting.

The Deadline is a bold story, but its audacity can be appreciated only when, as the translator puts it, 'the deor-bharjai relationship [is] foregrounded in its cultural context for a proper understanding of the translated story.' A dying young bachelor and his bhabhi, who is a mother and a friend to him, are jettisoned into a vortex when the young man is diagnosed with cancer. Against the backdrop of the deadline of six months fixed by the doctor, the family's torturous journey to the end, and the dying man's unfilled dreams and desires, the relationship transforms so drastically that the deor becomes a son, a brother and a lover to his bharjai. By overturning the traditional relationship, Prakash infuses an unmatched intensity and poignancy into the tragic tale.

In *Machhi,* the writer adopts yet another style. The story is told through four soliloquies by four principal characters. It also deals with the naxalite problem. *He is Not Jasbir* (Eh oh Jasbir Nahin) is a story about the militant phase in Punjab and is also featured in another anthology mentioned in this book.

Author

Prem Prakash (1932–) is one of the finest short story writers in Punjabi and edits a Punjabi Literary magazine called *Lakeer,* which he started with Surjit Hans, since 1971. Prakash has won many awards, including the Sahitya Akademi Award 1992, which was given for his book *Kujh Ankeha Vi*. His short story collections include *Kach-Kade*, *Namazee*, *Muktee*, *Shwetambar ne Kiha Si*, *Rangmanch te Bhikshoo* and *Sunde Khleefa*. Some of his stories have been adapted for films – *Bangla, Mada Banda, Docter Shakuntala, Goee* and *Nirvana* and has written four volumes of autobiographies – *Bande andar Bande*, *Aatm Maia*, *Meri Urdu Akhbar Naweesi* and *Dekh Bande de Bekh*. He has also written a novel *Dastavez* (The Document), which is on the Maoist–Naxalite movement in East Punjab. A postgraduate in Urdu from Panjab University, he has worked as a farmer, teacher and then as a subeditor with two local dailies.

Raghubir Dhand

- *Melting Moments* by Raghbir Dhand; Translated by Rana Nayar; Published by Unistar Books Pvt. Ltd.

Rana Nayar, in his brilliant Introduction, places the work of Dhand in the context of other diasporic writings and finds that Dhand was a pioneer of sorts among the first generation of Punjabi immigrant writers. Dhand always sought to negotiate the complex, ghettoized, feudal Punjabi identity through the mish-mash of racism, politics of exclusion, identity, language and culture. His stories deal exclusively with the problems of a dual identity.

The author vividly explores the world of the migrant Asian working classes and these stories capture the moment accurately. They unravel the intimate world of the people there as well as their joys, sorrows and concerns. The author weaves fiction around other communities too – the racism faced by migrants from Bangladesh, Pakistan, Africa and even Ireland.

Some of the stories are set on Indian soil but Dhand is at his best when crafting tales of the life and experiences in the Promised Land. His fictional world offers a great range in terms of variety of themes, ideas, techniques and craft, with economy of language, singleness of effect, unity of motives, action and impression.

The present book begins with *Bondage*, which is a multilayered narrative, structured around the principle of inverted racism and social hierarchy. The Indian owners of the store exploit poor and simple Peter, a white young man, who slogs for them. *Dustbin* is a famous story that is included in other anthologies too.

Leaves of Acacia deals with the neglect of parents by children in the United Kingdom and the post-Emergency phase of terrorism in Punjab. Isolated by their children and disillusioned with the materialistic culture of the West, two old friends, who have already retired, decide to return to India for good. Much to their discomfiture, they discover how their homeland is no longer the safe haven they had left behind but has now become strife-torn and eminently unlivable. Their final decision, which brings the story to its climax, leaves a bitter taste in the mouth, somewhat akin to chewing the poisonous 'leaves of acacia.'

In *Ode to Donkeys*, the author casts a nostalgic look at his land, recounting with enthusiasm his childhood obsession with donkeys. He desires to have a glimpse of his obsession. Ultimately, the much-desired encounter does take place but in an unexpected manner. The story leaves a characteristic sting-in-the-tail effect, making it an enormously comic experience.

Going beyond the narrow confines of Punjabi identity, *No Exit* focuses upon the problem of 'double identity' in relation to a Jamaican youth who shuttles relentlessly between and across cultures, unable to find his moorings or an anchor. In *Faultlines*, the futility of organized religions is brought out and is placed against the backdrop of Partition. In *Dying Embers*, the author, in a tongue-in-cheek manner, focuses on the tribe of pretentious authors. *Tapeworm* is a brutal assessment of some of the Indians who, while fighting racism in England, remain antagonistic to Muslims. *The Canker* is a very sensitive portrayal of Jeeti who, though living in England, is very much affected by the assault on the Golden Temple.

Dhand is scathing in his criticism of many Indians too. In *Bondage*, for instance, the character says, 'Real greatness of Indians is that they hate everything Indian.' In *No Matching Horoscopes*, when racially discriminated, one Indian asks another to give witness, the later refuses saying, 'The day I came to England I left my pride and dignity behind at the Palam airport. When we return, we'll collect it.'

Author

Dr. Raghbir Dhand (1934–1990) was born in District Sangrur (Punjab). He did his MA in History from Panjab University

Chandigarh before migrating to England in the early 1960s. Soon after obtaining his degree as a graduate in teaching from Leeds University, he started teaching at a local school. Often looked upon as a pioneer among the progressive writers of the Punjabi diaspora in England, he is believed to have inspired a whole generation of writers with his ideas as well as his craftsmanship.

During his relatively short career as a writer, he published around five collections of short stories namely *Boli Dharti* (Thus Spoke the Earth), *Us Paar* (Across the Shores), *Kaya Kalap* (The Metamorphosis), *Kursi* (The Chair) and *Shaan-e-Punjab* (The Pride of Punjab). In 1975, his collection *Us Paar* was given the first prize by the Department of Languages, Punjab, while in 1987, a few years before his pre-mature death, International Punjabi Sahit Sabha, Canada, bestowed the Manjit Memorial award on him. He was awarded a Doctorate by the Government of Cambodia in recognition of his work on Governance in Cambodia.

Rajendra Awasthy

- *Selected Punjabi Short Stories*; **Edited by Rajendra Awasthy; Published by Fusion Books.**

Fusion Books has published a series of anthologies of English translations of modern short stories written in the different Indian languages – a commendable work indeed.

The present anthology has stories from Punjab which are earthy, touching on themes like love, hatred, passion, reconciliation, rural life, suffering and, most important of all, the triumph of the human spirit.

Awasthy has selected 17 stories by different writers. He has fortunately not chosen the representative stories of the famous authors except Sujan Singh's *Love Play*, which is included in some anthologies as *Rass-Leela*, Santokh Singh Dhir's *Common Wall* and Kulwant Singh Virk's *Blades of Grass*. We are thus introduced to the lesser-known works of authors like Buta Singh and Mohan Singh Diwana.

The story, *The Guard of Many Loves* by Gurbaksh Singh Preetlari is very aptly about Preet (or love). Love gives courage to the young maiden Rukni to take on the most powerful in the village and, having lost her beloved, she vows to help all the lovers in her village. In time, the village comes to worship her as the guardian of lovers.

Dasaundha Singh by Devendra Satyarthi is one colourful Sikh bus driver who traverses over the entire country with his whims, his love for the bizarre and his colourful graphic language. The story is about one such journey where the perils of travel, the witty dialogues with his passengers, and even attempts to flirt with one of them, are all beautifully depicted. This is an utterly fascinating and unique story.

Buta Singh's *The Old Woman* is about Mai Sadhran who has turned grey from picking cinders from the railway yard. When young, she was a victim to firemen, drivers and watchmen. Rejected in her old age, she is keen on protecting her daughter-in-law, who is also widowed, from those lovers of flesh. But her stark poverty defeats her, and we have a tragic story.

Blades of Grass, the all-time-favourite story on Partition by Kulwant Singh Virk, is about the heroine who, despite her hardships and loss, still looks to pick up the threads of life. She is a true symbol of the will to survive and is a metaphor for all those who were uprooted. The writer compares these human beings to blades of grass who are uprooted root and blade but still, in few days, 'The earth breaks forth invisibly, irresistibly and the little blades of grass peep through again.'

Mohinder Singh Sarna's *The Shirt* is a voyage in nostalgia when Babu Lok Nath remembers his pre-Partition carefree days of youth and bachelourhood. In contrast, his post-Partition life is humdrum and full of family worries. He struggles to grasp the little pleasures of life, such as a freshly laundered shirt, but these too prove elusive.

The three prima donnas of Punjabi Literature again deliver very poignant woman-centered stories. *The Unfortunate One* by Amrita Pritam is about a young woman, ironically named Karmavalli (fortunate one), who has to leave her husband soon after marriage as he has another woman in his life. The author's setting of this story is very realistic as she finds this woman and gets to know her story in a dhaba while she is travelling. *A Season to Die* by Dalip Kaur Tiwana is on similar lines. Rachna, who is engaged to Arvind, decides to pay him a surprise visit, only to find her fiancé with another woman in his house. *The Coconut* by Ajeet Cour is about Juhi who has been used by many men and compares herself to a coconut that has been discarded after people have drunk out of it.

The volume includes stories such as *A Room 10 × 8* by K. S. Duggal, a story about how fate has its own way of getting back to you; *Metamorphosis* by Raghubir Dhand which is set during Emergency and shows how people's idealism falls down when it comes to their own creature comforts; *A Martyr's Body Never Tells a Lie* by Jaswant Singh Kanwal, which is a hard-hitting story of the lawlessness that prevailed during the militant phase in Punjab and is actually a chapter from his famous novel, *The Dawn of the Blood*.

Rajinder Singh Bedi

- *Rajinder Singh Bedi: Selected Short Stories;* **Selected and Edited by Gopi Chand Narang; Translated from Urdu by Jai Ratan; Published by Sahitya Akademi.**

Gopi Chand Narang, an eminent scholar, has compiled this anthology of 18 stories, which runs through the gamut of Bedi's writings and displays various phases of his development. Like with the anthology of Balwant Singh, the Sahitya Akademi has done a creditable job in getting this anthology prepared. Professor Narang has once again written a very erudite introduction to the book dealing with Bedi's art, style and his place in Urdu literature. He also compares Bedi's works to the three distinct stalwarts of Urdu literature – Premchand, Manto and Krishan Chander. The introduction gives valuable insights to the mythological influences in Bedi's work, which would otherwise escape a lay reader's attention.

In fact, the book also includes an essay written by Bedi himself – *A Note on the Creative Process and the Art of Short Story* that further highlights his craft and his observations on the growth of Urdu literature, especially the short story. He makes a very pertinent observation that, 'By laying undue emphasis on the so-called powerful expression in the short story we have done incalculable harm not only to the short story but to their writers too.' He adds, 'great stress was laid on diction […] and that the Urdu language has not developed to the extent as to cope with the demands made by short story on it; it has failed to carry this sophisticated art form in its stride.'

The themes of the stories are universal, and most of the stories are based in Mumbai as Bedi lived in Mumbai for most of his years. Further, some stories have autobiographical associations too, like

Garam Coat (The Woolen Coat) in which the poor protagonist constantly postpones buying a coat for himself to replace his old, tattered one. He does this in order to save money for his family. Or *Only a Cigarette,* a story of an estranged couple – because of the man's losses, his family has a very poor opinion of him, especially his son who thinks his father has no business acumen. The father, in turn, considers his son to be blindly in love with filthy lucre and nothing else. The brilliantly layered short story unravels relationships on the cusp of capitalism.

Another story is *Lajwanti* in which Bedi creates the immortal character of Lajwanti, who is subjected to the animal passions of perfectly 'normal' men motivated by the religious fanaticism or sexual desire unleashed by the communal horrors of Partition in 1947. But Lajwanti refuses to submit to her fate as the abducted wife now forced to live across the border in Pakistan. She wants to be rehabilitated and accepted as a loving wife when she is repatriated and expects her husband to listen to her tale of woe and resilience.

Another famous story is *Grahan* or *Eclipse*. Running parallel to the lunar eclipse is the story of Holi, a poor helpless woman at the mercy of her husband and his family. But tyranny of society is more diabolical than that of the husband. While escaping from her in-laws, she falls into the clutches of Ram who takes her home and forcibly tries to outrage her modesty. Her family was 'Rahu' and the other man was 'Ketu.' She is tarnished by one eclipse and ravished by another.

Lambi Ladki (Too Tall for Marriage) is a very delightful story of a granddaughter and her grandmother and so much more that happens in Punjabi families when girls start growing too tall, restricting their choice to get eligible grooms. *Diwala* (Bankruptcy) is the story of a Bhabhi and her nanad's (husband's sister) sexual mores in which Bedi has raised some fundamental questions about the institution of marriage. Set in a Marwari family where the men are busy buying linseed crop, the author's versatility comes to fore as it does in the next story *Jogia* which is set in Kalbadevi, Mumbai, and the characters attend JJ School of Art but cannot marry due to caste and class distinctions. In *Maithun*, Bedi weaves, through mythological characters, a story of a young helpless woman artist who is exploited by the crafty handicraft storeowner. *Intermittent Fever* is set in Calcutta where a famous theatre artist tries to run away from his home because his too pious wife has converted that home to a temple.

Speak up is a wonderful and complex story of a young man who is accused of kerosene theft. His fiancé has to sell herself to the policemen to get his bail. What unfolds next is a complex saga and a very beautifully crafted but disturbing story.

However, the story that excels is *Apney Dukh Mujhe De Do* (Give Me Your Sorrows). Replete with mythological connotations, the story is an example of selfless love and sacrifice where a woman gives herself fully to look after her husband's family. Bedi is at pains to impress upon the reader that woman drank the poison of life to make the ambrosia of life available to man. She suffers to bring joy in her husband's life. Bedi draws a composite image of a woman, scintillating with love, sacrifice, respect and purity – all drawn from our mythological traditions.

And the icing on the cake is a personal and candid account of his own life in the article titled *In Front of the Mirror* where the author, in his characteristic style, lays open his life bare for the readers. In all, this is a highly readable book.

Ranjit Singh

- *The Crossroads: Short Stories in Punjabi*; **Translated by Ranjit Singh; Published by Punjabi Academy, Delhi.**

This book is prefaced by an introductory note by The Punjabi Academy, which, until the publication of this book, was doing a lot of pioneering work in the publication of academic as well as creative writing of Punjabi writers. It was also translating famous English and other language works into Punjabi. This book, however, marks the Academy's first attempt to publish an English translation of Punjabi writing.

The translator, Professor Ranjit Singh has done a wonderful job as none of the stories in *The Crossroads* lose any of their typical Punjabi flavour.

The present collection has 15 stories and both Ranjit Singh and Gurbachan Singh Bhullar, who helped select the stories, deserve praise for including some upcoming authors along with the already well-established ones. Among the established authors are Raghubir Dhand, Gurbachan Singh Bhullar, Ram Sarup Ankhi, Mohan Bhandari, Baldev Singh and Sadhu Binning. With them, there are some truly beautiful stories from authors like Sukhwant Kaur Mann, Jasbir Singh Bhullar, Afsal Tausif, Iqbal Deep, Makhan Mann, Jinder, Jagroop Singh Datevas and Gurdev Singh Rupana. The inclusion of these authors is extremely welcome, because – although they have published a vast amount of work in Punjabi – not much has been translated into English. Thus, through this translation, the reader is introduced to their literary prowess and their extraordinary talent for story-telling.

There is one story by Ranjit Singh himself called *The White Rose*. It is a heart-warming story of a lady whose son is an army officer in Delhi and who requests her to come to Delhi from Ludhiana for his 25th birthday. On her way there, the lady befriends her taxi driver and soon finds out that he, too, was born on the same day in the same hospital at Ludhiana as her son. Both develop a bond and she tells him that, on his birthday, Pandit Nehru happened to be in Ludhiana. On a whim, he decided to visit that hospital and give a white rose each to all new mothers. The lady, an admirer of Panditji, was thrilled and still retained the flower in her diary. The startled Sikh taxi driver understands then why his mother too had been keeping an old flower in her gutka all these years.

The Nectar by Ram Sarup Ankhi is about the protagonist's visit to Pakistan that ends in a tearful reunion with his erstwhile neighbour from Kala, Jhelum, from where he was uprooted and fled to India during the Partition of India and Pakistan. *Two Alone* by G S Bhullar is a story about the neglect of old parents, while *A World Apart* by Sadhu Binning deals with an old man trying to live life as per his convictions. *Auntie was Right* (Jagroop Singh) and *So Near So Far* (Baldev Singh) are about the frustrations of married couples who do not get enough time and space in their small houses and about how the women bear the brunt of it. Jinder, in *Two Minutes More*, exhorts empathy as he writes about how we exploit our workers and try to squeeze the maximum from them without realizing that they too have houses and families to go back to.

Iqbal Deep's *The Rhythm And The Melody* is a beautifully tragic story about a father and a son who bond over a shared love of music. Raghubir Dhand writes about a similar bond and passion for music in *The Chair* but also uses his story to comment on the neglect of folk art while urban art seems to flourish. *Somnath Temple* by Mohan Bhandari is about how a father comes to terms with his daughter's love affair after a great deal of understanding and introspection. *Bequeathment* by Makhan Mann tackles the issue of trickery that is used in land deals in rural Punjab and its fallouts.

It is a very readable collection with a very wide variety of stories. The only flaw is that the book does not provide any biographical details about the contributing authors.

Ranjit Singh

- *Square One: Punjabi Short Stories*; **Translated by Ranjit Singh; Published by Punjabi Academy, Delhi.**

This is the second anthology translated by Ranjit Singh and it comes 12 years after the first one. Once again, it has the usual suspects – Gurbaksh Singh, Nanak Singh, Ram Sarup Ankhi, Sant Singh Sekhon, Sujan Singh, Gurmukh Singh Musafir, Devendra Satyarthi, Santokh Singh Dheer as well as those whose works are not readily available in English – S Saqi, Chandan Negi, Sukhjit, Nachhatar, Pritam Sandhu, Surinder Singh Oberai, Ranjit Singh Bhinder, Navtej Puadhi, Bachint Kaur, Gul Chauhan, Rajinder Kaur and Karanjit Singh.

All the stories chosen are masterpieces in their own right, covering a myriad of themes and subjects. Some of them are marital infidelity (*The Prayer Room* by Ranjit Singh Bhinder), corruption and double standards by the police (*The Game of Cards* by Nanak Singh), dealing with change as the old order becomes irrelevant (*The Broken Idol* by Devender Satyarthi), a young woman's plight after her husband joins the army (*Come Rain Come Sunshine* by Sant Singh Sekhon) and disputes between brothers about repairing a common wall (*The Common Wall* by Santokh Singh Dheer).

Rajinder Kaur, in *Old People's Home*, writes about the neglect of a mother when none of her three children are able to look after her. *Tattoo Marks* by Chandan Negi is a delightful story about a Pathan lady who had dared to elope with and marry a Hindu before Partition and in her old age visits Pakistan to 'touch the dust of my ancestral land, to breathe in the air of this country once again.' *Brothers by Choice* by Karanjit Singh is about how children in school break down caste and religious barriers and share food among each other. Ram Swarup Ankhi in *A Screwed Up Discussion* adopts a different style by way of dialogue between friends to whom he is trying to tell the story.

The book begins with the famous story *Bhabhi Maina* by Gurbakash Singh. The story is about a young Jain widow who develops a bond with a child living opposite her house. Because she is barred from having any worldly attachments, she finally renounces the world and becomes a Jain priestess, but her zest for life results in a tragic end.

S Saqi paints an excellent and insightful portrait of a man, Bishen in *Bishen Weeps Again*. It is about an elderly man, Bishen who comes to the community centre and regales the youngsters with his real-life stories. He also acts a counsellor of sorts, people share their joys and sorrows with him, and he helps mend many a relationship. *Romance of Portrait* by Surinder Singh Oberai is about a young man who loves painting but is pressurised to join the family's tobacco business and who finally leaves the house in search of his true vocation.

The Poachers by Ranjit Singh (the translator) is the only story with some humour, which is surprising. Punjabis have a great zest for life and an ability to enjoy despite terrible hardships, yet their literature is largely devoid of satire and humour. The stories are generally very bleak and gloomy. Thus, Ranjit Singh's story is a welcome break. Gul Chauhan in *Raag Maru Bihag* (Sombre Desert Tunes) also tries his hand at humour by writing about the travails of people seeking rented property and about the tyranny of landlords. He does not fully succeed, and the story is good only in snatches.

The next three stories deal with vastly different but very relevant issues. The story by Bachint Kaur (*The Dead End*) focuses on the issue of pedophilia when a poor eight-year-old girl is lured by her neighbour. *The Blizzard* by Sukhjit touches lightly on the delicate subject of incest when a brother–sister duo gets stranded on a cold wintery night in a car. In *The Broken Reed* by Nachhatar, a widowed woman tries to balance her relationship with her teenaged son and with an office colleague who provides a lot of help, care and support to her and with whom she develops an affinity despite her son not liking the budding relationship between them.

Pritam Sandhu, in *Antidote*, writes the story of an unrequited love and a long life of waiting; while the title of the anthology is derived from the story of the same name by Navtej Puadhia about a tonga walla (hand-drawn carriage driver) who ends up committing blunders and is soon back to square one.

Rana Nayar

- *Slice of Life: Punjabi Short Fiction 1901–200;* **Translation and Introduction by Rana Nayar; Published by Unistar Books Pvt. Ltd.**

Among the anthologies selected for this book, this anthology is a unique one. Most anthologies do not have a predominant theme except that they are stories of Punjabi authors or stories written by diasporic Punjabis. In this anthology, Rana Nayar has focused on the evolution and history of the Punjabi short story as a modern literary form. He has provided a very erudite introduction about the history of short story as a genre and the tradition of Punjabi short story in it.

Thus, while choosing the stories, Nayar has started from the earliest modern Punjabi short story writers like Charan Singh Shaheed (1887–1935) and Giani Heera Singh (1889–1965). He then proceeded chronologically, choosing subsequent writers like Gurbaksh Singh Preetlari, Nanak Singh and others. Finally, he chooses the latest Punjabi authors like Prem Gorki (1947–), restricting himself to authors who were born before 1947. Thus, in this book, the reader can see how the Punjabi short story has evolved from 1900 till 2000, in terms of both writing style and topics chosen.

Further, Nayar has tried to avoid the representative stories of the selected authors so that we get to read new stories by them. Even so, stories like *Bhabhi Maina* by Gurbaksh Singh Preetlari, *Bhua* by Nanak Singh, *Pemi's Children* by Sant Singh Sekhon, *Raas-Leela* by Sujan Singh and *The Miracle* by Kartar Singh Duggal continue to appear in this and many other anthologies included in this book. Nayar needs to be thanked for including stories by authors like Charan Singh Shaheed and Giani Heera Singh, as these are perhaps the only translations of their stories available in English, as far as my research shows.

Starting with ideological moorings, the short stories of Shaheed and Hira Singh tackled social issues from which they wanted the people, especially Sikhs, to be away from. Thus, in *The Divine Sight,* Charan Singh deals with a Baba getting the power of divine sight with which he could tell who was what in his/her previous birth. This causes untold misery and strife all round and the people realize the futility of such powers. In *Pir Galarh Shah* by Giani Heera Singh, the people discover that the venerated Pir and his tomb were not real but actually a hoax planted by some students.

And Thus Crashed the Idol by Devendra Satyarthi deals with rituals and ceremonies that surround a young girl's initiation into the world of spinning wheel. In a sense, it also marks her initiation into adulthood and youth. However, the author also uses the opportunity to discuss the raging debate of that time regarding use of home-spun khadi vis-a-vis the factory made and imported khadi.

Thursday Fast by Amrita Pritam, *Moments Hung on the Cross* by Ajeet Cour and *A Silent Wish* by Dalip Kaur Tiwana all deal with strong woman characters. Pooja in *Thursday Fast* marries against her parent's wishes but ends up in prostitution to help support her family. Karuna in *Moments Hung on the Cross* is a woman waiting for the courts order on her divorce as well as on the question regarding the custody of the child. While Gita in *A Silent Wish* on being abandoned by her husband, educates herself and becomes a schoolteacher. All three show exemplary poise in their respective circumstances to ride over the crises.

The Kareer Branch by Gurdial Singh is another story of a very strong, rebellious and fiercely independent woman who works herself into a kind of psychological trap when her husband manages to extract a promise out of her to not react to his parents. This promise gets stuck in her throat like a thorny bush of Kareer, and she is forced to suffer a lifelong journey of never-ending atrocities.

Hey, Your Milk This! by the master story teller Kulwant Singh Virk is a story about a woman who is left alone for long spells due to her husband's long tours and starts fantasizing about the young man who comes to deliver milk at her doorstep. It is a superb story of feminine sensibility and understanding of human character and psychology.

This anthology covering almost 100 years of Punjabi short story shows a lack of writing by Punjabi authors on two themes; one – The Sikh genocide of 1984 and second – humour. There is a brief attempt at humour in *Bhua* by Nanak Singh and satire in *The Wretched Fellow* by Prem Prakash but as Rana Nayar himself mentions – 'surprisingly, humour hasn't really had its chance with the Punjabi short story. Even when it's articulated, the treatment is so hesitant and reserved that it almost threatens to lose its distinctive appeal and effect.'

The lack of these however does not take away from the great reading that these stories provide, each of which is a treat to read. And the icing on the cake is Rana Nayar's incisive introduction, which puts things into perspective and leads to a better understanding of the stories.

Saadat Hasan Manto

- *Bitter Fruit: The Very Best of Saadat Hasan Manto*; **Edited and Translated by Khalid Hasan; Published by Penguin Books India.**

Bitter Fruit is the most exhaustive compendium of his works in English. It has 51 of his best short stories (including the ones for which he faced various court cases on obscenity charges), 32 sketches, 15 portraits, his famous series of nine *Letters to Uncle Sam*, the only stage play that he wrote, *In This Vortex* as well as the short and amusing piece that Manto wrote, not long before his death, on himself. Since *Bitter Fruit* contains mainly his short stories, a genre that was his favourite, it is included under short stories section in this book.

The volume also carries translated conversations about Manto, one amongst his daughters, his sister and his wife's sister, and the other amongst his friends. Khalid Hasan's introduction is a very informative one and it gives a glimpse of the person as well as his work and style.

But the icing on the cake is a highly personalized account of Manto, the person, by his nephew Hamid Jalal that was written during Manto's lifetime. He has focused on three important parts of Manto's life – his literary activities, home life and behaviour as a dipsomaniac. It is as bold an account of the author (especially of his last days) as Manto was in his writings. He points out that, from the beginning, Manto was alright with not being a normal person – he narrates his action of walking on fire and telling his publisher, 'Let it (his portrait) be drawn in such a way that it should provoke people to abuse me.' He further talks about Manto's expensive tastes, his unobtrusive hospitality, love for his

Bombay days, his addiction to cigarettes and whiskey (things that finally took his life) and his defiant attitude.

The book thus manages to present to us a complete account of Manto the author as well as Manto the person and is a highly readable one. As the blurb says, 'the short stories seduce; the sketches wring out the sharp brevity of truth; the biographical portraits entice with their candour; the letters to Uncle Sam drip with sarcasm; while the lone play smoulders with desire that finds fulfillment in death. His stories on Partition are considered the best.'

Writer Aakar Patel, in his introduction to the book *Why I Write*, feels that Manto was an Indian trapped in Pakistan and that was a real misfortune for both the countries. He reluctantly fled his beloved Bombay after Partition. As a writer of films, he was not a very great success but he earned well and made very good friends like Ashok Kumar, Shyam and Baburao Patel. But he excelled in producing his magical short stories. The liberal environment of British Bombay and its mixing of many cultures produced the fertile material that Manto needed for his writing, especially the short stories.

Author

The most widely read and the most translated writer in Urdu, Saadat Hasan Manto (1912–1955) constantly challenged the hypocrisy and sham morality of civilized society. He was born in Sambrala in Indian Punjab and died in Lahore. He showed little enthusiasm for formal education. He failed twice in his graduating examinations; ironically, one of the subjects that he failed was Urdu, a language in which he was to produce such a powerful body of work later in life. He entered college in Amritsar in 1931, but there too failed his first year examinations twice and dropped out. In 1934, he joined Aligarh Muslim University (AMU) and there too he did not do well as a student and left in nine months due to suspected tuberculosis.

From AMU, he went back to Amritsar and then Lahore where he took his first regular job with a magazine called *Paras* but soon shifted in 1936 to Bombay to edit a film weekly *Mussawar*. For more than a decade, between 1936 and 1948, Manto worked in Bombay's film industry, creating scripts, magazine articles and short stories.

He entered his best phase in screenwriting for films, which included *Aatth Din, Chal Chal Re Naujawan* and *Mirza Ghalib*. Some of his best short stories also came from this phase including *Kaali Shalwar, Dhuan* and *Bu*, which were published in *Qaumi Jang* (Bombay). He moved to Pakistan in January 1948 after the Partition of India in 1947. He produced 22 collections of short stories, one novel, five series of radio plays, one stage play, three collections of essays and two collections of personal sketches.

Read on
Other translated works of Manto in English:
- *Kingdom's End and Other Stories* (1987) is a collection of stories written by Saadat Hasan Manto, published by Penguin Books India.
- *Manto My Love: Selected Writings of Saadat Hasan Manto* – Selected and Translated by Harish Narang; Published by Sahitya Akademi.
- *Bombay Stories* – Translated by Matt Reeck and Aftab Ahmad; Published by Vintage International.
- *My Name is Radha* – Translated by Muhammad Umar Memon; Published by Penguin.
- *Mottled Dawn: Fifty Sketches And Stories Of Partition* – Translated by Khalid Hasan; Published by Penguin India.
- *Manto: Selected Stories* – Translated by Aatish Taseer; Published by Vintage Books.
- *Naked Voices: Stories & Sketches* – Translated by Rakhshanda Jalil; Published by Roli books.
- *No Man's Land: A Novel*; Published by Milad Publications India.
- *Why I Write: Essays by Saadat Hasan Manto*; Edited and Translated by Aakar Patel; Published by Tranquebar.

Books written on Manto
- *Dozakhnama: Conversations in Hell;* dialogue between Ghalib & Manto; by Rabisankar Bal; Translated by Arunava Sinha; Vintage.

Movies on Manto
- Pakistani director Sarmad Khoosat has made a biopic titled *Manto*.
- Indian Director Rahat Kazmi has made a movie called *Mantosthan* based on Manto's four short stories.
- In India, Nandita Das is making a movie on Manto's life titled *Manto*.

Sadhu Binning

- *Fauji Banta Singh and Other Stories* by Sadhu Binning; Translated from Punjabi by the author himself; Published by TSAR Publications, Canada.

The stories in *Fauji Banta Singh and Other Stories* were originally written in Punjabi but are a little more than merely the straightforward translation from the original. The author, who writes with equal felicity in both English and Punjabi, has recreated these stories in English himself and has even made some changes. He took these stories from two anthologies that he had published in Punjabi, *Kis da Kassor?* (Whose fault? 1982 and 2001) and *Off Track* (1994 and 2001).

Fauji Banta Singh is set among people who immigrated to Canada in the late twentieth century. These people faced racial animosity and economic insecurity even as they moved forward and their lives become more settled. It gives us rare glimpses into the private lives of Vancouver's Sikh community – the successes and failures, the growing and painful irrelevance of the old, changing values and the conditions of the women, the place of religion and tradition, and the ever-present echoes of distant Indian politics and national extremism. Unique and powerful, brutally honest yet compassionate, these stories present us with characters that are empathetic and vividly real.

In the stories, the economic hardship and multiple challenges of both young and old reflect a tug-of-war between 'home' and 'away.' From the elderly soldier Banta Singh, who recalls that he began as the only Punjabi mailman in his assigned neighbourhood to the high-school student Sito, who is used and betrayed by Kelly, a Punjabi boy, Sadhu Binning gives us multiple perspectives and responses to the dislocation and relocation of diaspora. Some stories are very short and are surprising in their brevity while some, such as *Off Track* and *The Accident*, relate disturbing stories of domestic and racially motivated violence that resound beyond the book's covers.

What stands out in this collection is the resilience of these characters and the connections they forge both within and outside their homes and neighborhoods. In *Father and Son*, the link (ironically) is economic exploitation and homelessness as, on the street, indigenous, local and immigrant develop an intense loyalty and mutual respect. Similarly, in *Eyes in the Dark*, we encounter Punjabi men working in Northern BC who marry indigenous women in order to gain official status.

Binning takes a sociological approach in this book. These are stories that look at how a community is shaped by its experiences, how it responds to change and how it tries to shape its own circumstances.

The stories not only look at what is going through people's minds but also at how cultural and feudal values change after immigrating to Canada. Binning based the book in the 1970s, '80s and '90s because Vancouver then had a different multicultural identity. While the stories are all fiction, they're based on real-life experiences.

Author

Sadhu Binning was born in India and immigrated to Canada in 1967. He has published more than 15 books including one novel, two short stories and four poetry collections. He edited a literary monthly *Watno Dur* from 1977 to 1982 and currently co-edits *Watan*, a Punjabi quarterly. Binning is the founding member of the Vancouver Sath and Ankur collective. He has co-authored and produced a number of plays about the Punjabi community. A retired Punjabi language instructor, Binning lives in Burnaby, British Columbia.

In 2012, Binning – the prominent leftist and atheist author – initiated dialogue on atheism within his community with his Punjabi book, *Nastak Baani* (Atheistic Verses). *Nastak Baani* is a collection of quotations from various world-renowned atheists, philosophers and thinkers who have questioned the concept of religion. It is dedicated to Bhagat Singh, the towering leftist revolutionary of India, who had written a powerful essay 'Why I am an atheist?' a year before his execution. Binning has spoken lucidly about atheism and wants to break a myth about the South Asian community being 'too religious.' In the past, Binning had written a poem praising Vancouverites after a survey revealed that a significant number of people in the city are non-religious. His short stories also give an idea about his secular views towards life and politics. As an editor of the Punjabi magazine *Watan*, he has written extensively on this subject.

A linguistic activist who has worked hard to promote Punjabi language in public schools, Binning has been conscious not to mix the language with religion. He believes that the Punjabi language does not belong to the Sikhs alone, as other communities speak it too. Binning is also staunchly opposed to casteism, though he is from a dominant Jat (Peasant) Sikh community.

Read on

- Sadhu Binning's Punjabi poetry collection titled *Watno Dur Nahi* has been translated into English as *No More Watno Dur*; Published by TSAR Publications, Canada.

Sujan Singh

- *Town And The Countryside* by Sujan Singh; Translated By Narinder Jit Kaur; Published by Sahitya Akademi.

Town and the Countryside is a translation of Singh's Sahitya Akademi awarded collection of 13 Punjabi short stories called *Shehar Te Garaan*, published in 1985. As the title suggests, some of the stories are based against an urban background whereas some of them have a rural set-up. As the translator in her translator's note explains, 'this aspect of the book refers to the changing contemporary contexts of that time. As Punjab witnessed great movement from the villages to the towns, these stories record the transition, which is not only the physical shift, but the transition that took place in the thinking, in the social and moral values and in the psyche of the people.'

Due to poverty, he had to work till quite late in his life, but his needs did not stop him from caring about the world. Called Principal Sujan Singh, he was a very respected teacher and he struggled against slavery, imperialism, capitalist's brutality and human exploitation. He worked for peace in the world and still made time to form literary societies. As a result of his association with communist parities, many of his stories represent that ideology. He even wrote against the militants in Punjab and suffered their threats.

The very first story in this collection articulates some of his beliefs. *The Power of the Pen* was written during the Emergency and depicts the writer's concern about the State's attempt to muzzle the pen. He was a part of a progressive group for whom literature was meant to serve a 'solid objective' and not just be 'for pleasure.' Similarly, the story, *Kalyan Sundari* deals with women's education as well as communal harmony. He further focuses on women's education and rights in stories like *The Stranger, Ramlila* and *The Full Circle*. In *Full Circle,* his focus is also on the menace of dowry.

In *Faith and Fallacy,* he demonstrates how education is an antidote to all the superstitions that the uneducated people follow in villages, once again promoting the cause of education. Through his stories, *Massacre of the Monsters* and *The Retribution*, his wish is to empower people so that they stand against injustice and do not suffer like they did before. His story, *Rai Sahab* deals with the silent dignity of a rickshaw puller. He works hard and appreciates his wife's hard work and sagacity. Moreover, he refuses to take any compensation from the government even though he had been displaced from Pakistan, had been rendered penniless, and was slowly rebuilding his life and educating his children.

Singh had great friendships with some of his contemporaries, especially Bawa Balwant and Ishwar Chitrakar. In the long-short story *The Nescient Muse*, he pays tribute to his close friend Bawa Balwant and also mentions Ishwar Chitrakar. The latter had died young, and Sujan Singh brought up his children. Thus, his socialism and humanism were not just present in stories but were practiced by him in his real life, despite his uncertain and difficult financial condition.

This book depicts the author's philosophy of life, the changes that Punjab witnessed after Partition and the changes brought about by the advent of education and urban migration.

Author

Sujan Singh (1909–1993) was born in Dera Baba Nanak, a town of Gurdaspur district of Punjab. He was brought up by his maternal grandparents and spent his early childhood days in Calcutta. After his grandparents' and father's death, he had a difficult time. He did his Bachelor of Arts from Khalsa College in Amritsar followed by Giani and Master of Arts in Punjabi through correspondence.

He worked as a bank employee, teacher, headmaster, lecturer and principal. He is known as a progressive writer. He was founder-president of Kendri Punjabi Lekhak Sabha and Lok Likhari Sabha, senior vice president of Punjabi Sahitya Academy Ludhiana, member of presidium of Progressive Writers Association of India and of Afro-Asian Writers Association.

Although he is known for his stories (he wrote seven collections of short stories), he wrote some essays too. His first essay, *Tawian wala Waaja* was published in the monthly magazine, *Likhari*. He published two collections of essays, *Jammu Jee Tusi Barhe Raa* and *Khumban Da Shikar*. His story anthologies include *Dukh Sukh, Dukh Sukh Ton Pichhon, Dedh Aadmi, Manukh Te Pashu, Kalgi Dian Annian* and *Shehar Te Garaan*.

He was awarded the Sahitya Akademi Award in 1987 for his story collection, *Shehar Te Garaan*. He was also awarded the Best Storywriter of Punjabi by the Language Department of Punjab in 1972. He wrote three books on the lives of Sri Guru Nanak Dev ji (*Wade Kian Wadiian*), Guru Amar Dass ji (*Amar Guru Rishman*) and Guru Gobind Singh ji (*Kalgi Dian Annian*).

Waryam Singh Sandhu

- *Selected Short Stories of Waryam Singh Sandhu*; Translated by Paramjeet Singh Ramana; Published by Punjabi University.

This is an anthology of Waryam Singh Sandhu's seven short stories, although some of them are 'long' short stories, a form that he has refined considerably. Paramjit Singh Ramana, a leading scholar in the field of translation and a professor of English, has translated the stories.

The collection includes stories like *The Golden Specks* (Sunheri Kinka), *The Return* (Wapsi), *Yours Forever* (Ang Sang), *The Pond* (Dumh) and *Everyone's Share* (Apna Apna Hissa), which give voice to the suffering, the pain and the harsh realities of the farming community of Punjab.

The story, *The Return* juxtaposes Kuldip Singh and Santa Singh and symbolically evaluates their two contrasting ways of life. Santa Singh, suspecting his wife's infidelity, abandons his family responsibilities and plunges into a religious life. His nephew, Kuldip turns into a revolutionary and, when he meets his uncle, raises several questions. Santa refuses to face these questions. Kuldip then requests Santa to tear his religious mask and return to his grieving family. Kuldip gets killed in an encounter with the police and Santa decides to 'return' to his village and family, bearing the heavy load of the ill-treatment of his family and of their suffering. Sandhu has rated *The Return* as one of his best stories.

The story *Yours Forever* is about the death of a poor farmer, Kartar Singh who used to live well with the money sent by his father from Singapore. Once his father died, the money stopped coming. Meanwhile, Kartar Singh had become an addict and was compelled to mortgage the tiny land, to steal household articles and to take on debts. His son, Amrik Singh feels sorry that he did not persuade his father to give up bad habits, but as the real extent of his father's deeds comes to his knowledge, he and other family members are secretly relieved at their father's death. This is the typical story of a farmer fallen on evil days.

The third story, *Everyone's Share* is about a one-time wrestler Ghuddu, now a farmer. His mother has died and he has no money for the death rituals. His two older brothers, who are very rich, arrive from the city but want him to share the expenses thus revealing their pettiness. Exasperated by their pettiness, Ghuddu tells them to leave his one-third share of the ashes with him and declares that he will do the needful when he has money. This is a very touching story that gives a true account of the individualism and money-mindedness of the people now as against the age-old familial bonds and social relations.

I Am Alright Now (Mein Hun Thik Thak Han) is a 'long' short story describing rural life as seen through the eyes of a God-fearing farmer. It is a reaction to the onslaught on the Golden Temple (1984) and the trials and tribulations that ordinary people had to bear from the security forces as well as from the militant youth.

Nine Twelve Ten (Nau Bara Dus) takes one to the heights of fantasy through the central character Ninder while, at the same time, revealing how poor simple farmers are exploited by the big ones and how differences of caste remain etched in people's mind.

Author

Waryam Singh Sandhu (1945–) is undoubtedly one of the best Punjabi short story writers today. He spent 50 years of his life almost exclusively in village Sur Singh near Amritsar where his parents migrated to in 1947, leaving all their ancestral land and property in Pakistan. His father was a small farmer, and the young Sandhu helped in farming even after he joined his job as a teacher and remained deeply involved with his village and farming community. He is deeply rooted in the cultural ethos of rural Punjab, particularly the Majha region, and all his stories bear testimony to this fact. His stories are very often inspired by real people and happenings. He had a brush with the leftist ideology during the Naxalite movement and he was also witness to the subsequent militancy era as Majha was one of the most affected regions. Sandhu, who holds a Doctor of Philosophy degree, retired as a lecturer from Lyallpur Khalsa College, Jalandhar, and is now settled in Canada.

He has published 34 stories. Some of these have been adapted into telefilms, radio plays and stage plays. He has also written poems, travelogues, a biography and an autobiography. His short story collections include *Lohe De hath, Ang Sang, Bhajian Bahin, Chauthi Koot, Til Phul* and *Chonvian Kahanian*. In 2000, he was awarded the Sahitya Akademi Award for his short story collection *Chauthi Koot*. He has bagged many other awards – Punjab Ratan Puraskar, Hira Singh Dard Award, Bhai Veer Singh Puraskar, Kulwant Singh Virk Puraskar and the Sujan Singh Puraskar. Although he writes in Punjabi, his works have been translated into Hindi, Bengali, Urdu, English and other languages.

Read on

- One more anthology of Waryam Singh Sandhu's translated short stories in English has been published by Sahitya Akademi – *The Fourth Direction and Other Stories* (2005); Translated by Akshey Kumar.
- A film by the name of *Chauthi Koot* (The Fourth Direction) is based on two stories, *The Fourth Direction* and *I am feeling fine now* from Waryam Singh Sandhu's short story collection. *Chauthi Koot* has been made by noted director Gurvinder Singh. It won the National Film Award for best feature film in Punjabi, Best Asian Feature Film at Singapore Film Festival and was screened at 2015 Cannes Film Festival.

Note on Exclusive Anthologies Dedicated to Punjabi Writers Settled Abroad[1]

Among the anthologies, there are three anthologies dedicated solely to Punjabis settled aboard. One of them, edited by Rana Nayar (*From Across The Shores*), deals with authors settled in the United Kingdom while the other one, edited by S. P. Singh for Guru Nanak Dev University (GNDU) (*Between Two Worlds*), has stories from Punjabi authors in the United Kingdom, the United States and Canada. Thus, the authors living in UK – Tarsem Neelgiri, Swaran Chandan, Kailash Puri, Pritam Sidhu, Dharshan Dheer, Shivcharan Gill and Raghubir Dhand are common to both the anthologies. And, in two cases, both the editors have chosen the same stories, although they are titled differently.

Thus, Tarsem Neelgiri's poignant story, titled *The Divided Shores* and *The Two Shores* in the two anthologies, is about Pakhar Singh who is fed up of the hard, lonely life full of racist taunts in the United Kingdom. He yearns to come back and settle in his native village in India. However, his family treats him like a moneymaking machine and wants him to continue work in the United Kingdom. His dilemma and angst is that of every

---

1 The last three short stories anthologies are dedicated to Punjabi writers settled abroad. Since they have some things in common, so before mentioning the three books, a short note is given to highlight the similarities.

immigrant. The other repeated story is by Pritam Sidhu, titled *In the Distant Lands* and *A Tragic Tale From Alien Shores,* respectively. It is about an aged man who is stuck in the alien land and is neglected by his son and daughter-in-law. He desperately wants to go back to his village and to his wife. It is a sad story of how some immigrant Punjabis mistreat their elders and are only concerned with earning more and more for themselves.

From Across the Shores (the book) has a critical introduction by Rana Nayar that tries to explain why, even while living in the United Kingdom, these authors continued to write in Punjabi despite a lack of readership there. He found that there were as many as 625 Punjabi writers living in the United Kingdom and what struck him was the indomitable courage and resilience of these authors. Hence, in a way, his book is a tribute to the efforts put in by them to survive in an alien environment and continue to serve their mother tongue. Most of their readership is in Punjab.

He also found that very little effort had been made to make the work of Punjabi immigrant writers available to the English readership, both in England and outside. So, these three volumes make an effort to bridge the yawning gap between the two languages – Punjabi and English. S.P. Singh too, in his introduction to *Between Two Worlds,* writes that the book 'contains realistic and poignant portrayals of oppressed and exploited working class immigrants of all ages. The appeal of the stories may not lie so much in literary ingenuity and technical craft, as in the possibility of identification and empathy with the pressures the common people face in foreign environment. The stories are coloured by the immediacy of first hand experience. One may read the book as a document of social as well as cultural history and psychological insight into immigrant consciousness.'

The third anthology, *The Lost Trail* is edited by Puran Singh, President of the Punjabi Sahit Sabha, London and has 16 stories from authors based in the United Kingdom, Canada and other countries.

Rana Nayar

- *From Across The Shores: Punjabi Short Stories by Asians in Britain*; **Edited and Translated by Rana Nayar; Published by Sterling Publishers 2002.**

From Across the Shores contains 16 stories of Punjabi settlers in the United Kingdom and is an anthology of translations into English from the original Punjabi. The authors have tackled a wide range of issues from the 'wayward ways' of the young generation who refuse to follow the 'old mindset' of their parents, to double standards, the inability of immigrants to fully assimilate within the British culture, race issues and women's issues among others.

Raghubir Dhand in *The Dustbin* shows the true face of the so-called educated people vis-a-vis the uncultured, rustic ones. The former are busy promoting themselves and would offer platitudes when actual help is required, while the latter are genuine people who are really there in times of need although they may not be as sophisticated. The narrator is advised by the well-wisher to not make his house a dustbin by inviting the former trash.

Baldev Singh's *A Wicked Girl* is the story of an old man who has a chance meeting with a young white girl who is facing a lot of personal issues and has taken to drinking. She reminds him of his own wayward manners and how it would have impacted his daughter. This is a gripping tale of fragile human emotions that is handled in a manner that is at once endearing and disarming.

Shivcharan Gill's *Samskaras* is also about a middle-aged Indian who finds himself being the object of love of a young white girl. He is a respected teacher and has a friend, Harry who has always stood by him because of his credentials. Harry is very candid in confessing that, despite his liberal views, the ingrained Samskaras (culture) of racial prejudice come out when he sees that girl cozying up to his Indian friend.

Gurdial Singh Rai was born in Assam and is perhaps the only one among the expatriate authors who is equally at ease with Hindi, Urdu, Punjabi, English, Bengali and Assamese. His story, *The Daughter of Eve* is focused on the Muslims among the Asian community. The girl, being considered a burden, is packed off in marriage to a close cousin despite her father knowing that the boy was a wayward. Their justification is that marriage would pull him back on track. Now divorced, the girl puts her sorrows behind and selflessly serves in an Old Age Centre providing the much-needed warmth and care to the occupants.

The four women authors in this anthology bring their unique perspectives to the immigrant experience. Kailash Puri's story *Behind Open Doors* casts a glance at the contradictions and unresolved paradoxes of an unorthodox open society. The Ahujas have spent a large part of their lives in India and find that, in England, they have not been able to fully accept their changed circumstances. The children move away from the codes of their parents. The author conveys the agony of the ageing parents and she handles the narration quite deftly.

Surjit Kaur Kalpana in *Two Long Years* deals with the treachery, greed and shamelessness of relatives who look to their expat relatives as cash cows. Gurbaksh Kaur Dosanjh is a second-generation writer who has come to terms with her adopted land and is interested in negotiating in its new spaces. In *Shifting Sands*, the middle-aged couple learns to assimilate with their British neighbours although not all of them are as keen. The illness of neighbours and the reminder of life's mortality also force them to reexamine their life and bring them closer and make them more understanding of each other. Veena Verma, in *A Soiled Sheet*, explores the commodification of women and their desires. Even when she is working and is apparently an independent woman, the man continues to dictate her terms of living and she continues to be used.

Harjit Atwal, in *The Smoke*, attacks the hypocrisy and duplicity of those who seek better economic opportunities in a highly industrialized world without making any effort to abandon their backward, regressive, feudalistic mindset.

Gurnam Gill, in *Trees of Kew Garden*, deals with the difficulty of assimilation in the new culture and with the racist attacks that are a part of the life of an immigrant. Life seems hunky-dory to their relatives in India but the daily grind makes them often wonder if it is all worth it.

Gurdeep Puri's *Crazy for Pounds* is a very touching story about certain Punjabis for whom earning more and more pounds is the only motive in life. Sabby, a character, explains that the moment she landed in London after marriage, she was put to work in a store. Her husband and her father-in-law also work tirelessly from morning to night in the store. They are well off now, yet there is no meaning to life. When she is told that she should rebel and make her own life, she exposes the hypocrisy of the narrator who is ready to give advice but lacks the courage to see it through.

Rana Nayar's translation is highly evocative and all the stories are beautifully rendered.

Rita Chaudhry and Harbir S Manku

- *Between Two Worlds: Pravasi Punjabi Short Stories*; Translated by Rita Chaudhry and Harbir S. Manku; Published by Guru Nanak Dev University, Amritsar, 2004.

Between Two Worlds is a collection of 14 short stories of writers from the Punjabi diaspora, dispersed across England, Canada and the United States. This manages to give a fair representation to major voices in short fiction emerging out of a certain section of the Punjabi diaspora. The editor, while defining the concept of the Punjabi diaspora, conceptualizes it in the broadest sense possible, saying that it is 'spread across Britain, Canada, America, Singapore, Dubai, Thailand, Australia, New Zealand, Denmark, Germany, Norway, Netherlands and Switzerland.' The leitmotif of Pravasi Punjabi short story is the call of the homeland that is translated into the urge to return to the roots. There is a evident struggle between the first-generation immigrants' desire to acquire Western privileges and the desire to retain their original identity and religion. The collection has wide-ranging themes and a wide variety of characters struggling hard to negotiate the space within the chains that bind them.

Besides the UK authors already mentioned in the 'Note...' above who are repeated here (albeit with different stories in all but two cases), we also have USA-based authors like Rani Nagendra and Jagjit Brar and Canada-based authors like Ravindra Ravi, Sadhu Singh, Amanpal Sara and Surjit Kalsi. Surjit Virdi is an addition to the U.K.-based authors list.

The Green Card by Rani Nagender is not only about the travails of immigrants who are working to get the most coveted Green Card but also about how the expatriates were deeply affected by the sad happenings in Punjab – the attack on the Golden Temple and Akal Takht, the police excesses on common people and the militancy.

The story of *Bachni* by Kailash Puri deals with the racist abuse of a Punjabi immigrant working in a factory and her struggle against racial discrimination in her workplace. Going back to India means going back to the smoke-filled hearth and claustrophobic house in Punjab where her mother-in-law makes all decisions for her. Facing this Hobson's choice, Bachni emerges as a sadly disoriented character.

Similar is the story in *Across the Divide* by Raghubir Dhand where the racial attitude and hatred of first- and second-generation English men and women is depicted. However, it is heart warming to see that the third generation rejects this divide and works alongside the Asians and Africans to bring unity into the society.

Jagjit Brar, in his story *Homecoming*, builds up a scenario of how people are compelled by hunger and poverty to seek a new life in foreign lands, only to face discrimination, violence and exploitation. The story is set in America and provides a clear picture of the tension caused by religion and roti (bread) in such an artistic way that it almost leads the reader to alter his/her perception and philosophy of life.

The Road to Marriage by Ravindra Ravi and *The Free Society* by Swaran Chandan both deal with the gap between the first- and second-generation immigrants. The first-generation parents continue to hope that their children will live up to their expectations of being ideal Indian children and not be decadent like those of the host country.

Tables are turned in *The Disowned* by Shivcharan Gill, where it is the first-generation immigrant who is not able to adjust in the alien country as he marries a white woman but they soon fall apart. He is lost to his own country *and* his host country and is thus 'disowned' by all.

Sadhu Singh (*Bridge Across the River of Fire*), Surjit Kalsi (*Who Shall I Tell My Sorrow To*) and Surjit Virdi (*Cancer and Flowers*) all deal with conflicts and dilemmas of the immigrant community from a psychological viewpoint. These are real-life issues beyond the homeland nostalgia and inter-cultural adjustments that are already present. In *Margharita* by Amanpal Sara, we see that the people in the West too are grappling with these issues of relationships with children and with other relatives.

Between Two Worlds is an important addition to the repertoire of the Punjabi diaspora available in the English language.

Puran Singh

- *The Lost Trail: Selected Punjabi Short* **Stories; Edited by Puran Singh; Published by Unistar Books Pvt. Ltd.**

First-generation immigrants always find it difficult to adapt to the socio-cultural diversity in the new places because they bring with them social norms and cultural values from their home country, while also engaging in assimilation and socializing in their new country. But very soon, they come face-to-face with intergenerational conflict owing to cultural differences between their parents' home-country values, norms and behavioiral patterns, as well as the mainstream culture of the immigrant country to which the children are exposed.

The Lost Trail, a collection of 16 short stories written by Punjabi writers settled in England, Canada and other countries, deals with this conflict between the two generations. Almost all the stories are written by first-generation writers, and so this collection deals with these issues from a single perspective.

One major worry of the parents and a potential source of conflict is the corrupt influence of mainstream culture, especially related to sexual relations. This is more acute with daughters – their choice of clothes, dates and their choices regarding marriage. Second-generation daughters often rail against their parents' surveillance, which places greater restrictions on them than on their brothers who are usually allowed much more freedom. Another source of conflict is parental pressure to marry within the ethnic group, which second-generation youngsters may resent.

These issues have been taken up by a number of stories like *Old Fashioned* by Gurnam Gill, *A Bit of Sun* by Balbir Kaur Sanghera, *Grocery* by Sathi Ludhianvi, *Mother* by Rattan Raheel, *Black Gold* by Major Mangat and *Water* by Jarnail Singh.

Another very important issue that has become a nightmare for the elderly generation is that of old-age management, maintenance and healthcare. This issue has two aspects – those parents who live in India and have their children living abroad prefer to stay on in India in their own homes, persevering independently for as long as they can. It is too much to expect them to start their lives anew in a foreign land. But their children insist that they come and stay with them, only to use them for their financial benefits and then leave them unattended and uncared for, as in *The Journey* by Santokh Dhaliwal, *The Thirsty Plants* by Darshan Singh Dhir and *Good Deal* by Aman Pal Sarna.

On the other hand, those who are first-generation immigrants themselves are neglected by their children, who have imbibed the lifestyle and behavioural patterns of their new country where youngsters have a right to lead their lives independently and shun the responsibilities of looking after their aged parents. This theme has been very aptly depicted in *Twilight* by Puran Singh, *A Bit of Sun* by Balbir Kaur Sanghera, *I Am Not That Lucky* by Maggar Singh Panesar and *Grocery* by Sathi Ludhianvi.

Though most of the stories present a pathetic picture of the life of immigrants, in some stories, support and consolation comes from unexpected quarters, thus breaking the myths that have made people so rigid in their thinking. In *Twilight,* a mother of seven sons and two daughters lives alone and buys vegetables and groceries for the whole family, creating an imaginary situation where all her children would come home asking for dishes of their choice. It is Christopher, a well-to-do English construction contractor, who fills the vacuum created by the absence of her children, and thus helps her snap the thin thread of the non-existent bond with them. In *A Bit of Sun,* an old lady who has been humiliated, insulted and abandoned by her children, finds a saviour in Richard, her English son-in-law, towards whom she earlier had reservations. *The Journey* depicts a different story where two elderly people, a man and a woman who met on a plane during their journey, are attracted to each other and, when they are badly treated by their respective children, find solace in each other's company.

Some of the stories deal with completely different issues. *The Golden Tooth* by Gurpal Singh talks about human greed even in death as one brother wants to extract the golden tooth from the dead body of his brother, misleading people with a fake superstition. *I Was Surprised* by Maggar Singh Panesar relates the story of a person who feels obliged to Adi Amin, the Ugandan President, who is otherwise known for his cruelties, for helping him out of a helpless situation. *A Church for Sale* by Dr. Swaran Chandan talks about religion as opposed to scientific temper and how religion has impacted Indian politics during the Babri Masjid demolition and its after effects. *The Ungrateful* by Puran Singh is about how petty communal interests turn the Sikh community so indifferent and heartless that they forget the good done by the British and lose no time in condemning and standing against the British authorities for a very small issue. In *The Sparrow*, Kuljit Mann has, through the allegory of the sparrow, talked about the very complex relationships between husband–wife, mother–daughter and father–daughter.

The stories have been translated by professional translators but no names have been given in the book.

Appendix 1:
Translation

Manjit Inder Singh in the introduction to his book –*Contemporary Punjabi Short Stories – An Anthology* states – 'One tends to agree with Salman Rushdie's remark that translation's go beyond the literary and the aesthetic, indeed, towards creating something exclusive that travels from one language, its milieu, to another. In a country like India rife with myriad forms of divisions – religious, linguistic, cultural, of class and caste – translation can contribute to form a kind of "literary democracy." Another view that I tend to subscribe to is that issues that go beyond art/literature/aesthetics need to figure in academic discussion on translation. There has been arguably a persistent need to forge commonalities in Indian languages towards an idea of India; and one of the most constructive ways to do that, to bring together distinct voices is through translation, that would certainly overcome the otherwise arbitrary barriers that have existed between English and regional Indian bhashas.'

He further adds, 'Sahitya Akademi's contribution has been remarkable in the history of translation in India, largely by using English as a conduit language. If one expands the argument, English and native languages present two post-colonial avatars today. Indian literature in English and the latter come from two different sets of assumptions: one an elite articulation of India and the other a more authentic representation of Bharat. Today, fortunately, translation into English has acquired an intellectual viability, even economic, so that publishers are ready to invest in it. At heart, however both in Indian literature in English and Indian language literature lies the shift in our attitude, our relation to English language, which not only appears our own, but is also (in this sense) eminently suited to convey our post-modern, post-colonial and post-global realities.'

Rana Nayar in the Introduction to the book – *Earthy Tones – A selection of Best Punjabi Short Stories – Gurdial Singh* says, 'However despite its usefulness it is a difficult task. Translation, as any translator worth his salt would easily concede, is not merely a game of finding linguistic equivalencies at the semantic or the syntactic levels. Often the local idiom is so deeply embedded in the cultural layers that any attempt at a simple rendering could, at best, turn into a contraction or reduction and at worst, a deflection, if not a total loss of meaning. Besides, the syntactic structures into the two languages viz., Punjabi and English operate so very differently that often the process of transmission from one to the other may threaten to become obfuscating, even non-communicative. Whichever way we choose to think about it, the loss is invariable of those cultural specificities that are intrinsically and inherently resistant to any act of translation, howsoever shrewd or strategic. While self-reflexivity is an inescapable fact of any translator's job, it doesn't always become a route to self-awareness. Even in those cases where it does become so, the practice of translation may often throw up challenges, which no amount of anticipation or awareness might actually be able to help tide over. Faced with some of these limitations, the task of a translator, especially if he is seeking to capture the "spirit of the original," may actually become not easy but all the more difficult, even formidable.'

For Amarjit Chandan who has translated the world's best poets into Punjabi, translation is as creative an endeavour as original writing. No way does he feel it hinders the creative process. 'On the contrary, it acts as an impetus, for it opens windows to other cultures, civilizations and thought processes,' says he.

Appendix 2:

The Monolingual Dystopia – Power Dynamics of Literary Translation – Change Magazine – 10 March 2017 By Anvita Budhraja

Ask people to name a few Latin American writers and they'll say Borges, Márquez, perhaps even Neruda. I'd be astonished if they mentioned Clarice Lispector.

New York City's Symphony Space recently held an event that celebrated Lispector's exceptional work. Her readers often call her Brazil's Virginia Woolf for her acute insights about a women's consciousness. And yet, she is outside the canon. Not due to literary demerit but because, until very recently, her works were not translated into the English language. I found it saddening to see how something so arbitrary could dictate literary recognition and fame. This means that if you are an English language reader, translators curate your reading tastes more than you would like to believe.

Once you start looking, you very quickly find that all is not well with literary translation. Structures of power already in place affect *what* is translated, *what language* it is translated into and also *how* things are translated. In her book, *The World Republic of Letters*, Pascale Casanova develops the idea of each language as a currency in the world literary market. Denouncing a rosy view of globalization and what that does to international literature, she explores how each language has a different value on the market (just like currency does), how that affects minor languages and literatures and how it shapes the tenuous translation market.

There is no denying that English enjoys unequalled power in this global literary market. The PEN report on The International Situation of Literary Translation concludes that because of the global nature of the English language (and its position as the second language of choice), a work translated into English reaches not only native English speakers but also a truly universal audience. As the language of the internet world and the language spoken in the world's current economic and political superpower, it is the most powerful language in the literary market. Finally, a compelling argument that the report makes is that even though Spanish and Chinese are among the top languages spoken in the world, native speakers of those languages are most likely bilingual with English, further proving its power on the global scale. Translation *into* English then becomes a yardstick for literary recognition. Consider – the Nobel Prize is not given to works that have not been translated into English.

Then there is asymmetrical translation – another consequence of this inequitable power dynamic. Most of the literature being translated now is translated *into* English, not the other way around. English language classics are not available in a lot of minor languages of the world. This professor of Punjabi has translated the greats of English into Punjabi to reach audiences who speak only that language; but instances like these are atypical and, as one goes down the hierarchy of relative language power, such efforts are independent and exceedingly rare. There is simply no impetus to translate *from* English – its global power affords its native speakers the privilege of remaining monolingual and having the rest of the world learn their language.

However, this power dynamic is seen not only in the unbalanced direction of translation but also in the manner in which translations occur. Lawrence Venuti is often credited with the idea of domestication, or the process through which, during translation, the cultural 'other' is domesticated or made more intelligible and familiar. Something 'foreign' (and therefore peculiar) in another culture – manifested through the language – is made 'less odd' and more like something speakers of the target language would recognize and accept. Gideon Toury further argued that the more powerful the language, the less weirdness it would accept. Thus, works translated into English are often smoothed out. The translation of ideas across cultures then becomes problematic because the foreign concept is tamed and not really conveyed in its gloriously complicated entirety. There is no way in which this bodes well for the international communication of ideas.

Finally, tangentially related but still intriguing is the idea of soft power or the ability to shape the likes and preferences of others through appeal and attraction rather than money or physical power. A few statistics for you: translations account for only an average of 3 percent of the books published in the United States and the United Kingdom (the primary English-speaking countries). Within this, French, German and Italian are the top three languages translated into English and their numbers exceed the other languages by a wide margin (PEN report). What does this mean for the influence that these three countries have on the English-speaking world? Surely, they enjoy a great deal of soft power – any college student in the United States can talk at length about the works and ideas of Camus or Nietzche, but you'll be hard-pressed to find someone who can tell you about Slovakian culture or Bangladesh's contributions to world literature.

It all goes to show that not even literary translation is immune to the power dynamics that have accompanied globalization. Ultimately, though, I don't believe that this is a fault inherent in the English language. Whatever the global 'lingua franca' may have been, these issues would have held true. Addressing them, then, does not undermine English; rather it seeks to prevent a move into a monolingual dystopia – one where ideas, concepts and cultural traditions become uniform and stagnant and where minor languages slowly become extinct.

Appendix 3:
What Ails Punjabi Writing?

While writing the book review of Fauzia Rafique's Skeena for Sikhchic.com, noted author Rupinderpal 'Roop' Singh Dhillon had an occasion to reflect on the malaises that are there in Punjabi Literature and why it needs to expand its horizons. He writes:

Techniques in how to write prose have moved on a lot in the last century or so. The other factor that has moved on is the subject matter and how honestly it is dealt with. What may have seemed great in Russian and English literature (other than Urdu and Hindi, the greatest influencers on Punjabi language in the last 100 years) in Victorian times, and pre-partition India is now stale, boring and irrelevant. There has been a malaise in Punjabi literature, confounded, I think by the following factors:-

- Male domination in writing
- Religious domination, but often the incorrect interpretation of the faith
- Sycophantic behaviour of the established writers
- Greedy Printer-Publishers
- Political strangulation of the artist
- The public itself not reading
- Writers' life experience only restricted to the village
- Conservative values

It is a well-known fact that society is judged culturally by two yardsticks: its religious beliefs and its art. Punjabi society puts little value on the latter, though it then bemoans why its language and rituals are being lost by the young, especially those in the diaspora.

Russian, English and Spanish societies, taking but three examples, put great emphasis on language and literature. The English worship Shakespeare, to the extent one thinks no one anywhere in the world or in any other language can write like him. Obviously a false premise, but one that shows how important literature is to reflect a society's wants, truths and desires.

The Russians treat their writers like demi-gods. What is more interesting is that in all of these societies, the greatest readers are the women. Not the men. So clearly, to ensure that one's literature is relevant and well read, one cannot ignore women. Yet, Punjabi has done so, never giving women writers (Amrita Pritam is the one true exception) a voice. Worse, the men do not have a clue what it is the women want to read or what experiences they need to read to fulfill their spiritual needs. This failure means that Punjabi writers can never be read that widely and how can any man really capture what has happened to a woman that well? Feminist literature is a necessity in Punjabi, a voice as important as the Dalits.

There are positive points in faith. Islam brings unity, encourages belief in one God. Hinduism brings order and Sikhism has placed all men of all faiths equal and, more importantly, women at the same level. The failure has come in interpreting and applying these faiths, or ignoring the real messages, or using them to suppress weaker members of society.

In Sikhism, it is clear that man and woman, apart from the obvious physical differences, are equal in rights. Yet in practice, Punjabi culture dominates, placing women as subservient.

This is even worse, when viewed through caste, as in Hinduism, much worse in Muslim society. Conservative values often clash with the democratic soul of art. Punjabi literature will not truly shine again until such conservative views are challenged, without the fear of a fatwa.

We have all forgotten what made Punjabi literature great. Guru Nanak was a rebel and all of his poems and writings in the Guru Granth are a direct assault on the established attitudes of organized religion. The same is true of Sufi literature. Yet if one was to do that now, the extremists will come down like bricks on you.

Appendix 4:

Reclaiming Punjabi by Mahmood Awan

Similarly the noted author **Mahmood Awan** has in a beautiful write-up in **The News International, Pakistan,** dated 19.2.2017 reflected on why Punjabi language continues to languish. Though the article has been written in context of West Punjab/Pakistan but what he has written is equally applicable to the situation in East Punjab/India. He writes:

As the world celebrates the Mother Tongue day on 21 Feb, let's admit that we have failed to make Punjabi language an issue for the common people of the Punjab or its political parties. Significant blame of this self-hate may lead us to our colonial past but let's try to avoid any excuses on this mother language day and dig a little deeper in analysing issue of Punjabi language, which to me is primarily a class issue. From 1849 to 2017, we have faced 168 years of official demeaning of our language (ironically it was on 21 February 1849, when the British defeated the Punjabis at the Battle of Gujarat). Punjab has already lost at least five generations without any formal education in their mother language. It's an immensely huge gap that haunts not only us but will impact our forthcoming generations too. Therefore, we need to take a holistic view of options currently available to us to reclaim our identity that is pivoted in our mother language.

Punjabis still have Punjabi speaking as part of our daily lives. We are a large vibrant global community but it's also true that parents of even our labour classes prefer to talk with their children in Urdu now with their eyes already targeted on English mediums. The same trend is visible across all our villages.

It may not be an exaggeration to say that the next generation of Punjabis (especially working classes) will learn Chinese, and the conscious romanticism for the mother tongue will be left to those few who have secured their careers through non-Punjabi-related professional degrees and have the insight, leisure and privilege to 'preach' and 'practice' Punjabi. An option not available to many others who inspite of their love and longing for the language are struggling to make both ends meet, and Punjabi language and culture is nowhere on their priorities' list.

Therefore, as a first compulsory step, all flag bearers of Punjabi cause, activists, and writers must lead by example, starting from their own homes. They shouldn't do what Punjabi Marxists, scholars and professors did in the past when they were advocating the case of Punjabi to an entire world outside, but – inside their homes – they were encouraging their children to learn English and Urdu.

The next step should be to lobby with the Punjab Government and private educational institutions to have Punjabi classics and history of the Punjab included in primary school's syllabus across Punjab. And if we can convince them to start a dedicated Punjabi language subject, then that will be a huge success. As we know few private schools in Lahore are already offering Punjabi to their students.

Let's first admit that we have failed to make Punjabi language an issue for the common people of the Punjab or its political parties. Even those classes who don't know any other language except Punjabi are unwilling to own it or fill the streets for its cause. Therefore, we need to shift our focus to those target groups who have the economic capacity to take the 'risk' in the name of Punjabi. If we can influence that socio-political class of the Punjab, someday that Punjabi ownership may trickle down to those classes and groups who are linked to or are socio-economically dependent on them.

I strongly believe that the future route to reclaim Punjabi language runs through Punjab studies, Punjabi films and music. To put it crudely, we need to make Punjab and Punjabi fashionable! Punjab is a unique phenomenon, blessed with the power to fascinate and transform anyone who comes closer to it. Those who will take Punjab studies even in English will ultimately come to Punjabi, as any research on Punjab is incomplete without understating its language and literature. We need to convince ourselves that there is no greater pride than owning our roots and celebrating our thousands of year's old heritage and civilization that has grown global. There is hardly any city in the world where you will not find a fellow Punjabi with a broad smile and a welcoming heart irrespective of their religion or caste. Let's reclaim that all through an all-inclusive culture and language.

About the Translators[1]

Aga Shahid Ali
Aga Shahid Ali is a Kashmiri poet. His collections include *A Walk Through the Yellow Pages*, *The Half-Inch Himalayas*, *A Nostalgist's Map of America*, *The Country Without a Post Office* and *Rooms Are Never Finished*, the latter a finalist for the National Book Award in 2001. Ali taught at the MFA Program for Poets & Writers at University of Massachusetts Amherst, at the MFA Writing Seminars at Bennington College as well as at creative writing programs at University of Utah, Baruch College, Warren Wilson College, Hamilton College and New York University. He died of brain cancer in December 2001 and was buried in Northampton, Massachusetts.

Ajmer Rode
Writer, dramatist and translator Ajmer (1940–) was born in the village Rode of Punjab, India. After completing his degree in engineering, he migrated to Canada in 1966 and became a full-time writer in 1994. He has published more than 20 books of poetry, plays, non-fiction and translations from Punjabi and English and has won several prizes. *Leela*, co-authored with Navtej Bharati, is more than 1000 pages and is his most well-known work and is considered one of the most outstanding works of the 20th century Punjabi poetry.

His first book *Vishava Di Nuhar* published in 1966 expounds Einstein's Theory of Relativity in fictional form. Similarly his first poetry book *Surti* is credited with introducing concrete poetry in

---

[1] No information could be obtained for some of the translators despite even contacting the publishers and writers.

Punjabi. Ajmer's *Stroll in a Particle* is one of the eight international English poems inscribed in bronze on a public wall outside the new office complex of Bill & Melinda Gates in downtown Seattle. Ajmer is the founder of Canadian Punjabi Drama and has written 10 plays. His one-act play *Dooja Passa* was the first Punjabi play written in Canada and his full-length play *Komagata Maru*, recently published online by Canada's Simon Fraser University, was the first full-length Punjabi play written and staged in Canada.

Amin Mughal

Amin Mughal was born in the Punjab in 1935 and has lived in England as a political exile since 1984. He is a critic of Urdu and Punjabi literature. He taught English at Islamia College and Shah Hussain College in Lahore. As a leader of the National Awami Party, he was imprisoned a number of times. He worked for the weekly magazine *Viewpoint* in Lahore and was editor of *Awaz*, an Urdu daily published in London.

Anand

Anand, a former print and broadcast journalist, has translated Yashpal's major novels, from Hindi into English, as well as his short stories into English and French. He was the editor of the fourteen-volume *Collected Works of Yashpal*, published in 2008. He has also translated Canadian writers Alice Munro, Mordecai Richler and Hugh MacLennon into Hindi.

Anwar Dil

Anwar Dil was born in Jullundur, Punjab, and was raised in Abbottabad in North-West Frontier Province. Dr. Dil has been Professor of Language, Science and Communication at United Sates International University in San Diego, California, since 1973. Earlier he was a teacher of English at various colleges in Pakistan. He is author and editor of over 35 books including 19 volumes published in a series by Stanford University. His books include *Humans in Universe*, co-authored with Buckminster Fuller; *Norman Borlaug on World Hunger;* and *Towards a Hunger-free World:*

Life & Works of M.S. Swaminathan. His calligraphic and abstract paintings are in the collections of connoisseurs around the world.

Arvinder
Arvinder taught English at Government College for Girls, Chandigarh. She is multi-lingual. She writes in English as well as in Punjabi and Hindi. She is the author of a book of Punjabi poetry. She has also translated a book on memory improving methods into English and is currently working on a project on writing skills in English.

Avtar Singh Judge
Avtar Singh Judge (1929–) is a translator in English and Hindi. He has translated Surendra Prakash's Sahitya Akademi Award winning short story collection *Baaz Goyi* into English, apart from both the seminal works of Ram Sarup Ankhi – *Kothe Kharak Singh* & *Partapi* as well as Rajinder Singh Bedi's *Ek Chadar Maili Si*.

B. M. Razdan
B. M. Razdan started his career as a lecturer in the erstwhile PEPSU and Punjab Education Service. He taught at the Punjabi University, Patiala, in the early 1960s when the university was in its formative years. One of the most impactful teachers, 'Bijee,' as he was affectionately called by his colleagues and friends, was selected by the U.S. Education Foundation in India (USEFI) to teach as a Fulbright Professor in Berkeley campus of California University in America. On the completion of his U.S. assignments he returned to join the faculty of Punjab University, Department of English, in Chandigarh, where he stayed till his retirement.

Christopher Shackle
Christopher Shackle (1942–) is a master of Urdu and Punjabi and has done considerable work in both languages. He is a retired professor of Modern Languages of South Asia at the University of London, Department of the Languages and Cultures of South Asia, and also professor, Department of Study of Religions at that

university. He is furthermore the head of the Urdu department at the School of Oriental and African Studies of London, project leader at the Arts and Humanities Research Council's Centre for Asian and African Literatures, and a member of the Centre of South Asian Studies. He is an expert on the Saraiki language, which he learned from Mehr Abdul Haq. He has written several books on Saraiki literature and on Khwaja Ghulam Farid.

He has written many books and published over 19 books and journal articles in the field of Urdu literature. He has won many awards including Fellow of the British Academy in 1990, 2004 Award of the Royal Asiatic Society and Pakistan's highest award for the arts, the Sitara-i-Imtiaz in 2005.

Gita Rajan

An MBA and a qualified company secretary, Gita Rajan took voluntary retirement from government service to pursue a keen interest in Indian literature, Indian mythology, translation, philosophy and to travel. A former Katha editor, she has also translated *Parthiban's Dream* by R. Krishnamurthy, better known as Kalki, credited with pioneering the historical novel in Tamil literature. She lives in Delhi.

Gopi Chand Narang

Gopi Chand Narang, born in Dukki, Balochistan, is an Indian theorist, literary critic and scholar who wrote in Urdu and English. Narang taught Urdu literature at St. Stephen's College (1957–58) and went on to become professor of Urdu at Delhi University. In 2005, the university named him a Professor Emeritus.

In addition to being a teacher, Narang was vice-chairman of the Delhi Urdu Academy and the National Council for Promotion of Urdu Language, as well as vice-president and president of the Sahitya Akademi.

He is a recipient of many awards including the President of Pakistan's National Gold Medal for his work on Allama Iqbal and a Padma Bhushan and Padma Shri from India. Narang received the Sahitya Akademi Award in 1995 as well as its highest honour, the Fellowship, in 2009. Narang has published more than 60 scholarly and critical books on language, literature, poetics and cultural studies; many have been translated into other Indian languages.

Gurbhagat Singh

Gurbhagat Singh is one of the most respected thinkers, interpreters and scholars with a deep study of international philosophy and literature. Gurbhagat Singh was one of the most Westernized scholars in Punjab in terms of his rich knowledge of Western thought, and, at another level, the most non-Westernized in terms of his emphasis on indigenous sources of knowledge. Singh joined the Department of English of Punjabi University, Patiala. in 1976–77 where he eventually became a professor and chair of the Department of English and dean of the Languages before retiring in 1998. Singh was deeply influenced by the French philosophers of the post-modernist, post-structural and post-colonial schools of thought. He wrote a number of books on criticism including *Poetry as Meta-consciousness*, *Western Poetics and Eastern Thought*, *Literature and Folklore after Post-Structuralism*, *Sikhism and Postmodern Thought*, and *The Sikh Memory: Its Distinction and Contribution to Mankind*. Singh took up the task of transalting the Guru Granth Sahib, but unfortunately, he could complete only 1208 pages before his death in April 2014.

Gurdial Singh Aarif

Gurdial Singh Aarif retired as a teacher and did freelance writing in Urdu and Punjabi as well as translations. He held various posts like Secretary, Chandigarh Sahitya Academy, Member, Punjab Arts Council, and President, Chandigarh Lekhak Sabha amongst others. He won the Gurmukh Singh Musafir Award from Punjab Government and wrote many books in Urdu and English.

Gurpal Sandhu

Gurpal Sandhu is professor of Punjabi in Department of Evening Studies – Multi Disciplinary Research Centre at Panjab University,

Chandigarh. He has done his masters in Anthropological linguistics and Punjabi and Ph.D on *The Semiological Study of Punjabi Novel* from Punjabi University, Patiala.

Gurshminder Jagpal

Born in 1961 at Ludhiana, Gurshminder Jagpal grew up in various Indian Air Force bases across the country, where his father remained posted during his long stint with the AF. A postgraduate in English Literature from Panjab University, Chandigarh, he obtained his M. Phil from Jammu University. He is associate editor of *Urdu Alive* – a bi-annual journal. He also has to his credit articles published in leading newspapers and magazines in English – the subject he has been teaching since 1987. He is presently principal, Partap Public School, Ludhiana.

Harbans Singh

Harbans Singh was an educationist, administrator and a scholar. He had a vital and pervasive influence in the field of religious studies, with special reference to Sikhism. Singh received his schooling at Khalsa Secondary School at Muktsar and started his career as a lecturer of English at the Khalsa College in Amritsar in 1943.

He wrote his first book on the history of the State of Faridkot, depicting its rulers' sponsorship and enshrinement of Sikh traditions. He also wrote a history of the Sikh rule under Maharaja Ranjit Singh and a book on aspects of Punjabi Literature.

Among his other books are *Guru Gobind, The Heritage of the Sikhs* and *Guru Nanak and Origins of the Sikh Faith*. All through, he kept up with his scholarship in Sikh history and literature by writing books, contributing articles to journals and newspapers, translating Punjabi authors, and editing collections of short stories, essays and conference papers. Singh also wrote an autobiographical essay in Punjabi.

The culmination of his life's work was the momentous *Encyclopedia of Sikhism*, the first in the English language. This comprehensive work covers different aspects of Sikh history, literature and philosophy. He received an honorary degree of Doctor of Letters from Guru Nanak Dev University and continued working on his project till his death. He was honoured by the SGPC, and during the Khalsa Tercentenary Celebrations he was posthumously invested with the Order of the Khalsa. The Punjabi University honoured him by prefixing his name as Professor Harbans Singh. Singh was a sage-like figure who stayed away from the limelight, selflessly pursuing his literary and scholarly interests.

Harbir Singh Manku

Harbir Singh Manku is a professor in English at the Guru Nanak Dev University, Amritsar.

Hina Nandrajog

Hina Nandrajog joined as a lecturer at Vivekananda College, Delhi, and rose to be its acting principal. She taught Contemporary Literature, Nineteenth-Century British Literature, Modern European Drama, and her areas of interests are Partition Literature, Cultural Diversity in India and Translations.

She is a prolific translator from Hindi and Punjabi into English. She has translated seven Punjabi books – *Inheritors of a New Age* (Navein Yug de Waris) by Mohinder Singh Sarna; *The New Breed* (Navein Lok) by Kulwant Singh Virk; *It is Light and other plays for children* (Chaanan Hoya atei hoar baal naatak), a collection of children's plays by Dr. Prabhjot Kulkarrni; *Kahaniyaan da Shahar* by Rukminin Banerjee; *The Elusive Fragrance and Other Stories* by Dr. Jaswinder Singh; and *Gadar Party Hero: Kartar Singh Sarabha* by Chaman Lal. She co-translated *Santalinama: Partition Stories*. Ed. Anna Sieklucka and S.S. Noor. She has also translated numerous Punjabi stories in anthologies.

Jai Ratan

Jai Ratan (1917–2012) was born in Ludhiana and was educated at the Forman Christian College in Lahore. Translating literary works from languages such as Hindi, Punjabi and Urdu was a passion for him.

A founding member of the Writers' Workshop in Kolkata, Winner of the Sahitya Akademi Award for Translation, and the Devi-Vageesh Prize, Jai Ratan could easily be one of the most prolific translators in the country and has translated almost all famous writers like Premchand, Upendra Nath Ashq, Kamleshwar, Dalip Kaur Tiwana, Bhisham Sahni, Balwant singh, Krishan Chander, Abdus Samad, Nirmal Verma and many others. He not only translated 600 short stories into English but also penned many original stories. He has over 60 books to his credit.

Jamal J Elias
Jamal J Elias is associate professor of Religion at Amherst College.

Jane Duran
Jane Duran (born 1944) is a Cuban-born poet. She has published four collections – *Breathe Now, Breathe* (1995), *Silences from the Spanish Civil War* (2002), *Coastal* (2006), and *Graceline*, all published by Enitharmon Press. *Breathe Now, Breathe* won the Forward Poetry Prize for Best First Collection, and in 2005, Duran received a Cholmondeley Award.

Jasdeep Singh
Jasdeep Singh is a translator, blogger and software engineer. He has worked as an additional dialogue writer and translator for two critically acclaimed Punjabi films *Annhe Ghore Da Daan* and *Chauthi Koot*. His blog www.parchanve.wordpress.com is an eclectic mix of Punjabi poetry translation, short stories and audio renditions. He lives in Chandigarh, India.

Jasjit Mansingh
Jasjit Mansingh is a freelance writer, broadcaster, editor and translates from Punjabi to English. She has co-authored a biography, *Lt Gen P S Bhagat*; written a memoir, *Oona Mountain Wind*, a book on environmental issues using the work experience of her late daughter, Oona; done a transcreation of the *Japjee*; compiled and

translated short stories from Punjab; and contributed articles in magazines and journals. She also scripts and voices for All India Radio. Her interests are birding, trekking, gardening and tennis. She lives in Delhi.

Jasminder Dhillon

Jasminder Dhillon is associate professor in English at Punjab University. He did his Ph.D on *The Nature of Violence in the Novels of Toni Morrison* from Punjab University, Chandigarh. He is an avid scholar of contemporary literary theory with a voracious penchant for research and studies in English literature. He has presented about two dozen research papers in national and international seminars and conferences and also published extensively on eco-criticism, post-colonialism, etc. in leading research journals. He has worked in major UGC-sponsored research projects and was also associated with a project of Punjabi University of translating *Mahan Kosh: An Encyclopedia of Sikhism* into English.

Jaspal Singh

A former diplomat, Dr. Jaspal Singh occupied the coveted position of Vice-Chancellor of Punjabi University, Patiala, from 2007–2017. During his stint as India's High Commissioner to Mozambique and Swaziland, Singh played the stellar role of identifying newer areas of cooperation for enhancing the scope and vistas of understanding among the countries concerned.

After securing his Master's degree in Political Science from Aligarh Muslim University, he did his Doctorate from Panjab University, Chandigarh. He taught for 23 years at colleges in Delhi. Singh has authored well-acclaimed books including, *Raj da Sikh Sankalp, Sikh Dharam te Rajniti* and *Sri Guru Granth Sahib: Sadivi Prerna Sarot*, besides over 200 articles on Sikh history, religion and on issues of national and international politics thus establishing him as a erudite scholar and exponent of Sikh theology and its practice.

He has been bestowed with many fellowships, awards and honours by various national and international institutions including Best Prose Award by Punjabi Academy, Delhi, Vismad Naad Fellowship, Nishan-e-Khalsa, Punjabi Parchar Parsar Award.

Dr. Singh has also remained General Secretary of Delhi Sikh Gurudwara Management Committee, Founder Member of Punjabi Academy, Delhi, Member, Board for Centre for Dalits and Minorities Studies, Jamia Millia Islamia, New Delhi and Chairman, Harkrishan Public School, New Delhi.

John Berger

John Berger was born in London in 1926. His many books, innovative in form and far-reaching in their historical and political insight, include *To the Wedding* King and the Booker Prize-winning novel, *G*. Amongst his outstanding studies of art and photography are: *Another Way of Telling*; *The Success and Failure of Picasso*; *Titian: Nymph and Shepherd* (with Katya Berger); and the internationally acclaimed *Ways of Seeing*.

He lives and works in a small village in the French Alps, the setting for his trilogy *Into Their Labours* (*Pig Earth, Once in Europa and Lilac* and *Flag*). His collection of essays *The Shape of a Pocket* was published in 2001. His latest novel, *From A to X*, was published in 2008. *About Looking*, published by Bloomsbury in April 2009, is the follow-up to the seminal *Ways of Seeing*, one of the most influential books on art.

John Welch

John Welch was born in 1942 and lives in London. He edited *Stories from South Asia*, an anthology for school and college use, published by Oxford University Press in 1984. For around 25 years he ran the Many Press, publisher in 1993 of Amarjit Chandan's pamphlet collection *Being Here*. His own publications include *Collected Poems* and *Visiting Exile*.

Julia Casterton

The poet and teacher Julia Casterton graduated from the University of Essex with a first-class degree in comparative literature in 1975; Julia joined the editorial board of the London-based journal *Red Letters* in the early 1980s. From 1986 to 1996, she published poetry and reviewed for Ambit poetry magazine. Among her many teaching jobs, her long association with London's City Lit was one of the most important; beginning in the early 1980s, she taught creative writing to students of varying abilities. The fruits of her wide teaching experience came with the book *Creative Writing* and *Writing Poems: A Practical Guide*.

J. S. Anand
Dr. J.S. Anand, an Indian author who has excelled in English poetry, fiction and non-fiction. His works include *Beyond Words*, a collection of his poetry.

Kiran Heer
Kiran Heer is working as a performance management analyst at Royal Bank Canada Insurance Toronto, Canada. Born in London in a Punjabi emigrant family, Kiran Heer has passed her B.A. Hons. in business administration from Middlesex University, London, the United Kingdom and moved to Toronto in 1999. She is a keen reader of Punjabi and English literature, particularly, of fiction and translates Punjabi short stories into English.

Khalid Hasan
Khalid Hasan – journalist, writer and translator – was born in Kashmir. Besides translating most of Manto's work, he has also translated the stories of Ghulam Abbas and the poetry of Faiz Ahmad Faiz. His own publications include *Scorecard, Give us Back our Opinions, The Umpire Strikes Back, Private View* and *Rearview Mirror*.

Khushwant Singh
Khushwant Singh (1915–2014) was an Indian novelist, lawyer, journalist and politician. He studied law at St. Stephen's College, Delhi, and King's College London. After working as a lawyer in Lahore Court for eight years, he joined the Indian Foreign

Service upon the Independence of India from British Empire in 1947. He was appointed journalist in the All India Radio in 1951 and then moved to the Department of Mass Communications of UNESCO at Paris in 1956. These last two careers encouraged him to pursue a literary career.

As a writer, he was best known for his trenchant secularism, humour, sarcasm and an abiding love of poetry. His name is bound to go down in Indian literary history as one of the finest historians and novelists, a forthright political commentator, and an outstanding observer and social critic. He was a prolific writer. Among the several works he published are a classic two-volume history of the Sikhs, several novels (the best known of which are *Delhi, Train to Pakistan* and *The Company of Women*), and a number of translations and non-fiction books on Delhi, nature and current affairs.

He served as the editor of several literary and news magazines, as well as two newspapers, through the 1970s and 1980s. Between 1980–1986, he served as Member of Parliament in Rajya Sabha. He won numerous awards including the Sahitya Akademi Fellowship Award, Lifetime achievement award from TATA Literature Live, Punjab Rattan, etc. He was also decorated with the Padma Bhushan in 1974. But he returned the award in 1984 in protest against Operation Blue Star (Union Government's siege of the Golden Temple at Amritsar). In 2007, he was awarded the Padma Vibhushan, the second-highest civilian award in India.

Lucy Rosenstein
Lucy Rosenstein did her MA in Indology at Sofia University (Bulgaria) and came to SOAS, University of London to further her knowledge of Hindi in 1991 by doing an MA and a PhD in Hindi.

Madhumeet
Dr. Madhumeet works in the English Department at Kanya Maha Vidyala, Jalandhar. She has translated stories of renowned authors like K. S. Duggal and Prem Parkash. Dr. Madhumeet has been regularly translating Punjabi literature into English and has

translated books for the British Centre for Translation and for the Sahitya Akademi.

Manjit Inder Singh
Professor Manjit Inder Singh has been Professor and the Head, Department of English, Punjabi University, Patiala. His teaching and research career spans well over 40 years, in which he has specialized in numerous literary, critical and theoretical fields, among them, Modern literature and theory, post-colonial writing and literary studies, literary theory, Indian writing in English, translation studies, diasporic literature and interdisciplinary approaches to diasporic studies, Punjabi literature, etc. Professor Singh has travelled and published widely, with over eight published critical volumes on above-mentioned areas and dozens of research papers in prestigious journals and anthologies, and the most popular of them are: *V S Naipaul* (Rawat, 1998) and *Contemporary Diasporic Literature* (Pencraft International, 2010). After teaching of literature for such a long span, he has moved to diaspora studies; he is presently coordinator, UGC Centre for Diaspora Studies, Punjabi University, Patiala (Punjab).

Manmohan
Punjabi poet and critic Manmohan's debut Punjabi novel *Nirvaan* won the Sahitya Akademi Award 2013. An Indian Police Services (IPS) of Bihar cadre, he is now the inspector general, police with Intelligence Bureau at Chandigarh. Born and brought up at Amritsar, Manmohan holds a doctorate on mythological poetry of Guru Gobind Singh, the 10th Sikh Guru. He has written eight anthologies of poems in Punjabi and one in Hindi. He has also translated three books from English to Punjabi like *Shikari diaan yadaan, Aakhri Ticket* and *Indira Gandhi*.

Masooma Ali
Masooma Ali is senior lecturer in the English Department of Miranda House, University of Delhi. She has edited a popular Hindi magazine *Chitrank*, published from Bombay in 1978–79. She

has contributed extensively to literary magazines and books and has participated in talks and discussions on All India Radio. She was one of the editors of a two-volume encyclopedia on Kim II Sung, the President of the Democratic People's Republic of Korea. She has also assisted in designing the costumes of a T. V. serial *Akbar the Great*.

Moyna Mazumdar
Moyna Mazumdar is an editor and occasional translator based out of Kolkata with an interest in literary translation.

NarinderJit Kaur
NarinderJit Kaur is a prolific translator and writer based in Patiala, who taught at Mohindra College, Patiala. She has translated five very significant books from Punjabi into English (all of which are incidentally included in this compilation), including *Voices in the Back Courtyard*, a collection of short stories of Punjabi Women Writers, *Town & Countryside* By Sujan Singh, *Anndatta* By Baldev Singh, *On the Trails of Fire* by Inder Singh Khamosh and *Twilight* by Dalip Kaur Tiwana. Her own short stories and poems in English and Punjabi have been published in various newspapers and magazines and she has her own blog (narinderjit.com). Currently, she is translating a collection of Shahmukhi (Punjabi) stories by Pakistani Women Writers.

Navdeep Suri
Navdeep Suri is a career diplomat and currently serves as India's High Commissioner to Australia. He joined the Indian Foreign Service in 1983 and speaks French and Arabic and has served in diplomatic missions in Cairo, Damascus, Washington, Dar es Salaam, London, and Johannesburg. His father, Kulwant Singh runs a reputed publishing house in Amritsar and is head of the Punjabi Publishers Association. His mother, Attarjit Kaur is a professor of Punjabi literature who taught Punjabi to college students for almost 30 years and is the author of an authoritative biography of Nanak Singh.

Suri is the grandson of Nanak Singh and cherishes childhood memories of bedtime stories narrated by Punjab's greatest storyteller. He has translated two of Nanak Singh's classic books, *Pavitra Paapi* and *Adh Khidya Phul*.

Naveed Alam
Naveed Alam is a poet and translator. His first collection of poems, *A Queen of No Ordinary Realms*, won the Spokane Poetry Prize and his works have been published in a number of literary journals and magazines including the *Prairie Schooner, American Poetry Journal* and *Poetry International*, among others. He currently lives in Lahore, Pakistan.

Navtej Sarna
Navtej Sarna, IFS is an author-columnist and diplomat and has served in Moscow, Warsaw, Thimphu, Geneva, Tehran, Washington DC, Israel and the United Kingdom and is currently the Ambassador to the United States. He was joint secretary at the Ministry of External Affairs (MEA) and holds the distinction of being the longest-serving spokesperson of the ministry, and also served two prime ministers, three foreign ministers and four foreign secretaries. He also writes short stories and book reviews. His published works include *Folk Tales of Poland, We Weren't Lovers Like That, The Book of Nanak, The Exile* and *Second Thoughts, Winter Evenings* and a translation of Guru Gobind Singh's *Zafarnama*.

Neer Kanwal Mani
Neer Kanwal Mani has translated a variety of literary and nonliterary texts. Her 12 books in translation include the comic *Du-Rex ke Jalwe* for United Nations Development Programme, four books from *The Chronicles of Narnia* series by C.S. Lewis, two novels by Paulo Coelho along with folk narratives and oral epics for IGNCA, New Delhi. She translated Kerstin Ekman's *Blackwater* as a part of Indo-Swedish Writers Union Project in 2001–02. An associate professor in English, Neer has been engaging students in

literature, critical theory and translation for 26 years. To many, her approach is life altering; her methods, thought-provoking and multi-layered.

Niranjan Tasneem

Retired as professor of English from Govt. College, Ludhiana, Niranjan Tasneem has contributed 10 novels and 10 books of literary criticism. He is a former Fellow of Indian Institute of Advanced Study, Shimla. He has translated a large number of Urdu and Punjabi poems into English. He has received the Sahitya Akademi Award in 1999 and Punjab Sahit Ratan Award in 2016.

Nirupama Dutt

Nirupama Dutt is a poet, journalist and translator who writes in Punjabi and English. She received the Punjabi Akademi Award for a book of poems, *Ik Nadi Sanwali Jahi (A Stream Somewhat Dark)* that has been translated into English, Hindi, Kannada, Bengali and Urdu and featured in various anthologies. She is a veteran in the arena of Punjabi poetry and short fiction. A senior journalist with over 28 years of experience, she is the Features Editor of *The Tribune*. She has two anthologies of short stories by Pakistani writers and has co-edited with Ajeet Cour, an anthology of SAARC poetry, *Our Voices*. She has translated short stories, plays and poetry of many contemporary writers of Punjabi, Hindu and Urdu. She is convener of a women's study group called Hamshira.

Paramjeet Singh Ramana

Paramjeet Singh Ramana teaches comparative literature and is Dean of Language, Literature & Culture, Central University, Bathinda. He has six books of translation and literary criticism to his credit including the English translations of eminent Punjabi writers such as Gurdial Singh, Waryam Singh Sandhu, Mohan Bhandari, Ajmer Singh Aulakh and Pakistan writer Bushra Ejaz. He has published more than 50 research articles and papers in different literary journals.

Paul Smith

Paul Smith, who was born in Melbourne, Australia, in 1945 is a poet, author and translator of over 150 books of Sufi poets of the Persian, Arabic, Urdu, Turkish, Pashtu and other languages, including Hafiz, Sadi, Nizami, Rumi, 'Attar, Sana'i, Jahan Khatun, Obeyd Zakani, Mu'in, Amir Khusrau, Nesimi, Kabir, Anvari, Ansari, Jami, Omar Khayyam, Rudaki, Yunus Emre, Mahsati, Lalla Ded, Bulleh Shah, Shah Latif, Makhfi and many others, as well as his own poetry, fiction, plays, biographies, children's books and a dozen screenplays. Not many people in the entire Indian Subcontinent can boast of such a magnitude of flawless translation.

P.K. Nijhawan

P.K. Nijhawan started his career with Public Relations, Punjab and shifted to the Ministry of Family Planning, Government of India. A man of considerable literary caliber, he has written both in English and Hindi on a variety of subjects like current affairs, poetry, criticism, translation, thought and fiction. His *Sri Guru Gobind Singh Gita* and *Hinduism Redefined* earned him fame. His lifelong quest had been to be well-known as a good Punjabi. That is why he translated Shah Mohammed's *Janganamah* into English and Hindi to enable most of the Punjabis to read and appreciate it.

Rajendra Awasthy

Rajendra Awasthy is the editor and translator of this anthology. He started his writing career as a Hindi poet with the pen name of *Trishit*. He started with the Hindi daily, *Nav Bharat* and went on to edit *Sarika* before joining the Hindustan Times group as the editor of *Nandan*, *Kadambini* and *Saptahik Hindustan*.

Awasthy's writing includes short stories like *Lamse-na* and *Dagarpole* and the novel *Jungle ke phool*, which earned the President's award. He wrote eight novels and was the recipient of many national literary and media awards including the

Mahapandit Rahul Sankrityayana Puraskar, Mahadevi Verma Samman and Sahitya Bhushan Samman.

Raji Narasimhan

A journalist, writer and translator, Raji Narasimhan has published five novels – *The Heart of Standing is You Cannot Fly*, *Forever Free* (shortlisted for the Sahitya Akademi Award), *Drifting to a Dawn*, *The Sky Changes* and *Atonement*. Her writing includes a volume of short stories, the *Marriage of Bela and Other Stories*, and a work of literary criticism, *Sensibility Under Stress: Aspects of Indo-English Fiction*. She has translated Maitreyi Pushpa's *Alma Kabutari* and Rajee Seth's *Unarmed*, from Hindi to English for Katha and Macmillan India, respectively. She also writes articles and review for journals and newspapers. She lives in Delhi.

Rana Nayar

Rana Nayar is professor and former chairperson, Department of English and Cultural Studies, Panjab University, Chandigarh. A practicing translator of repute, he has rendered around 10 modern classics of Punjabi into English, ranging over novels, short stories and poetry. He was awarded First Prize, in an All India contest, organized by Sahitya Akademi, New Delhi, for his translation of Baba Farid's Shlokas into English. Among other works, his translations include those of Gurdial Singh, Mohan Bhandari, Raghbir Dhand and Beeba Balwant. He has one collection of poems *Breathing Spaces* and three critical books, i.e., *Edward Albee: Towards a Typology of Relationships*, *Inter-sections: Essays on Indian Literatures, Translations and Popular Consciousness*, and *Gurdial Singh: A Reader* to his credit. Moreover, he has directed over 20 major, full-length productions and acted in almost as many.

Ranjit Singh

Professor Ranjit Singh is a prolific writer of short stories in Hindi and Punjabi. He has also translated some Punjabi poetry in a book called *Quatrains*.

Rita Chaudhry
Rita Chaudhry is a professor in English at the Guru Nanak Dev University, Amritsar.

Satjit Wadva
Satjit Wadva, part-Grewal, had a traditional upbringing in Punjab. She taught at Guru Harkrishan Public School, New Delhi, for two decades and has translated Osho and other metaphysical writing besides *Aa Behn Fatima*, an award-wining story for Katha.

S. C. Narula
S. C. Narula, a professor of English at the Delhi University has translated the book, *A Light Within*. He has translated many works from Punjabi into English and has done extensive research in the comparative literature of Hindi, Punjabi and English.

Shashi Joshi
Shashi Joshi has a PhD in History from Jawaharlal Nehru University. She began her academic career lecturing at Miranda House, University of Delhi, was senior fellow at the Nehru Memorial Museum and Library, New Delhi and, during 1983–1997, was co-director at an Indian Council of Social Science research project. She is currently senior fellow at the Institute of Advanced Study Shimla. She has several publications to her credit including a three-volume work co-authored with Bhagwan Josh entitled *Struggle for Hegemony in India: 1920–47*. She has also published a play based on the Mountbatten Papers, *The Last Durbar: The Division of British India*.

Shiv Nath Dar
Shiv Nath Dar was an officer of Defence Audit and Accounts services and a voracious reader and collector of books. Before Partition, he had a collection of around 20,000 books at Lahore, which was fully lost during Partition. He wrote three books, *Culinary Art and Culture of India and Pakistan*, *Housing Patterns*, and

Costumes of India and Pakistan, out of which only the last seems to have been published as the manuscripts of the other two were apparently lost. He worked hard on translation in verse of Waris Shah's *Heer* but could not get it published in his lifetime. One of his friends, Mr. Sudhir K Sopory finally got it published after Mr. Dar's untimely death.

Stephen Watts

Stephen Watts is a poet with a number of books to his name. He was born in 1952 and lives mostly in London and the Western Isles, with close cultural roots in the Italian Alps. He has worked extensively in hospitals and in schools as a poet and recently was the first 'embedded poet' writing on issues of suicide in the Highlands and Islands. For a number of years, he helped run the Multicultural Arts Consortium in London. With Ana Jelnikar he co-translated *Six Slovenian Poets* and has also co-edited four anthologies of translated poetry.

Supriya Bhandari

Dr. Supriya Bhandari, M.A. (Eng.) UGC-NET is Professor in English at Guru Nanak College, Moga.

Swaraj Raj

Swaraj Raj is working as associate professor and head, Department of English at Govt. Mohindra College, Patiala. He got his Ph.D on Diasporic Consciousness in the Selected Novels of Salman Rushdie, Rohinton Mistry and Bharati Mukherjee from Punjab University, Patiala. Presently, he is actively involved in deconstructing the fundamental issues of theory and interpretation of cultural studies, translation studies, media studies and literary theory and translating Punjabi plays into English. He has about two dozen research publications to his credit including translation of Prof. Pritam Singh's stupendous article *Punjab, Punjabi and Punjabiyat* and remarkable short stories of Punjabi, i.e. Maninder Kang's *Bhaar* (The Burden), Sukhdev Sindhu's *Barkate* (Barkate), Sant

Singh Sekhon's *Pemi de Nianey* (Pemi's Children) and Kartar Singh Duggal's *Karamat* (Miracle) from Punjabi to English.

Tara Meenakshi Sekhri
Tara, a Tamil Brahmin who married a Punjabi, is a graduate in Sanskrit and speaks Tamil, Hindi, Urdu and Punjabi fluently. She has worked closely with Amrita Pritam and translated her work in *Fifty Fragments of Inner Self*. She has a post-graduate diploma in Linguistics from Delhi University.

Tejinder Kaur
Tejinder Kaur is professor of English at Punjab University, Patiala, India. She has headed Department of Distance Education and currently holding the office of dean, Faculty of Languages in Punjabi University. She has presented papers and delivered key-note and valedictory addresses in more than 100 national and international conferences and seminars. Having, a book on critical theory entitled *R.S. Crane: a Study in Critical Theory*, two co-edited books: *Perspectives on Diaspora Indian Fiction in English* and *Perspectives on the Partition Fiction of the Indian Sub-continent* and more than four dozen articles and research papers to her credit, she has also published four collections: *Reflections*, *Images*, *Expressions* and *Perceptions* of her poems in English. She has keen interest in translation and has translated few short stories of Punjabi into English.

Tejwant Singh Gill
Professor Tejwant Singh Gill taught English at Guru Nanak Dev University, Amritsar. He was the editor of many English and Punjabi magazines. He has published 10 books in Punjabi on language, literature and culture of the region and three books in English.

He is a prolific translator having translated works like *Kafis* of Shah Hussain, *Jangnama* by Shah Mohammad, poems of Pash as *Reckoning with Dark Times*, Sant Singh Sekhon's *Selected Writings*,

Sohan Singh Seetal's *Yug Badal Gia*, poems of Mohan Singh as *Dreams and Desire* and Manjit Pal's poetic play *Sundran*.

He is currently working as language editor for revising the *Encyclopedia of Indian Literatures*, writing *History of Modern Punjabi Literature* in five volumes and working on *Punjab: Its Language and Literature*.

T. C. Ghai

T. C. Ghai taught English language and literature at Deshbandhu Evening College, New Delhi, from where he retired a reader in 2002. He is the writer of *Patterns and Significance in the Novels of R. K. Narayan* published by Sahitya Akademi. He has also published two short novels, *The Stricken Moth* and *Alone in the Wilderness*. He has published some poems in *The Journal of the Poetry Society (India)* and *Poetry India: Voices for the Future*. He published a Hindi translation of his short stories, *Adamboo* originally written in English. He has translated Punjabi poems of Dr. Puran Singh Kanwar's anthology, *Rattan di Rut* into Hindi and English.

Vishav Bharti

Vishav Bharti is a journalist working with *The Tribune* in Chandigarh.

Bibliography

1. Punjabi Literature: The Journey So Far
   - Nayar, Rana. *Slice of Life: Punjabi Short Fiction, 1901–2000.* Chandigarh: Unistar, 2006. Print.
   - Tasneem, N. S. *Studies in Modern Punjabi Literature.* New Delhi: Avishkar Prakashan, 1980. Print.
   - Nayar, Rana. 'The Backdrop of Punjabi Literature.' *Folk Punjab.* 31 July 2012. Web. <www.folkpunjab.org>. Article originally published on cultivation.org, which is now offline.
   - Awan, Mahmood. 'Scripted Wall of Punjabi.' *The News on Sunday (TNS).* 22 June 2014. Web. <http://tns.thenews.com.pk/scripted-wall-punjabi-gurmukhi-or-shahmukhi/#.WSp9ihhh28U>.
   - Dutt, Nirupama. 'Waiting for Spring.' *Himal Southasian.* Apr. 2010. Web. <http://old.himalmag.com/component/content/article/138-waiting-for-spring.html>.
2. Beeba Balwant: Nayar, Aruti. 'The Poet Who Keeps Open House.' *The Tribune, India.* 25 Oct. 2003. Web. <http://www.tribuneindia.com/2003/20031025/windows/zero.htm>.
3. *Skeena*: Dhillon, Rupinderpal Singh. 'Skeena, A Book Review.' *SikhChic.* 9 June 2011. Web. <https://sikhchic.com/article-detail.php?id=2490&cat=11>.
4. Mohan Singh: 'Mohan Singh (1905–1978).' *The Sikh Encyclopedia.* Web. <https://www.thesikhencyclopedia.com/biographies/famous-sikh-personalities/singh-mohan-1905-1978>.
5. Mazhar Tirmazi:
   - Rabe, Nate. 'A rare gem from Pakistan: A lifetime on tiptoes.' *Scroll.in.* 6 Mar. 2016. Web.

- https://scroll.in/article/804656/timeless-pieces-a-lifetime-on-tiptoes
- http://mazhartirmazi.com
6. Jaswant Singh Zafar: Singh, Jasdeep. 'Jaswant Singh Zafar: Two Poems.' *International Writing Program, University of Iowa.* Web. <https://iwp.uiowa.edu/91st/vol9-num1/jaswant-singh-zafar-two-poems>.
7. Ram Sarup Ankhi: Chandan, Amarjit. 'Ram Sarup Ankhi: An Obituary.' *Academy of the Punjab in North America.* Web. <http://apnaorg.com/articles/amarjit-22/>.
8. Appendix 1:
    - Singh, Gurdial. *Earthy Tones: A Selection of Best Punjabi Short Stories.* Trans. Rana Nayar. Delhi: Fiction House, 2002. Print.
    - Singh, Manjit Inder, ed. *Contemporary Punjabi Short Stories: An Anthology.* New Delhi: Sahitya Akademi, 2011. Print.
9. Appendix 2: Budhraja, Anvita. 'The Monolingual Dystopia: Power Dynamics of Literary Translation.' *Change Magazine, Columbia.* 10 Mar. 2017. Web. <http://change-magazine.org/2017/03/the-monolingual-dystopia/>.
10. Appendix 3: Dhillon, Rupinderpal Singh. 'Skeena, A Book Review.' *SikhChic.* 9 June 2011. Web. <https://sikhchic.com/article-detail.php?id=2490&cat=11>.
11. Appendix 4: Awan, Mahmood. 'Reclaiming Punjabi.' *The News on Sunday (TNS).* 19 Feb. 2017. Web. <http://tns.thenews.com.pk/reclaiming-punjabi/>.
12. General information about authors and books taken from:
    - www.wikipedia.com
    - www.sikhchic.com
    - www.britannica.com

Index

A

Aakar Patel, 284-285
Aatish Taseer, 285
Abbas Athar, xxxviii
Abdullah, xxvii, 124, 129, 245
Abdus Samad, 330
Aftab Ahmad, 285
Afzal Ahsan Randhawa, xxix, xxxi, 231-232
Afzal Saahir, xxxi
Afzal Tauseef, 231-232
Aga Shahid Ali, 135, 323
Ahmad Rahi, xxxi
Ahmad Yar, xxxvi
Ahmed Salim, xviii, 262
Ajaib Kamal, xxx, xxxvii
Ajeet Cour, v, vii, xvi, xix, xxii, xxix, xxxiv, 2, 13, 210, 212, 228, 232, 237, 241, 260, 270, 281, 338
Ajmer Aulakh, xli, 196
Ajmer Rode, xvii-xviii, xxx, 118, 323
Ajmer Sidhu, 250, 252
Akhtar Husain, xxxii
Ali Haidar, xxxv
Amandeep Sandhu, xiii, 99, 176
Amanpal Sara, 302, 304
Amar Jyoti, xxxvii
Amarjit Chandan, vi, xiii, xix, xxii, xxx-xxxii, xxxvii, 118-119, 154, 156, 171, 310, 332
Amin Mughal, 118, 324
Amrik Singh Kanda, vii, 213-214
Amrik Singh, vii, 171
Amrita Pritam, v, xvi, xviii-xix, xxii-xxiii, xxviii, xxxi, xxxiii-xxxvi, 5, 22, 24-25, 27, 31, 66, 161, 211, 228-229, 232, 237-238, 241-242, 259, 261, 270, 281, 316, 343
Anand 112, 114, 324
Anked Saleem, xxxviii
Anna Sieklucka, 230, 329
Anvita Budhraja, viii, xxi, 311
Anwar Dil, 163, 324
Arpana Caur, 211, 237
Arunava Sinha, 286
Arvinder Kaur, xiii, 26, 325
Asif Javeed Mir, 43
Atamjit, vii, xiii, xxx, xli, 194-195
Attar Singh, xxxi, 73-75
Attarjit, xliii
Avtar Singh Judge, 83, 88, 91, 325
Azad Gulati, 13
Azra Wakar, 262

B

B.M. Bhalla, 179
B.M. Razdan, 158, 325
Baba Farid/Fariduddin Ganjshakar/ Sheikh Farid, x, xxvi, xxvii, xxxi, xxxii, xxxv, 42, 121, 169, 172, 183, 188, 200, 326, 340,
Bachint Kaur, v, 8, 10, 13, 87, 259, 277-278
Balbir Kaur Sanghera, 305-306
Baldev Singh Dhaliwal, vii, 216, 218
Baldev Singh/Baldev Singh Sadaknaama, 29, 152, 232. 237, 238, 276, 299, 336,
Balraj Sahni, xxxi, 38, 73, 84, 110
Balwant Gargi, xvii, xxx, xxxii, xl, 93, 171, 228-229, 241-242, 255, 261-262
Balwant Singh, vii, xviii, xxii, 33, 54, 124, 126, 219-220, 242, 272, 330
Balwinder Brar, 259
Balwinder Singh Grewal, 250
Bawa Balwant, xxxvii, 257, 291
Beeba Balwant, vi, 125, 340, 345
Bhagwant Rasulpuri, xviii, xliii,
Bhai Jaito, xli
Bhai Vir Singh, v, xxxvi, 32-35
Bhisham Sahni, xxii, xxiii, 36, 330
Bhupinder Singh, 40-41, 169, 194, 239
Bimal Kaur, 32
Bushra Ejaz, 222, 338
Buta Singh, xvii, 237-238, 269-270

C

Chaman Lal, xxii, 25, 329
Chandan Negi, xviii, xxxix, 277
Charan Das Sidhu, xli
Charan Singh Shaheed, xxix, xxxix, 280, 281
Christopher Shackle, 128, 325

D

D. R. Goyal, 50
Dalip Kaur Tiwana, v, xviii, xxiii, xxix, xxxii, xxxiv, 11, 13, 39-40, 87, 232, 259, 270, 281, 330, 336
Daljit Ami, 99
Damodar Das, xxxi-xxxii
Darshan Khatkar, 156
Darshan Singh Awara, xxxi
Darshan Singh Dhir, 306
Des Raj Kali, xliii
Dev 134-135
Devendra Satyarthi, xvii, xxxii, 134, 232, 269, 277, 281
Devinder Daman, 196
Devinder Kaur Assa Singh, 210, 238
Dhani Ram Chatrik, xvii, xxviii
Ditt Singh Giani, xlii
Diwan Singh, xxviii
Dominic Rai, 204

E

Elizabeth A. Siler, 40

F

Faiz Ahmad Faiz, xxxviii, 333
Fakhar Zaman, v, xxix, xxxviii, 24, 42-43
Fauzia Rafique, xiii, xxii, xxxv, 315
Fazal Shah, xxiii, xxviii, xxxv

Index | 349

G

Gagan Gill, vi, xxxvii, 138-139
Ghulam Abbas, 333
Gian Singh Shatir, xxii
Giani Heera Singh Dard, xxix, xxxix, 89,295,
Gilani Kamran, 43
Gita Rajan, 68-69, 326
Gopi Chand Narang, xxiii, 219, 272, 326
Gul Chauhan, 277-278
Gulzar Mohd Goria, 262
Gulzar Singh Sandhu, v, 50-51, 243, 247
Gurbachan Singh Bhullar, 89, 93, 231, 275
Gurbaksh Garcha, 204
Gurbaksh Kaur Dosanjh, 300
Gurbaksh Singh Preetlari, xvi, xxii, xxxix, 17, 228, 229, 231, 269, 277, 280
Gurbhachan Singh Bhullar, xxxix, 89,93, 231, 250, 275, 276,
Gurbhagat Singh, 132-133, 327
Gurdas Ram Alam, xliii
Gurdeep Puri, 301
Gurdev Singh Rupana, xiii, 262, 275
Gurdial Singh Aarif, 225, 327
Gurdial Singh Phul, xl
Gurdial Singh Rai, 300
Gurdial Singh, v, xvi, xviii, xxiii, xxxii-xxxiv, xl, xliii, 13, 16, 18-19, 31, 48, 225, 231, 281, 300, 310, 327, 338, 340

Gurmukh Singh Jeet, 241
Gurmukh Singh Musafir, xvii-xviii, 12, 228, 232, 277, 327
Gurmukh Singh Sehgal, v, 53, 55
Gurnam Gill, vii, 225, 227, 301, 305
Gurpal Sandhu, 233, 235, 327
Gurpal Singh, 307
Gursharan Singh, xxx, xl
Gurshminder Singh Jagpal, xiii, 151, 186-187, 328
Guru Arjan Dev, xxvii, 76
Guru Gobind Singh, xxvii, 207, 292, 335, 337, 339
Guru Nanak Dev/Baba Nanak, xxvi, xxvii, xxviii, xxxi, xxxii, 6, 32, 106, 121, 133, 143, 148, 151, 160, 172, 292, 317, 328, 337
Gurvinder Singh, xix, 18, 118, 295

H

Habib Jalib, xxxi
Hafiz Barkhudar, xxiii, xxviii
Hamid Jalal, 283
Harbans Singh, vii, xviii, xxiii, 228-229, 328-329
Harbhajan Halwarvi, xxxvii, 140,
Harbhajan Singh, vi, xix, xxiii, xxxvi, 124, 139, 142-144, 146, 161, 250
Harbir S. Manku, 302
Harcharan Singh, xl
Hardev Grewal, xxix
Harish Narang, 285
Harish Trivedi, 115
Harjeet Atwal, xiii, xvii, xxx, xl

Hartej Kaur, 250
Hashim Shah, xxiii, xxviii, xxxv
Heera Singh Dard, xxix, xxxix
Hina Nandrajog, vii, xiii, xviii, 230, 239, 250, 329

I

Iliyas Ghuman, 231, 262
Imroz, v, 6-7, 26-28, 126
Inder Singh Khamosh, v, 56-57, 216, 336
Iqbal Deep, 275-276
Iqbal Qaiser, xxxi
Ishaq Mohammad, xliii
Ishmeet Kaur, xiii, 224
Ishwar Chitrakar, 291
Ishwar Nanda, xxx, xl

J

J. S. Anand, 78, 333
J. S. Rahi, 143, 144
Jagdish Chander, 195
Jagjit Brar, 302-303
Jagjit Kaur, xxxi
Jagroop Singh Datevas, 275
Jagtar, xvii, xxxi, xxxvii, 128
Jai Ratan, xviii, 11, 38-39, 41, 61, 219, 244, 272, 329-330
Jamal J Elias, 183, 330
Jane Duran, 138, 330
Jarnail Singh, vii, 233, 235-236, 245, 250, 305
Jasbir Singh Bhullar, 275
Jasdeep Singh, 151, 330
Jasjit Mansingh, vii, 210, 237, 330

Jasminder Dhillon, 233, 235, 331
Jaswant Deed, vi, xxxvii, 148, 150, 230
Jaswant Singh Kanwal, vi, xxviii, xxxiii, 58-59, 271
Jaswant Singh Neki, xxxvii
Jaswant Singh Virdi, 237-238
Jaswant Zafar, vi, 151
Jasweer Singh Rana, 250
Jaswinder Singh, vii, 239-240, 250, 329
Jatinderpal Singh Jolly, xxxi
Javed Boota1, xxxi
Jinder, xxxi, 251, 275-276
Joga Singh, xxxvii
John Berger, 118, 332
John Welch, 118, 332
Joshua Fazal Deen, xxix, xxxix
Julia Casterton, 118, 332

K

Kabir, xxvii, 144, 148, 171, 339
Kailash Puri, 297, 300, 303
Kamleshwar, 330
Karanjit Singh, 277
Karnail Singh Thind, xxxi
Kartar Singh Duggal, xvi, xviii, xxii, xxx, xxxii, xxxiii, xxxiv, xix, xl, 61, 130, 198, 228, 229, 237, 241, 242, 247, 250, 262, 270, 280, 334, 343
Khalid Hasan, 42, 283, 285, 333
Khushwant Singh, 5, 22,81, 171, 210, 241, 333
Khwaja Ahmed Abbas, 241, 242
Kirpal Kazak, 250
Kishan Singh Arif, xxxv

Krishan Chander, xxii, 221, 244, 272, 330,
Krishen Singh Dhody, 237
Krishna Gorowara, 5
Krishna Sobti, vi, xvi, xxii-xxiii, 65-66, 68-69
Kuljit Mann, 307
Kuljit Singh, 250
Kulwant Singh Virk, vii, xviii, xxx, xxxii, xxxix, 190, 228, 232, 237-238, 247-248, 250, 269-270, 282, 295, 329
Kumar Sushil, 222

L

Laeeq Babri, xxxviii
Lal Singh Dil, vi, xxxii, xliii, 119, 154, 156
Lochan Singh Bakshi, 232
Lucy Rosenstein, 138, 334

M

Madho Lal Hussain/Shah Hussain, 172
Madhumeet, xviii, 148, 250, 334
Madhuri Chawla, vii, 230, 250
Maggar Singh Panesar, 306, 307
Mahmood Awan, viii, xiii, xxi, xxx, 319
Major Mangat, 305
Makhan Mann, 275-276
Malik M Zamurrad, 42
Manjit Inder Singh, vii, xxi, 250, 309, 335
Manjit Pal Kaur, vii, 201, 203
Manjit Rana, xxxv
Manjit Tiwana, vi, xxxvii, 158-159

Manmohan Bawa, 196, 237
Manmohan, 196, 335
Maqsood Saqib, xxxi
Masha Simrat Kaur, 247
Masooma Ali, 2, 335
Matt Reeck, 285
Mazhar Tirmazi, vii, xxx, 204-205, 345
Mir Tanha Yousafi, xxix
Mohammad Baksh, xxxv
Mohammad Buta Gujarati, xxxvi
Mohammad Idris, 224
Mohammad Mansha Yaad, 262
Mohan Bhandari, vii, xxxix, 231, 253-255, 275-276, 338, 340
Mohan Kahlon, xxxiv-xxxv
Mohan Lal Philauria, 262
Mohan Singh Diwana, xvii, 172, 269
Mohan Singh, vii, xvii, xxviii-xxix, xxxi, xxxvi, 17, 63, 110, 128, 144, 160-161, 228-229, 344-345
Mohanjit, xxxvii
Mohinder Singh Joshi, 228-229, 231
Mohinder Singh Sarna, vii, xxiii, 230, 256-257, 270, 329
Mohmammad Safdar, xxxviii
Moyna Mazumdar, 65, 336
Muhammad Umar Memon, 285
Mulk Raj Anand, xxii
Munir Niazi, vii, xxix, xxxviii, 163-165
Muqbil, xxxv
Mushtaq Soofi, xxxii

N

N. Kaur, 259
Najm Hosain Syed, xviii, xxix, xxxii
Namdev, xxvii

Nanak Singh, vi, xvi-xvii, xxiii, xxviii-xxix, xxxii-xxxiii, xxxix, 55, 70-73, 87, 102, 105, 228-229, 257, 261, 277, 280, 282, 336-337
Nandita Das, 286
Narain Singh, xxxv
Narendrapal Singh, xxxiii-xxxiv
Narinderjit Kaur, viii, xiii, 56-57, 259, 336
Natasha Tolstoy, 72
Naurang Singh, 232
Navdeep Suri xxiii, 70, 73, 336
Naveed Alam, 172-173, 337
Navtej Puadhi, 277
Navtej Sarna, xxiii, 256, 337
Navtej Singh, 228, 231
Neelam Man Singh Chaudhury, xli
Neer Kanwal Mani, 65, 337
Nikky Guninder Kaur Singh, xxiii
Niranjan Tasneem, xxii, xxxii, xxxiv, 151, 338
Nirmal Verma, 330
Nirupama Dutt, viii, xiii, xviii, xxi, xxxvii, xli, 154, 161, 261, 338
Nizami, xxxv, 339
Nonika Singh, 31
Norah Richards, xl

O
Om Prakash Gasso, vi, xxxiv, 78-79

P
P. K. Nijhawan, 175, 176, 339
Pal Kaur, vii, xxxvii, 201, 203
Pali Bhupinder Singh, 194
Paramjeet Singh Ramana, xviii, 64, 254, 293, 338
Parvesh, 53
Pash/Avtar Singh Sandhu, xxxii, xxxvii, 119, 156, 166, 343
Paul Smith, 121, 339
Pawan Gulati, 140
Peero Preman, xli
Pir Hadi Abdul Mannan, xxix
Prabhjot Kaur, xvii, xxxvii
Prem Gorkhi, xviii, xliii, 262
Prem Prakash, viii, 237-238, 264-265, 282
Pritam Sandhu, 277, 279
Pritam Singh 'Safeer, xxxvii
Prof. Puran Singh viii, xxviii-xxix, xxxii, xxxvi, 134, 202, 307, 344
Puran Singh 298, 305

Q
Qadaryar, xxviii, xxxvi, 179, 202

R
Rabisankar Bal, 286
Raenee, 222
Raghubir Dhand, viii, xviii, 266, 270, 275-276, 297, 299, 303
Rahat Kazmi, 286
Raj Gill, 237
Rajendra Awasthy, viii, 269, 339
Rajesh Sharma, 196
Raji Narasimhan, 68-69, 340
Rajinder Kaur, 277
Rajinder Singh Bedi, vi, viii, xxii, xxxv, 81-83, 221, 241-242, 245, 272, 325
Rajinder Singh, vi, xiii, 3, 10, 41, 85, 87, 213

Index | 353

Ram Sarup Ankhi, vi, xxxiv, 30, 80, 88-89, 91-92, 231, 275-277, 325, 346
Ramindra Ajit Singh, 237
Ramnita Saini Sharda, 197
Rana Nayar, viii, xi, xiii, xviii, xxi, xxv, 18-19, 125-126, 195, 253, 255, 266, 280, 282, 297-299, 301, 310, 340, 346
Rani Nagender, 303
Ranjit Singh Bhinder, 277
Ranjit Singh, viii, xiii, 8, 175-178, 202, 208, 248, 275, 277-278, 328, 340
Rattan Raheel, 305
Ravi Deep, 80
Ravidas, xxvii
Ravinder Ravi, xiii, xxxvii
Reverend J. Newton, xxviii
Rita Chaudhry, viii, 143-144, 302, 341
Rupa Bajwa, xxii
Rupinderpal Dhillon, xiii, xxi, xxx, 45, 315, 345, 346,
Ruth Garcha, 204

S

S. C. Narula, 41, 341
S. Tarsem, 262
S.N.Dar, 189, 190
S.P.Singh, 297
S.S. Misha, xxxii
S.Saqi 277, 278
Saadat Hasan Manto, 220, 221, 241, 242, 245, 255, 272, 283, 333
Sadhu Binning, viii, xiii, xxii, xxx, 45, 275-276, 287-289
Sadhu Daya Singh Arif, xlii

Safi Safdar, xxxviii
Safir Rammah, xxxii

Sandeep Singh Virk, 247
Sant Gulab Das/Gulab Singh Nirmala, xxxv, xlii
Sant Ram Udasi, xliii, 156
Sant Singh Sekhon, xviii, xxii, xxiii, xxx, xxxiii, xxiv, xxix, xl, 58, 94, 189, 207, 228, 231, 250, 261, 277, 280, 343
Santokh Dhaliwal, 306
Santokh Singh Dhir (Dheer), xxxii, xxxvii, 169, 228, 231, 269, 277
Sanwal Dhami, 250, 252
Sarmad Khoosat, 286
Sathi Ludhianvi, 305-306
Sati Kumar, xxxvii
Satjit Wadva, 210, 238, 341
Satnam, vi, 85, 97-99
Shafqat Tanvir Mirza, xxix
Shah Mohammed, vii, xxvi, 175-177, 220, 339
Shareef Kunjahi, xxix, xxxviii
Shashi Joshi, 118, 341
Shiv Kumar Batalvi vii, xvii, xxviii, xxxvi, 161, 179-82, 187-188, 202, 255
Shivanath, 69
Shivcharan Gill, 297, 299, 303
Shivcharan Jaggi Kussa, xxx, 100, 297,299, 303
Sibtul Hasan Zaigham, xxxi
Snehlata Jaswal, 197
Sohan Singh Seetal, vi, xxviii, 103-104, 344

354 | Index

Sohinder Singh Wanjara Bedi, vi, 106
Stephen Watts, 118, 342

Sudhir, 210, 342
Sujan Singh, viii, xviii, xxxix, 231, 269, 277, 280, 290-291, 295, 336
Sukhjeet, 250
Sukhwant Kaur Mann, xviii, 232, 251, 259, 275
Sultan Bahu, vii, xxvii, 7, 130, 172, 183-185
Supriya Bhandari, 196, 342
Suresh Kumar Singla, 93
Surinder Singh Narula, xxxiii, 228
Surinder Singh Oberai, 277-278
Surjit Kalsi, xvii, xxx, xxxvii, 302, 304
Surjit Kaur Kalpana, 300
Surjit Patar, vii, xxviii, xxxii, xxxvii, 186-188
Surjit Singh Sethi, xxxiii-xxxiv
Surjit Virdi, 302, 304
Sutinder Singh Noor, 87, 230
Swaraj Raj, 197, 235, 250, 342
Swarajbir, xiii, 195
Swaran Chandan, vi, xxii, xxxix, 109-110, 297, 303, 307

T

T.C.Ghai, 166, 344
Talwinder Singh, xxxi, 250, 252
Tara Meenakshi Sekhri, 238, 343
Tarsem Neelgiri, 297
Tauquir Chugtai, 237
Tejinder Kaur, 235, 250, 343
Tejwant Singh Gill, xiii, xviii, 96, 160-161, 168, 201, 207-208, 343

U

Uma Trilok, 26
Upendra Nath Ashk, 242
Usha Mahajan, 241-242
Ustad Daman, xxviii

V

Vasudha Dalmia, 69
Veena Verma, xvii-xviii, xl, 250, 259-260, 263, 300
Vineeta, xxxvii
Vishav Bharti, 97, 344

W

Waris Shah, vii, xix, xxiii, xxviii, xxxv, 6-7, 129, 148, 162, 172, 177, 189-191, 208, 220, 257, 263, 342
Waryam Singh Sandhu, viii, 232, 293-295, 338

Y

Yashpal, vi, xvi, xxii, 112-116, 150, 241-242, 324